Essays and Studies 2020

Series Editor: Ceri Sullivan

The English Association

The English Association is a membership body for individuals and organisations passionate about the English language and its literatures. Our membership includes teachers, students, authors, and readers, and is made up of people and institutions from around the world.
Our aim is to further the knowledge, understanding and enjoyment of English studies, and to foster good practice in their teaching and learning at all levels, by

- encouraging the study of English language and literature in the community at large
- working toward a fuller recognition of English as core to education
- fostering discussion about methods of teaching English at all levels
- supporting conferences, lectures, and publications
- responding to national consultations and policy decisions about the subject

More information about the Association is on our website: https://www2.le.ac.uk/offices/english-association

Publications

The Year's Work in English Studies – published annually, *The Year's Work in English Studies* is a qualitative narrative bibliographical review of scholarly work that year about the English language or literatures in English, from Old English to contemporary criticism.
The Year's Work in Critical and Cultural Theory – a companion volume in the field of critical and cultural theory, recording significant debates in a broad field of research in the humanities and social sciences.
Essays and Studies – published since 1910, *Essays and Studies* is an annual collection of essays on topical issues in English, edited by a different distinguished academic each year. The volumes cover a range of subjects and authors, from medieval to modern.
English – published quarterly, *English* is a forum for people who think hard and passionately about literature and who want to communicate those thoughts to a wide audience. It includes scholarly essays and reviews on all periods of literary history, and new work by contemporary poets.

English 4 to 11 – published three times a year, this magazine contains material produced by, and for, the classroom leader. It is a reader-friendly magazine, backed by sound pedagogy, offering ideas for developing classroom practice.

The Use of English – published three times per year, this journal's articles and reviews are designed to encourage teachers to further their own interest and expertise in the subject.

Newsletter – produced three times per year, the *Newsletter* contains topical articles, news items, and interviews about English studies, and updates about The English Association's activities.

Benefits of Membership

Unity and voice – members join others with a wealth of experience, knowledge, and passion for English, to foster the discussion of teaching methods and respond to national issues.

Resources – members can access high quality resources on the Association's website, and in its volumes, journals, magazines, and newsletters.

Networking – members can network with colleagues and leading practitioners, including joining national special interest groups and their local Regional Group. Members also are given reduced rates for the Association's conferences and other events.

Essays and Studies 2020

Literature and Ageing

Edited by
Elizabeth Barry
with Margery Vibe Skagen

for the English Association

D. S. BREWER

ESSAYS AND STUDIES 2020
IS VOLUME SEVENTY-THREE IN THE NEW SERIES
OF ESSAYS AND STUDIES COLLECTED ON BEHALF OF
THE ENGLISH ASSOCIATION
ISSN 0071-1357

First published 2020
D. S. Brewer, Cambridge

D. S. Brewer is an imprint of Boydell & Brewer Ltd
PO Box 9, Woodbridge, Suffolk IP12 3DF, UK
and of Boydell & Brewer Inc.
668 Mt Hope Avenue, Rochester, NY 14620–2731, USA
website: www.boydellandbrewer.com

ISBN 978-1-84384-571-3

A CIP catalogue record for this book is available
from the British Library

The publisher has no responsibility for the continued existence or accuracy of
URLs for external or third-party internet websites referred to in this book, and
does not guarantee that any content on such websites is, or will remain, accurate or
appropriate

This publication is printed on acid-free paper

Printed and bound in Great Britain by
TJ Books Ltd, Padstow, Cornwall

MIX
Paper from
responsible sources
FSC® C013056

Contents

Notes on Contributors

David Amigoni is Professor of Victorian Literature and Pro Vice-Chancellor for Research and Enterprise at Keele University. He specializes in life writing, literature and science and, since 2009 when he started to work on the "Ages and Stages" project (funded by the cross-council New Dynamics of Ageing scheme), age studies. He co-edited, with Gordon McMullan, *Creativity in Later Life: Beyond Late Style* (2019), based on their Arts and Humanities Research Council-funded international research network.

Elizabeth Barry is Reader in English at the University of Warwick. She is the author of *Beckett and Authority* (2006), has edited issues of *International Journal of Cultural Studies*, *Journal of Beckett Studies*, and *Journal of Medical Humanities*, and has published several essays on literature and ageing. She is a partner on the interdisciplinary age studies project run by the University of Bergen, "Historicizing the Ageing Self." She has also held two Arts and Humanities Research Council awards to work with doctors on using modernist literature to investigate disorders of self.

Sarah Falcus is Reader in Contemporary Literature at the University of Huddersfield. She is interested in the intersection of ageing studies and literary studies, and is the co-author (with Katsura Sako) of *Contemporary Narratives of Dementia: Ethics, Ageing, Politics* (2019). She has published in journals such as *Feminist Review*, *Women: A Cultural Review*, and *Ageing and Society*. She co-edited a special issue of the *European Journal of English Studies* (2018), focused on the intersection of English studies and ageing studies. Her current work centres on two main areas: children's literature and ageing; and ageing/the life course in science and speculative fiction. She is the Primary Collaborator on the project "Ageing and Illness in British and Japanese Children's Picturebooks 1950–2000: Historical and Cross-Cultural Perspectives," funded by the Japan Society for the Promotion of Science. She is the co-director of the Dementia and Cultural Narrative Network.

Margaret Morganroth Gullette, an internationally known age critic, is the author most recently of *Ending Ageism, or How Not to Shoot Old People* (2017), which won both the US Modern Language Association Prize for

Independent Scholars and the American Psychological Association's Florence L. Denmark Award for Contributions to Women and Aging. She is the first non-psychologist to win the American Psychological Association Award. *Agewise* won a 2012 Eric Hoffer Book Award. *Aged by Culture* (2004) was chosen as a Noteworthy Book of the Year by the Christian Science Monitor. *Declining to Decline* (1997) received the Emily Toth Award as the best feminist book on American popular culture. Gullette also writes for mainstream media, feminist, literary, academic, and cultural studies journals. Her essays are often cited as Notable in Best American Essays. A recipient of National Endowment for the Humanities, American Council of Learned Societies, and Bunting Fellowships, Gullette is a Resident Scholar at the Women's Studies Research Center, Brandeis University.

Jacob Jewusiak is a lecturer in Victorian literature at Newcastle University. His first book, *Aging, Duration, and the English Novel: Growing Old from Dickens to Woolf*, was published by Cambridge University Press in 2019. He is currently working on a second book, titled *The Aging of Empire: Networks of Dependence from Young England to Young India*, which examines how models of imperial expansion derived their power from a tacit comparison to the development of a human life. His articles have appeared in journals such as *Novel: A Forum on Fiction*, *ELH*, *Textual Practice*, *Victorian Literature and Culture*, *SEL*, and *Nineteenth-Century Gender Studies*.

Margery Vibe Skagen is Associate Professor in French Literature at the University of Bergen. She has published extensively on Baudelaire and has co-authored and co-edited several collections in the field of Literature and Science. Currently working in the interface of literature, cultural history, psychology and gerontology, she is preparing a monograph on late life genres and reverie from Montaigne to Baudelaire. She leads the Norwegian Research Council research project "Historicizing the Ageing Self: Literature, Medicine, Psychology, Law."

Helen Small is Merton Professor of English Language and Literature at the University of Oxford. She is the author of *The Long Life* (2007; winner of the Truman Capote Prize for Literary Criticism, 2008, and the British Academy's Rose Mary Crawshay Prize, 2008), and several subsequent essays on literary and philosophical aspects of ageing. She is a member of the advisory board of *Age, Culture, Humanities: An Interdisciplinary Journal* (launched 2014).

Emily Kate Timms is a PhD student in the School of English at the University of Leeds. She is supervised by Dr Clare Barker and Professor John McLeod and her work is sponsored by the White Rose College of the Arts and Humanities. Her thesis examines postcolonial representations of age and ageing in Aotearoa New Zealand and Caribbean fiction and film, and investigates how such representations can intervene in the disciplines of critical gerontology and ageing studies. She is the current editorial assistant for *Moving Worlds: A Journal of Transcultural Writings* and co-founder of the New Voices in Postcolonial Studies network.

Peter Svare Valeur is Associate Professor in Comparative Literature at the University of Bergen. He has published many articles on European Romanticism and Modernist poetry. He is a member of the research networks Historicizing the Aging Self, Christianity and Modernity, and Theories of Compilation in the 18th Century. His PhD was titled "Romantic Figures of Old Age. Readings of Chateaubriand, Eichendorff and Wordsworth" (University of Oslo, 2013).

Kathleen Woodward is Lockwood Professor in the Humanities and Professor of English at the University of Washington, Seattle, where she directs the Simpson Center for the Humanities. She is the author of *Statistical Panic: Cultural Politics and Poetics of the Emotions* (2009), *Aging and Its Discontents: Freud and Other Fictions* (1991), and *At Last, the Real Distinguished Thing: The Late Poems of Eliot, Pound, Stevens, and Williams* (1980). She is also the editor or co-editor of three interdisciplinary collections of original essays on ageing: *Figuring Age: Women – Bodies – Generations* (1999), *Memory and Desire: Aging – Literature – Psychoanalysis* (1986), and *Aging and the Elderly: Humanistic Perspectives in Gerontology* (1978). Focusing on assisted living, frailty, and disability, Woodward's recent work appears in *International Journal of Ageing and Later Life, Occasion: Interdisciplinary Studies in the Humanities*, and *Age, Culture, Humanities*.

Acknowledgements

Our debt is great to the many people who have helped to inspire, elicit and contribute to this volume. We would first like to thank Ceri Sullivan, who, as general editor, invited us to contribute a volume on 'ageing' to this estimable series. Thanks to Rebecca Fisher of the English Association, and Caroline Palmer and everyone at Boydell & Brewer who have helped us to bring it into being. Thanks, of course, to all the contributors here for their rich and varied insights and eloquence on the topic of literature and ageing. Thanks to the Norwegian Research Council, whose support has allowed much of this research to happen and who have generously supported the development of this volume and some of its essays through the project "Historicizing the Ageing Self: Literature, Medicine, Psychology, Law" (https://www.uib.no/en/project/ageing). Thanks to the University of Bergen and the University of Warwick, who have hosted research events which contributed to the conception and development of the work. Thanks to our friends and colleagues Sarah Falcus, Vivan Joseph, and Katsura Sako, who have commented on drafts of the work. Special thanks to post-doctoral fellow Soledad Marambio and PhD candidate Solveig Helene Lygren at UiB for working so hard and so professionally on the volume, putting everything aside the week before submission to unify the style, format and references of the essays. And finally, very warm thanks to our families, for their support and great patience throughout the process.

Elizabeth Barry and Margery Vibe Skagen

1

Introduction:
The Difference That Time Makes

ELIZABETH BARRY WITH
MARGERY VIBE SKAGEN

Ageing eludes literary and critical representation in a number of ways.
It is, for one thing, a moving target: a process of continuous biological
and biographical change rather than a discrete object of attention.
Those who study age prefer to think in terms of growing *older* than
in terms of an absolute state of being *old*. It is also difficult in practice to determine and compare age categories: chronological age does
not always align with expected quality of health, physical capacity or
mental acuity. With greater longevity, as well as more fluidity in the
shape of careers and variance in childbearing age, the idea of fixed life
stages has given way to a more relativized conception of old age, its
boundaries and its limitations. It might be as well, as Rüdiger Kunow
suggests, to think of ageing not "as essence, biological, chronological
or otherwise," but as difference itself: "*the difference that time makes*"
(Kunow 295).

The subjective experience of ageing is also particularly difficult to
capture. It is hard to represent, let alone give compelling narrative
shape to what Kathleen Woodward has described as an "infinitesimally
incremental process of the subtraction of strengths" (*Aging and Its
Discontents* 38). In this sense, ageing is grindingly linear – an inexorable
process with no dramatic arc. Conversely, however, it is also bafflingly,
unpredictably non-linear. We may feel creaky one day, and sprightly
the next. We can feel old at forty and young, at least temporarily, at
seventy. Simone de Beauvoir famously observed just such an "insolu-
ble contradiction" between the clarity of the feeling that "guarantees
our unchanging quality," and the "objective certainty of our [external]
transformation" (323). Only at a very advanced age, perhaps, is one
– as Ursula Le Guin observed in her memoir of old age – unable to
maintain this contradiction: "If I'm ninety and believe I'm forty-five,
I'm headed for a very bad time trying to get out of the bathtub" (Le
Guin 9). A new knowledge of our intractable materiality asserts itself

just at the moment when our material selves start to feel stranger and less compliant with our will.

These sociological shifts in the definition of old age, and the perplexing experience it can represent first-hand, both make it a fascinating crux for literary representation. It can be, as Kunow goes on to say, a "highly charged but … opaque signifier" (Kunow 296). Literary narrative, attending by definition – albeit in a myriad of ways – to the difference that time makes, might be able to offer some elucidation. As Margaret Gullette has written, almost all literature tells us what it is like to get older, "if only a day or a few hours older" (*Safe at Last* 30). What does ageing mean for those characters living it, and to what dramatic or symbolic use is it put by the author? The work in this volume will explore just how this ageing – this difference – registers.

Ageing in literature can also be an equivocal signifier for the scholar. In one sense, it seems to be resoundingly literal. Mike Featherstone has argued of the body in general that its tangibility and visibility are seen to give it "a higher degree of realism and indexicality: as if the body has slipped under the guard of discourse … bodies [being] things which are self-evidently what they seem to be" (Featherstone and Wernick 3). This in itself can offer a challenge to those who come to conceptualize it, however. Kathleen Woodward has suggested that the *ageing* body in literature, in its distance from what it 'ought' to be, offers an even more 'real' form of realism, "the bedrock of the real, in Lacanian terms" (*Aging and Its Discontents* 19) – the pre-eminent example of unmediated, untheorizable experience. If ageing is hard to represent, how much more difficult might it be to theorize and how might literary studies – or any form of gerontology – approach it?

If writers can find ageing hard to conceptualize or even represent, our culture has plenty to say about it. There are many cultural expectations of ageing, and these are increasingly negative – the idea that old age might be venerable giving way in the cultural discourse to a litany of losses and exclusions. We do not, in this volume, seek to emulate the insistence that can be found, in countering this view, on 'successful ageing' or 'positive ageing.' The essays here offer a range of perspectives, as they examine a range of concepts and representations. As Helen Small has warned us in *The Long Life*, every generalization about ageing can be countered with its opposite (2). We encounter age in these pages as identified with knowledge and with cognitive decline, displaying rigidity and playfulness, as loss and acquisition. Old people figure as both the resource that might preserve the future, and the symbol of its disappearance. What is common to the examples considered here is that they confound our expectations. These essays show, first and foremost, that ageing and its representations submit to theorization and critique in intriguing and surprising ways.

* * *

This volume is one manifestation of a new era in literary age studies, in which scholars seek new critical and conceptual possibilities in the literary treatment of ageing – an assertion to which we will return below. It also aims, in drawing attention to age, to open up new concerns and approaches in the field of literary studies. Stories of middle or even older age are now becoming common to literary production, a story for our time as the Bildungsroman or heroic quest may have been in earlier eras, and they are now, if belatedly, receiving their due. It is not simply – though this is a factor – the dominance of literary realism in the nineteenth and twentieth centuries that accounts for this development. Representing old age, it is true, has been a badge of honour for the realist writer, representing daring candour or bold disregard for readerly taste, and it is notable that George Gissing, John Updike, and William Trevor began their careers as young men with novels (*The Nether World* (1889), *The Poorhouse Fair* (1959) and *The Old Boys* (1964), respectively) not just about an ageing protagonist but whole communities of older people.

Even modernist writing, however, identified as it may be with futurist slogans about the young or what Jed Esty has called "unseasonable youth," reveals a surprisingly widespread concern with older age. Virginia Woolf's call for a new kind of writing in her essay "Mr Bennett and Mrs Brown" (1924) entreats the would-be novelist to imagine the life, thoughts and trajectory not of the young man on the train but the old woman. Woolf herself, like Eliot, Yeats, Jean Rhys, Colette and Beckett, to name just a few, gives as much space to older voices as young ones, and the anxiety over ageing (or in Beckett's case, the relish) is often embraced when these writers are still very young. Since then, with greater longevity the norm, novels about old age have proliferated (see, for example, Rooke 244): more writers live to see middle and older age, and remain well enough to reflect on the experience.

Ageing also takes its place in speculative fiction (from Trollope's *The Fixed Period* (1882), to Ursula Le Guin's *Tehanu* (1990), to the examples of P.D. James and Tawada in Falcus's essay in this volume): older people can be conspicuously absent in the organization of future societies, or positioned so as to reflect critically on what may have vanished from these seemingly utopian – or plainly dystopian – social orders. Age is often the grit in the oyster: the warning sign that shadows totalizing ways of thinking about the future, or – more problematically for age studies – represents the loss of the very possibility of futurity. Ageing as an experience also becomes prominent along with the rise of life writing: the move of autobiography or autofiction from margin to centre of literary production sees an increase in literary reflection on the life course and the possibilities and challenges of its narrativization (see notable exponents Diana Athill and Lynne Segal). Ageing is a particular test case in discussions of the value of *experience*: age studies, like feminist studies before it, calls attention to the structures of feeling by which we live, at once determined by socioeconomic conditions and unfolding in embodied, emotional, habitual lives.

* * *

Given the complexity of ageing – the modifications brought about by age at all levels, from cell senescence to ageing population, as well as over time – gerontology has always encompassed more than one discipline, drawing on biological, social and human sciences. A scientific conception of ageing as we know it originated in the late nineteenth century with discoveries about cell ageing, and the first ventures into geriatric medicine in the 1880s (with Charcot's "Lectures on Senile and Chronic Diseases" in 1881 at the vanguard). Ageing itself began to be defined explicitly as a medical risk, and the condition of frailty a vulnerable and unpredictable state. Conversely, this was the period when changes in public health and the advent of state pensions (in 1908 in Britain) began to make possible a longer life in health. Historical and social approaches to gerontology have seen the character of old age change in the twentieth century, to admit the possibility of a period of later life offering freedom, leisure and self-realization (Peter Laslett's third age), as well as a last possible phase of decline (the fourth age; that of dependency – see Gilleard and Higgs). This more positive narrative came to be qualified, however, as the twenty-first century began, by ever-increasing media attention to the issue of dementia, and by the effects of the economic downturn, meaning that the prospect of a large retired population too often figures in the cultural imaginary – in what Kathleen Woodward has termed a kind of "statistical panic" – as a grey tsunami threatening to overwhelm the resources and deplete the economic reserves of the working population (*Statistical Panic*). Gerontologists in social science have continued to work to analyse and improve upon care, but the resources for its continuance, let alone its development, are felt to be threatened. Representations of ageing have, as a result of these fears, proliferated in the media, without these having necessarily gained more nuance. And, as has been seen, it is the case that any generalizations about the nature of age, positive or negative, are unwise. There are vast disparities in income, education, health and support amongst older people (Thane), a factor already central to the argument of Simone de Beauvoir's pioneering *Old Age* fifty years ago. A historically and conceptually nuanced approach is necessary in any examination of what it is to be old.

While age has long been the poor cousin to other forms of identity politics, ageist attitudes have been a matter of public concern for several decades, resulting in age discrimination legislation informed by the findings of geriatric psychiatry and social psychology in the 1970s. A turning point came when psychiatrist Robert Butler won a Pulitzer Prize for his book *Why Survive: Being Old in America* in 1976, making the concept of 'ageism' common currency. The urgency of finding social solutions for a crisis in care, and a corresponding concern over the rights and welfare of older people, has long been recognized. In this context, it arguably becomes more rather than less important to think about the symbolic aspects of ageing – the 'cultural imaginary' that determines the way that old age is conceived of and treated in both the private and public sphere. Critical, literary and narrative approaches from the humanities are therefore finding ever greater purchase in the field of gerontology. A caveat might be offered here, however. Literary studies as a field does not, as Sarah Falcus has written about literature itself, "provide answers to questions about ageing." It does not, nor should it, seek to "illustrate gerontological concepts" (Falcus 53). What it can do, however, is to maintain the "crucial complexity of growing old," as Sally Chivers has put it, because literature, as its object, can "encompass contradictions, and even gain [its] aesthetic strength from them" (Chivers x). This volume, historically bounded to reflect these modern conceptions of age, seeks to explore the way that literature represents and critiques the various parallel stories of age that have co-existed in the late nineteenth, twentieth and twenty-first centuries. If ageing is defined by difference, a discipline is needed that can read discourse of all kinds closely, and, in Gillian Beer's words, reveal "the apparent ease with which, in language, we inhabit multiple, often contradictory, epistemologies at the same time, all the time" (174). This is one of the defining aspects of the experience of ageing, and one of the guiding observations for these essays.

* * *

It is not simply a coincident emphasis on experience and representation that gives literary age and feminist studies a connection. Feminist scholars, alert to the double exclusion that ageing and gender could represent (as identified by Susan Sontag's "double standard of ageing"), were often responsible for the early instantiations of literary age studies. It was no accident that it was Simone de Beauvoir who published the first modern philosophical essay on old age in 1970, citing a range of literary authors and thinkers to denounce the treatment of older women and men as pariahs in modern society. Other celebrated feminists who have brought the topic of ageing into the foreground include Betty Friedan and Germaine Greer. Despite this, sociologist Stephen Katz remarked at the turn of the millennium upon the way in which gerontology, "a haven for women scholars and practitioners, and for the interests of older women," had been criticized by women's studies for being "gender-blind" and "theory-poor" ("Charcot's Older Women" 112–13). The first decades of the twenty-first century have seen the recognition of the two fields' common concerns, and leading exponents in both have instigated new and productive interdisciplinary approaches. Age studies has also expanded its purview as conceptions of gender have become more nuanced and inclusive. Literary considerations of ageing owe much to those who have 'thought queer,' as demonstrated by the appropriation of the concept of 'reproductive futurism,' coined by queer theorist Lee Edelman in *No Future* (2004) and then reapplied to age studies by Cynthia Port ("No Future?") in 2012. This idea is given enlightening deployment again in this volume by Sarah Falcus and Emily Kate Timms (and see also Linda Hess's broader study on queer ageing in literature).

Katz, writing in an editorial in the inaugural issue of the journal *Age, Culture, Humanities* in 2014, noted that literary age studies might enter a second wave akin to that in feminist literary scholarship – both finding their *raison d'être* in a concern with representations and identifications, but then moving into a more conceptual phase. Literary gerontology began, as it should have, looking at the ways in which age was repre-sented – developing a trenchant form of political reading that identi-fied stigma, othering and exclusion. Crucial work, but work that might also make room to accommodate a second wave of approaches: a wave more critical of its own practices; more concerned to theorize the given representations; looking to define the role of literature in the histori-cal, social and political consciousness of older age. One might find age studies scholars concerned to identify a poetics, or stylistics, of ageing and late life production (see Amigoni and McMullan for one example). Scholars might reflect on the processes of writing, reading and re-reading as older producers and consumers (see, for instance, Port, "Rereading the Future"). Literary age studies must also, of necessity, include intersec-tional approaches, and read age – as several pieces in this volume do – in relation to race, geopolitics, and class as well as gender.

This second wave has already begun, then, and those writing in this volume are its exponents. It has sought to recover age from its customary place as an "unacknowledged shadow," as Sarah Falcus (53) has put it, of more established approaches such as critical race and gender studies, and make it central to them. It is, we might note in passing, also timely that the social and political meanings of ageing should be scrutinized at a moment when public discourse seems particularly reliant on unexamined and polarizing conceptions of life stage and generation: the unthinking nostalgia of the reactionary voter; the selfish hedonism of the boomer; the simultaneous greed and burdensome need of those in retirement; the indolence, entitlement and whiny self-absorption of the millennial. Literary scholars – professional readers – can historicize, critique and improve upon these characterizations.

* * *

Literature and Ageing includes contributions from scholars who shaped the field from its inception. Margaret Gullette, who closes this collection, could be said to have opened the literary conversation with age studies in the first place. It was her essay in Anne Wyatt-Brown and Janice Rossen's 1993 collection on age and gender, "Creativity, Ageing, Gender," that brought the concept of 'age studies' into being by *fiat*, issuing a clarion call (45–6) for a theoretically informed, socially engaged movement on the model of gender studies and critical race studies. This would follow the model of her own 1988 literary study *Safe at Last in the Middle Years*, which used literary, psychoanalytic and sociological concepts to bring to light an unexamined genre, the 'midlife progress novel,' and examine its sociocultural significance. This genre, exemplified by Saul Bellow, Margaret Drabble, Anne Tyler and John Updike, introduced a counterpoint to the more customary 'decline narrative' of ageing: its protagonists faced the trials of middle age, real as they may be, with a confidence and psychological literacy that offered the possibility of self-cure.[1] Later, Gullette's field-defining *Aged by Culture* (2004) explored the reasons for personal ambivalence and social vilification towards the old, reading culture and lived experience in the light of social conditions in the USA and Western Europe that put pressure on midlife and older age. A formidable body of work, including *Declining to Decline: Cultural Combat*

---

[1]   See, for instance, Bellow's *Herzog* (1964) and *Humboldt's Gift* (1975), Drabble's *The Realms of Gold* (1975) and *The Middle Ground* (1980), Tyler's *The Accidental Tourist* (1985), and Updike's *Rabbit Is Rich* (1981), all works discussed by Gullette in *Safe at Last*.

and the Politics of the Midlife (1997), *Agewise: Fighting the New Ageism in America*, in 2011, and most recently *Ending Ageism, or How Not to Shoot Old People* (2017), as well as a huge body of scholarship, journalism and public oratory since, have established her as an age activist, translating her cultural analysis into a social movement.

Kathleen Woodward produced three of the earliest works of literary age studies in the form of her essay collections with Stuart F. Spicker and David Van Tassel, *Aging and the Elderly: Humanistic Perspectives in Gerontology* (1978), and with Murray Schwartz, *Memory and Desire* (1986), and her monograph *Aging and Its Discontents: Freud and Other Fictions* (1991), the latter two informed by a psychoanalytic framework. *Aging and Its Discontents* offers a subtle exploration of why we – and the discipline of psychoanalysis itself – might repress ageing more completely than we do death, and how images of ageing in fiction may nonetheless be read alongside Freud to draw out the psychology of ageing and our complex forms of resistance to it. Woodward's work, belying any narrative that sees the early days of age studies as dealing in transparent representation, reads Proust, Woolf, Beckett, Barthes, Eva Figes and Freud himself as writing 'scenes' in both a psychoanalytic and literary sense that stage our ambivalence towards our own ageing, introducing such generative concepts into the field of literary age studies as the 'mirror stage of old age.' Psychoanalysis has continued to be a rich framework for thinking about ageing in literature, notably in Amelia De Falco's *Uncanny Subjects: Aging in Contemporary Narrative* in 2010, and as an intermittent but illuminating presence in Lynne Segal's influential critical memoir, *Out of Time* (2013).

Woodward's edited collection *Figuring Age: Women, Bodies, Generations* in 1999 also broadened the scope of the field in inviting prominent feminist literary and cultural theorists to consider the intersection of gender and ageing, not just in terms of stigmatizing representations but also women's own complex set of identifications between generations as well as across cultural forms. Anne Wyatt-Brown and Janice Rossen's pioneering *Aging and Gender in Literature* (1993), mentioned above, has been followed by further work in feminism, gender and age studies, encompassing issues such as care and illness, by Chivers (2003), King (2013) and Hartung (2016) among others. More recently, Roberta Maierhofer (2007) developed the concept of 'anocriticism,' on the model of Elaine Showalter's 'gynocriticism,' as a theoretical framework within which to theorize age as socially constructed, and identify the ways in which one is aged in and by culture.

Sociologist Mike Hepworth's 2000 *Stories of Ageing* was notable for putting literary studies more directly into conversation with gerontology (as represented by approaches from sociology, anthropology and psychology), recognizing the value of narrative and symbol to the understanding of physical and psychosocial change as we age. Scholars such as Aagje Swinnen, Sally Chivers, Ulla Kriebernegg and Valerie Barnes Lipscomb have also thought about the social as well as the aesthetic power of stories of ageing, using literature, film and theatre in more applied contexts to explore the ecological experience of literature among older readers, consider the negotiations of identity in the Senior Theatre movement, and help to reconceive care policy and care practice. The intersection of age studies and disability studies has often been critical in these scholars' work and that of others (see, for example, the influential work of Lucy Burke and Amelia De Falco).

If psychoanalysis had had ageing as a blind spot, the same was true, Helen Small argued in her 2007 *The Long Life*, for most of the long history of Western philosophy. Pairing classical and Anglo-American moral philosophy with literary works, Small explored the big conceptual issues that lie at the intersection of philosophy and literary studies – identity, vulnerability, narrative modes of defining and evaluating the life course, moral responsibility towards one's past and future selves, attitudes to the end of life – through nuanced and mutually illuminating close readings of both canons. The condition of advanced age, Small contends, can cause difficulties for "any general theory" of living (266), and as such is a touchstone for thinking through our most fundamental intellectual and social attitudes – and the difficult questions that they occlude or suppress.

A prominent recent concern in age studies, engaging some of the conceptual and ethical 'difficulties' to which Small alludes, is the representation of dementia, a disease which, in depleting memory and language, also presents particular challenges to literary representation. Martina Zimmermann (2017) was among the first to write about dementia narratives, considering the medical, political and poetic dimensions of dementia in recent life writing. Rebecca Bitenc (2019) focused on the potential for narrative to reconceive of and increase empathy in care, and Sarah Falcus and Katsura Sako (2019) looked at contemporary literary narratives, relating ethics and aesthetics across a range of genres. Marlene Goldman (2017) has also applied literary critical tools to the culture and public discourse of Canada, dissecting the Gothic disease model at work in its often stigmatizing representations of the disease. Sarah Falcus and Raquel Medina have also recently established a 'Dementia and Cultural Narrative' network dedicated to researching the cultural and social dimensions of dementia, which puts literary studies into productive conversations with other disciplinary approaches to the disease and its cultural imaginary –

just one among a number of initiatives that allow literary age studies to look and reach outwards towards the lived experience with which it is always concerned.

* * *

The authors in this volume represent the span of strengths involved in literary age studies, from early career scholars reshaping the discipline in exciting ways, to its founders and leading exponents, reliably mentioned in any history or survey of the field. These are also esteemed and established figures in literary studies more broadly, active not simply as scholars, but in academic service, reshaping the way that we do humanities research and recognizing their responsibilities to subsequent generations of scholars and to the wider community – endeavours where a sensitivity to age and ageism is constitutively important. Their work on ageing, as has been suggested, reaches beyond the seminar room, library or academic convention – recognizing that scholarship on this topic, in particular, can command public interest and has a place in combating anti-ageist stigma, shaping social policy, improving medical and care practice, and promoting social inclusion.

The essays here demonstrate the scholars' expertise not only with their own disciplinary conventions, but also with the methods of other humanities disciplines (philosophy, history, race theory, environmental studies). The work also itself reflects critically on thinking age alongside and in these frameworks. How, Helen Small asks, should the individual stories encountered in the humanities interact with the data-driven empirical approaches of social science? Can we, as we age, avoid being crushed by the slew of negative statistical predictions – societal and epidemiological – while still maintaining our concern for those ageing in less favourable conditions than our own, and who may have a different relationship to these big-picture predictions than we do? How should we *feel* about ageing as individuals? And how might this change and we nonetheless anticipate a future with a dementia diagnosis? Small takes Mary Mothersill's philosophical address on "Old Age" in 1998 as a stimulus to thinking through these conceptual questions, and reads Alice LaPlante's 2011 novel *Turn of Mind* for a literary model in how to feel about a circumscribed individual future.

Kathleen Woodward also considers the affects of ageing in her reading of Margaret Drabble's *The Dark Flood Rises* (2016) in the next essay. Here the solitude of a neoliberal existence cuts its protagonist off from the existential meaning of her life, and so the worldly concern needed to cherish future generations and the threatened world they will (if they are lucky) inherit. To address climate change, we must also feel its effects, if not immediately on ourselves, imaginatively for future generations – and this perspective needs to be embedded in the theorizing, as well as the creative writing, that we do. This essay thus offers a provocative new way of thinking age in relation to climate change in the conditions of the Anthropocene, expanding the critical horizons of both age studies and environmental criticism in the process. In both these essays, ageing provides a compelling means to think through questions of scale, and futurity, offering a model for how the humanities can think back and also forward in time as confidently as the big-data disciplines do – but differently – to reconcile individual and societal perspectives.

While Drabble's novel finds disturbing signs that the feared future of climate apocalypse is at hand – the sense of an ending more immanent, in Frank Kermode's terms, than imminent (6) – Falcus explores this idea explicitly through her reading of two works of speculative fiction, P.D. James's *Children of Men* (1992) and Yoko Tawada's *The Last Children of Tokyo* (2014), in the third essay in the volume. These are novels in which progress and the promise of the future are disrupted by threats to generational continuity. Ageing is seen as key to these – and many other – works of dystopic fiction. While the figure of the child is often symbolically tied to hope in the future, the old have a more complex presentation than simply corresponding fearfulness. They can often represent contingency and instability, rather than the reproduction of the 'self-same' of existing social forms. To explore the generational anachronism in these novels, Falcus uses the concept of 'reproductive futurism,' as we have seen, where the old (like the queer) are ideologically positioned as standing outside mainstream temporalities and in the way of, rather than contributing to, the future. This concept also features in Emily Kate Timms's reading of Merle Collins, who, like Falcus's authors, is also writing in a speculative mode in reconceiving her native Grenada as the fictional Paz. Timms sees Collins critique the investment in masculine youth and Marxist revolutionary ideology in Grenada, a form of this 'futurism,' which has trapped it in a cycle of traumatic upheaval at the expense of intergenerational (and female) forms of knowledge and care.

Age relations are used to structure interactions, symbolize historical legacies and frame political change in both colonial and postcolonial fictions. In the former, addressed by Jacob Jewusiak in Chapter 5, intergenerational relationships are used ideologically to circumvent the tensions created by colonial occupation in India: what Jewusiak calls grandpaternalism – a benevolent, non-threatening, playful form of power – is envisioned as taking the place of an oppressive, inflexible paternalism to reconceive the colonial relationship in Kipling's 1901 novel *Kim*. In the latter, represented in Timms's essay (Chapter 6) by Merle Collins's *The Colour of Forgetting*, the older woman is not the type of the nurturing grandmother or black matriarch which persists in neo-colonial contexts (and whose unpaid care work props up neo-colonial economic exploitation). Older women are tricksters, refusing colonial authority and revolutionary masculine ideology alike, to represent and deploy embodied knowledge and canny, playful, shapeshifting forms of identity. These women at the crossroads – the crossing points – of past and present, mythical landscape and political territory, thereby elude and so survive the doctrinaire political structures that come and go in violent and traumatic cycles.

At the other end of the scale, but central to the history of both literary studies and age studies, is the changing conception of the individual self, brought into focus by the experience of radical cognitive impairment in dementia. Elizabeth Barry follows Small's lead in using the insights of Anglo-American philosophy to inform her analysis, considering the differing accounts of personhood – and its termination – in recent thought. Ronald Dworkin's idea of critical interests and Alasdair MacIntyre's narrative unity underpin a conception of the self as rational, stable and able to think in narrative terms about its own life – a selfhood at such risk from cognitive impairment as to be felt to be 'annulled,' with implications for treatment at the end of life. Barry reads Matthew Thomas's 2014 novel *We Are Not Ourselves* as offering a different and more expansive conception of the self, seen through Agnieszka Jaworska's philosophical account of critical *values* as opposed to interests, and considered in terms of a 'shared lifeworld' rather than a unitary consciousness. This debate has profound implications for how we conceive of the whole life course, as well as its end, qualifying our understanding of any life and any death. David Amigoni, in Chapter 8, also posits a more outward-facing conception of selfhood, with or without a dementia diagnosis – a self constituted through relationships of care and communicative technologies which can help it withstand the depletions of capacity entailed in dementia. He reads a recent first-person dementia memoir, Wendy Mitchell's *Somebody I Used to Know* (2018), as modelling this mobile and resourceful self, and compellingly situates this account in a history of self-help literature which has, despite its connotations of liberal Victorian self-sufficiency, advocated a relational self – and, indeed, foregrounded the process of ageing – from its beginnings with Samuel Smiles's *Self-Help* of 1859.

Finally, Peter Svare Valeur uses a more classical set of philosophical ideas than Small or Barry to read ageing in Samuel Beckett's *Krapp's Last Tape* (1958) in relation to the concept of non-identity, drawing on Augustine's 'region of unlikeness' and its origins in Platonic thought.

Krapp, like the protagonists in Barry and Amigoni's examples, renounces the idea of a coherent narrative self with stable interests. If he cannot maintain a stable sense of self over time, however, his fluid conception of identity makes for a more positive set of possibilities than might first be imagined, as he plays with different age-identities given material forms in his different tapes, and – in a fitting end to this volume attuned to the varied and sometimes surprising affects of age – finds a certain happiness in doing so.

* * *

In the introduction to *Figuring Age*, Kathleen Woodward has observed that age is *"the one difference we are all likely to live into"* (x). It is in this respect, as Rüdiger Kunow suggests, "a difference 'out there' that will, in due time, become a difference 'in here'" (Kunow 305). This lived property has contributed to its lack of theorization – its 'bedrock' status as a reality outside of conceptual frameworks. Difference that manifests itself over time (unlike, say, race: we do not *become* black or white) is usually temporary, inessential (Kunow 306); ageing, on the other hand is (if we're lucky) inevitable and universal.[2] In this sense, as an identity we grow into, shaped by culture, it complicates distinctions between what is natural and what is cultural, and has required an interdisciplinary approach to understand. Literary studies can offer a critical perspective on these issues, venturing where other disciplines have feared to tread in addressing the multiple, contradictory and often uncomfortable *meanings* that ageing has for us as individuals and for our culture. And in turn ageing can, as we hope this volume shows, open up established and nascent critical avenues in literary studies to a complex new set of questions and thematics that challenge and extend their very terms.

---

[2]   Sexual difference, itself bound up with growing and so ageing, of course complicates this distinction, one of the reasons why queer theory has been so generative in conjunction with age studies.

Works Cited

Amigoni, David, and Gordon McMullan, editors. *Creativity in Later Life: Beyond Late Style*. Routledge, 2018.

Athill, Diana. *Somewhere Towards the End*. Granta, 2008.

Beauvoir, Simone de. *Old Age* [1970]. Penguin, 1977.

Beer, Gillian. *Open Fields: Science in Cultural Encounter*. Oxford UP, 1999.

Bitenc, Rebecca. *Reconsidering Dementia Narratives: Empathy, Identity and Care*. Palgrave Macmillan, 2019.

Burke, Lucy. "Introduction." *Journal of Literary and Cultural Disability Studies*, vol. 2, no. 1, 2008, pp. i–iv

———. "'The Country of My Disease': Genes and Genealogy in Alzheimer's Life-Writing." *Journal of Literary and Cultural Disability Studies*, vol. 2, no. 1, 2008, pp. 63–74.

———. "On (Not) Caring: Tracing the Meanings of Care in the Imaginative Literature of the 'Alzheimer's Epidemic.'" *Popularizing Dementia: Public Expressions and Representations of Forgetfulness*, edited by Aagje Swinnen and Mark Schweda. Transcript Verlag, 2015, pp. 23–41.

Chivers, Sally. *From Old Woman to Older Women: Contemporary Culture and Women's Narratives*. Ohio UP, 2003.

Chivers, Sally, and Ulla Kriebernegg. *Care Home Stories: Aging, Disability, and Long-Term Residential Care*. De Gruyter, 2017.

De Falco, Amelia. *Uncanny Subjects: Aging in Contemporary Narrative*. Ohio UP, 2010.

Falcus, Sarah. "Literature and Ageing." *Routledge Handbook of Cultural Gerontology*, edited by Julia Twigg and Wendy Martin. Routledge, 2016, pp. 53–60.

Falcus, Sarah, and Katsura Sako. *Contemporary Narratives of Dementia: Ethics, Ageing, Politics*. Routledge, 2019.

Featherstone, Mike, and Andrew Wernick. *Images of Ageing: Cultural Representations of Later Life*. Routledge, 1995.

Gilleard, Chris, and Paul Higgs. "Aging without Agency: Theorizing the Fourth Age." *Aging and Mental Health*, vol. 14, no. 2, 2010, pp. 121–8.

Goldman, Marlene. *Forgotten: Narratives of Age-Related Dementia and Alzheimer's Disease in Canada*. McGill's-Queens UP, 2017.

Gullette, Margaret Morganroth. *Safe at Last in the Middle Years: The Midlife Progress Novel*. U of California P, 1988.

———. "Creativity, Ageing, Gender." *Aging and Gender in Literature: Studies in Creativity*, editors Anne Wyatt-Brown, and Janice Rossen. UP of Virginia, 1993, pp. 19–48.

———. *Declining to Decline: Cultural Combat and the Politics of the Midlife*. U of Virginia P, 1997.

———. *Aged by Culture*. U of Chicago P, 2004.

———. *Agewise: Fighting the New Ageism in America*. U of Chicago P, 2011.

———. *Ending Ageism, or How Not to Shoot Old People*. Rutgers UP, 2017.

Hartung, Heike. *Ageing, Gender and Illness in Anglophone Literature*. Routledge, 2016.

Hepworth, Mike. *Stories of Ageing*. Open University Press, 2000.

Hess, Linda A. *Queer Aging in North American Fiction*. Palgrave, 2019.

Katz, Stephen. "Charcot's Older Women: Bodies at the Interface of Aging Studies and Women's Studies." *Figuring Age: Women, Bodies, Generations*, edited by Kathleen Woodward. Indiana UP, 1999, pp. 112–27

———. "What Is Age Studies?" *Age, Culture, Humanities*, no. 1, 2014. https://ageculturehumanities.org/WP/what-is-age-studies/

Kermode, Frank. *The Sense of an Ending: Studies in the Theory of Fiction*. Oxford UP, 2000.

King, Jeanette. *Discourses of Ageing in Fiction and Feminism*. Palgrave Macmillan, 2013.

Kunow, Rüdiger. "The Coming of Age: The Descriptive Organization of Later Life." *Representation and Decoration in a Postmodern Age*, edited by Alfred Hornung and Rüdiger Kunow. Universitätsverlag Winter GmbH Heidelberg, 2009, pp. 295–309.

Laslett, Peter. "The Emergence of the Third Age." *Ageing and Society*, vol. 7, no. 3, 1987, pp. 133–60.

Le Guin, Ursula. *No Time to Spare*. Houghton Mifflin Harcourt, 2017.

Lipscomb, Valerie Barnes. *Performing Age in Modern Drama*. Palgrave Macmillan, 2016.

Maierhofer, Roberta. "An Anocritical Reading of American Culture: The Old Woman as New American Hero." *Journal of Aging, Humanities and the Arts*, vol. 1, 2007, pp. 23–33.

Port, Cynthia. "No Future? Aging, Temporality, History, and Reverse Chronologies." *Occasion: Interdisciplinary Studies in the Humanities*, vol. 4, 2012, pp. 1–19.

———. "Rereading the Future." *PMLA*, vol. 133, no. 3, 2018, pp. 640–6.

Rooke, Constance. "Old Age in Contemporary Fiction." *Handbook of the Humanities and Aging*, edited by T.R. Cole, D.D. Van Tassel and R. Kastenbaum. Springer, 1992, pp. 241–57.

Segal, Lynne. *Out of Time: The Perils and Pleasures of Old Age*. Verso, 2013.

Small, Helen. *The Long Life*. Oxford UP, 2007.

Sontag, Susan. "The Double Standard of Aging." *Saturday Review*, 29 September 1972, pp. 29–38.

Thane, Pat. *Old Age in English History: Past Experiences, Present Issues*. Oxford UP, 2000.

Woodward, Kathleen. *Aging and Its Discontents: Freud and Other Fictions*. Indiana UP, 1991.

——— editor. *Figuring Age: Women, Bodies, Generations*. Indiana UP, 1999.

———. *Statistical Panic: Cultural Politics and the Poetics of the Emotions*. Duke UP, 1999.

Woodward, Kathleen, and Murray Schwartz, editors. *Memory and Desire: Aging, Literature, Psychoanalysis*. Indiana UP, 1986.

Wyatt-Brown, Anne, and Janice Rossen, editors. *Aging and Gender in Literature: Studies in Creativity*. UP of Virginia, 1993.

2

On Not Knowing How to Feel

HELEN SMALL

Cultural criticism produced under the aegis of the 'positive ageing' movement draws a clear line of separation between the general social picture of late life, made visible in statistical data from the social and medical sciences, and the potential quality of our lives as we inhabit them. For the quantitative researcher, understanding old age entails tracking collective patterns of experience and examining the social structures shaping those patterns. That work is essential to social gerontology and geriatric medicine. In outline, its key observations are familiar to everyone: increasing care needs and burdens across the developing world; frailty, dementia, isolation; historically high life expectancy, of late plateauing, and in the US and UK now decreasing. There are more pleasant stories to tell – marriage and co-habitation among those over sixty-five have risen in the UK, for example, somewhat mitigating exposure to loneliness – but, even where guided by the insights of positive gerontology, the quantitative research concentrates on general social trends and their implications for policy-making. The contrary choice to downplay the data and focus on individual exceptions, qualitatively apprehended, is characteristic of much writing about old age in the humanities, especially dominant in literary and cultural studies and in creative arts today. There is an obvious cultural rationale: a corrective offered to ageism; welcome encouragement for personal optimism.[1]

It is in this context that I go back to an essay first published in 1999, and familiar to philosophers of old age, though little discussed beyond philosophy: Mary Mothersill's Presidential Address on "Old Age," delivered to the Eastern Division of the American Philosophical Association

---

[1]   The papers presented at the 2019 British Academy "Narratives of Old Age and Gender" conference, from which this volume partly derives, indicate how deep-rooted an orthodoxy such approaches have become within literary and cultural studies. Constellating around new (or old but newly valued) stories and images of ageing, they demonstrated little interest in the data-driven approaches that would dominate a social-scientific or medical set of essays on the same topic (Pat Thane's analysis of the recent social history of ageing being a partial exception).

in Washington, DC in December 1998.[2] The relevance of that lecture, written at a moment when the influence of the 'successful' and 'productive ageing' movements on gerontology had become evident, and the concept of 'positive ageing' was quickly gaining institutional traction,[3] is that it identifies a difficulty peculiar to the subject of old age for which, Mothersill argues, neither 'positive gerontology' nor the more 'negative' gerontology it substantially displaced has an adequate answer. The difficulty arises from the mismatch of perspectives between what we know about old age based on the data (quantitative information that dominates the demographic and public-policy conversation) and our first-person outlooks. Reconciliation of individual hopes and expectations with the general social tendencies is rarely straightforward, but in Mothersill's view there are special difficulties attaching to late life. As she presents it, the problem is less one of method than of emotional orientation: "We do not know how to feel" (Mothersill, "Old Age" 18).

Mothersill acknowledged her first-person familiarity with her subject at the start of the Presidential Address ("Old Age" 7, 9–23).[4] She was seventy-five at the time, and had retired five years earlier from her position as Professor of Philosophy at Barnard College and the Graduate School of Arts and Sciences at Columbia University, New York. As election to the presidency indicated, she remained, in retirement, a prominent and active presence in the American philosophical community, continuing to publish until just two years before her death in 2008. It is germane to the questions raised by "Old Age" that her reputation was (and remains) primarily based on her classic work of aesthetic theory, *Beauty Restored* (1984), in which she sought, as the punning title has it, to 'restore' the category of beauty to contemporary philosophical discussion, pushing back against the anti-aesthetic tendencies that followed from widespread adoption of ordinary language philosophy and linguistic theories of art.

---

[2]   As the main publication by Mothersill, though not the first listed, references to this piece will appear without further bibliographic information in the main body of the text after the first citation.

[3]   For a helpful account of the developments within gerontology, see Johnson and Mutchler. And for an exemplary consideration on the problem of sustaining a 'positive ageing' approach when dealing with age-related impairments, McGrath.

[4]   The last publications listed on her PhilPapers page are an essay on "Make-Believe Morality and Fictional Worlds," appearing in Bermúdez and Gardner's *Art and Morality* (2002), "Beauty and the Critic's Judgment: Remapping Aesthetics," in *The Blackwell Guide to Aesthetics*, edited by Peter Kivy; and "Art and Emotion" [review of Derek Matravers's *Art and Emotion* (Oxford UP, 1998)] in *International Studies in Philosophy* in 2005.

Her writings, whether on morality or on aesthetics, convey a vivid understanding of the importance of pleasure to our lives, without recourse to rule-based utilitarianism; also a frank recognition of how much, in questions of morality and art, remains messy, not to be satisfactorily dealt with through formal philosophical reasoning. She was an enlightening and witty reviewer, looking to keep academic philosophy in contact with other fields of inquiry, including literary criticism. Her 1975 review of three early works by Stanley Cavell, for example, provides a lucid characterization of the differences between modern philosophy and modern literary criticism, before wrestling with the unusual attractions and occasional irritations of Cavell's "philosophical criticism" (Mothersill, "Review").

Mothersill's writing seems to me hard not to like, but "Old Age" may be an exception. At a seminar discussion on the text a few years ago in Pittsburgh,[5] with a mixed but predominantly male audience drawn from across the university, including the medical faculties, a majority of participants expressed respect for the impeccably serious aims of the essay but reacted against the objections Mothersill raises to 'the new gerontology''s emphasis on 'successful aging'[6] and (what they took to be) the negativity of her outlook. I disagree on the negativity, but will come to that in due course. A likely explanation for why the essay got under some skins was that it brings the limitations and problems of 'successful ageing' directly home to the circumstances of the academic who seeks critical insight into old age but is implicated, as most of us are, in the subject matter. (The exceptions will be those readers with reason to believe they will not make it into old age, and whose relationship to the topic will be compromised in other ways.)

Mothersill spoke simultaneously as a moral philosopher familiar with contemporary gerontology and an individual woman advancing into her later seventies. Much of her text adopts the first-person plural, but the agents designated are not consistent: sometimes "we philosophers," sometimes "we oldies," occasionally "we academic emeriti." The provocations the address offers from these mobile, intermittently joined, perspectives are, I propose, worth going back to, over twenty years on, in thinking about how the general critical conversation about old age now looks, what place gender holds in that conversation, and what is involved (for all of "us") in mediating between the sociological picture of old age and

the specificity of personal experience. In the first part of this essay I set
out the main claims of "Old Age," and consider critically the problem of
"not knowing how to feel about a future that most of us hope for" (18). I
look, briefly, at the changing parameters of some of the quantitative data
through which collective social expectations for old age are articulated,
and the implications for a first-person plural perspective on old age. I
then turn to Alice LaPlante's *Turn of Mind* (2011), a novel focused on a
woman's efforts at navigation between the predictable trajectory of her
ageing with dementia and the particularity of her personality, her disposition, and her context.[7]

The literary text is not a direct match for Mothersill's essay: that is,
I do not select *Turn of Mind* on the basis that it reflects extensively on
the sociological and medical challenges of an ageing society. Other works
might serve better, in that regard – Margaret Drabble's *The Dark Flood
Rises* (2016), for example, discussed in this volume (Woodward), with
its tenacious exploration of the perspectives of educated older men and
women variously prompted to reflect on their relationship to the wider
social and demographic situation. *Turn of Mind* is an experimental work:
a surprising adaptation of genre fiction that probes the problem of how to
feel about old age while holding the reader back from any easy assumption
of sympathy. Like Mothersill's address, this is an approach to the subject
of old age at once strongly vested in the idea of a 'rational attitude' and
closely attuned to how emotion co-exists with reason. Awarded the third
Wellcome Trust Book Prize (2011) for an outstanding work of fiction
or non-fiction on the theme of health and medicine, LaPlante's novel
intensifies and helps to elucidate what may be involved in narrating the
individual experience against the recognized facts of late life, putting intelligent pressure on the idea of "how to feel about a future" that must, other
things being equal, become incrementally exposed to the "ills ... peculiar
to old age" (20).

* * *

Observing a surprising lack of engagement by gerontology to date with
philosophy, Mothersill sets herself the task of defining what the salient
questions about old age should be for both fields. Her opening gambit

---

[7]   Beyond praising reviews on first publication, *Turn of Mind* has not, to my
knowledge, attracted a significant critical literature as yet – though see Martina
Zimmermann, *The Poetics and Politics of Alzheimer's Disease Life-Writing*, ch. 1,
for brief acknowledgement of its interest as a contribution to the growing literary
sophistication of imagined dementia patient narratives.

is a blunt assertion that ageing possesses greater philosophical interest than death: "talk of death, though it may have poetic power, is embarrassingly trivial," she remarks, "end[ing], sooner rather than later, in a blind alley, in a dead end" (9). The justification for holding that view is straightforward: much of the philosophical discussion about whether death does or does not harm the person who dies rests on intuitions about an afterlife or its absence which can never be anything *more* than intuitions. Philosophical consideration of old age need not be similarly "otiose." Yet, despite extensive sociological and medical evidence of "a pressing and increasingly severe socio-political problem," gerontology has shown little interest. Mothersill considers the "consequences that flow" (9): not enough has been done by 1999 (or since) to move public opinion in a progressive direction by challenging "deeply rooted, often unacknowledged convictions" that lead Americans to reject "obvious remedial measures" for the problems of old age (9) – by increasing taxes, for example; tightening age discrimination legislation; enacting a "reasonable national health insurance bill"; incentivizing employers to provide transition measures from full-time working to full retirement; and so forth (13).

Mothersill starts her philosophical reasoning about old age from the question of how to relate temporality to value: "Is longevity, other things being equal, a positive good?" and is it "possible to speak here of a rational attitude" (10). "True goods and ills" seem to her to be "related only contingently to age" (19): she sees nothing intrinsically good or bad about longevity; pleasures and pains are pleasures and pains whenever they occur in our lives. (This view is, I argued in *The Long Life* (chs 2 and 3), vulnerable to a range of objections, but that is not my subject on this occasion.) What is *distinctive* about old age, she claims, is the liability of the mind to connect pain with the thought "I am soon going to die. This is the beginning of the end" (20): although a terminal diagnosis or hypochondria at any age may have the same effect, closer proximity to death makes old age in her view unlike other stages of life. Proximity (even if the notion lacks precision) is a certainty, and dislike of it is to be expected on a normative view of psychology. Mothersill thus returns to the question from which she started – whether death is bad and if so why, "hoping that [her] second thoughts are better than [her] first" (10). She puts her argumentative weight behind the well-known but often derided Epicurean thesis that we can rationally put our fear of death aside and take much of the unhappiness out of ageing by recognizing that "as long as we exist, death is not with us and when death comes, we do not exist" (10, 20).

The tone, when Mothersill comes to discuss her personal relationship to the pathogenic conditions that cluster in old age, is good-naturedly stoical, somewhat quizzical rather than resentful. "Isn't there," she asks, "when you come to think of it, something redundant in the expression 'successful aging'? Given the alternative, then as long as I keep chugging along, getting older and older and older, I'm ahead of the game, am I not?" (16). Here we come to the ground of my disagreement with members of the Pittsburgh audience over Mothersill's negativity. To deploy the notion of a "game" comically is, as I read it, strategic: it points us to the way in which the individual looking for a rational perspective on their own achieved or anticipated old age must cut a path through subject matter where outcomes are to a large extent socioeconomically predictable as well as biologically predictable without being known. The tension between these things is the problem, in one sense, but also the opportunity for Mothersill – allowing her (via irony) to acknowledge the negative indicators, but also hold on to (what may or may not be) the saving effects of contingency. It is also to acknowledge, and ward off, a thicket of cultural valuations, positive and negative: talk of ageing is, as Mothersill often reminds us, replete with dogmatisms, both old and new. Like (I imagine) most of us, she is attracted by the cases that flout expectations or bend the rules, even if they do not, strictly, falsify them: "(Think of that lady in Paris who died at the age of one hundred and twenty, far outliving the man to whom in a shrewd manoeuvre she had promised to leave her apartment)" (19).[8] Comedy, irony, game-playing are all ways of keeping one's feet amid so many invitations not just to bleakness but to banality. Though some of the rules are set, there is considerable latitude in how one acts within them and how much attention one pays to them. But to say this much leaves still unaddressed the degree to which the latitude is less expansive in old age than with many other forms of social experience and social identity.

"Old Age" has some significant though brief further remarks to offer on the subgroup to which Mothersill belongs: that is, the academic profession as it shapes her relationship to the wider social situation. There are advantages that go with being a retired, but formerly tenured, member of the academic profession, she acknowledges. She enjoys some security, "reasonably good health," and ongoing projects to which she is committed. (Presumably she was familiar with Beauvoir's *La Vieillesse* (1970), translated as *The Coming of Age* (1972), and echoes here its closing

<hr/>

[8]   And see www.nytimes.com/1995/12/29/world/a-120-year-lease-on-life-out-lasts-apartment-heir.html.

injunction to pursue projects that take one out of oneself and ward off demoralization (Beauvoir 540–1), though Beauvoir is neither cited nor referenced.) The picture is not all rosy: the academic world is characterized, as Mothersill sees it, by an "even-handed and unattractive *ethos*" of competition (18). To be a retired academic, but still active (as academia, attractively, permits many of its members to be), is to encounter the brutal edge of that ethos. She has noticed "a slight but noticeable lack of interest on the part of some junior colleagues" (18), a development she sources less to ageism than to their correct assessment of the diminishing clout she wields in assisting them into permanent employment. (Taking on the presidency of the Eastern Division no doubt brought some retrieval of status.) In any event, the life of the ageing tenured academic is far better supported than the life of the average care worker.

It is salient to my purposes that, though this compacted account of Mothersill's essay makes no mention of gender (nor does her own summary), gender plays a significant role in the delivery of the argument. "I fault the feminists," she writes (14), in one of her most arresting claims. There is, surely, humour in the gambit: I take Mothersill to be an ironic player of the blame game, just as I take her 'negativity' to be held in a balancing act with a more positive or hopeful outlook on old age. What she faults the feminists for (what she faults them/us/herself for) is failure to act on some obvious social injustices – the constituency of the carer community among them – for which ameliorative collective action should be relatively easy to formulate. The women's movement has "paid insufficient attention to the fact that the pressing problems of old age are predominantly women's problems. Not only are there more of us – hence more who require care – but the caregivers themselves, family members or professionals, are overwhelmingly women" (14). There are, in other words, inequalities in the social experience of ageing that go beyond, though they include, first-person expectations for, and experience of, one's own later life. The inequalities impact down the generations and across the social field. Ninety per cent of nurses' aides in America are female, she observes; 30 per cent are black, Hispanic or Asian (14). They do poorly paid work with little training required – not even, in Ohio, a basic requirement of literacy; often, they enjoy no medical benefits of their own. Until the big socioeconomic picture is remedied, it is no wonder that women like herself who can avoid being in institutional residence guard their independence as long as possible (15). Worse, she suggests, feminism and the new gerontology seem to have entered into a kind of unhealthy alliance of interests (she does not put it quite so strongly, but the implication is clear enough): insofar as the gerontologists construe 'successful ageing' as, in essence, an ethical project in care of the self, they fail to make common cause with feminism to address the structural problem. Unless or until feminism stretches its focus from an individualist interest in ageing to a systemic consideration of attitudes, conditions, resources and identification of the mechanisms required to effect change, Mothersill suggests, the experience of old age will go on being, by and large, pretty miserable for the majority of people in contemporary society and especially miserable for women as a social group made visible by the sociological data.

The mode of argument here, activating the question of gender to expose a larger problem of imperfect fit between the general social picture and the individual writer's experience, is worth pausing over, coming from a philosopher who places a high value on rationality and is strongly inclined to distrust "dogmatic" generalizations (10). A theoretical attraction of the subject of ageing for Mothersill is the degree of contingency attending any individual's experience of it (hence the ironic invocation of the idea of a "game"). It is not just the outlying cases, like the old lady in Paris, that appeal to her. Generalities such as *to be old is to be experientially enriched* or *old age is to be "pitied (or shunned)" because it brings inevitable loss of biological fitness* are, she notes, of limited use to any of us individually. "Not all of us are pitiful wrecks" (implicitly, "I am not"), she observes, and those inclined to harp on their own experience are liable to become "sententious bores" (18). And yet the physiological "prognosis" is undeniably "gloomy": "we" (that beckoning first-person plural again) are increasingly susceptible to bone fractures, cancer, heart disease, arthritis, infections. And then there are the cognitive impairments: "loss of memory, deterioration of problem-solving ability. Not all of us will be Alzheimer's victims, but predictably all of us will suffer some form, mild or severe, of senile dementia" (15). So grim are the data, in this regard, that it is difficult, Mothersill suggests, not to suspect old-style gerontology of "a certain gloating" tendency on these matters; we can thank the positive gerontologists for shifting the "tone" (15), but the unwelcome "facts" (9) remain.

Unlike so many writers in literary and cultural criticism, Mothersill is not much interested in cultural stereotypes and pernicious cultural narratives *per se*, though she acknowledges their power. Stereotypes and negative stories do damage (she does not deny this), but her low-level ironization of old age as a proffered social identity (first "we, the oldies" (13), then "we, the hapless oldies" (15)) points the reader to a problem: how do we know which conventions have force for people and which don't? How do we know for whom (which individuals? which groups?) the types and stereotypes are 'dominant,' and why? These are questions of method for which social science has tools, albeit imperfect ones; they are not questions cultural criticism tends to trouble itself with much – and the castigatory attitude of much literary and cultural criticism toward stereotyping of old age is often, as a result, unrevealing, failing to ask the harder questions. To employ a familiar narrative or characterological stereotype is not necessarily to *credit* it – representation can be ironic, sarcastic, comic, even just lame – so how can we be confident about the degree of authority invested in repeating old tropes? Hardline cultural determinists will say that any use of a negative narrative or stereotype maintains its currency and should therefore be avoided, but Mothersill's persistent use of the first-person plural in that terrain asks us to think harder about the *critical* function of stereotyping in making old age visible to us as a collective identification that we will, at various points, have to work around and cannot simply wish away.

What, then, should we make of a self-styled 'rational' argument that puts pressure against generalizing about the ageing process while equally "faulting the feminists" for failing to address the general sociological picture? It would not, I think, be going too far to suggest feminism is a kind of holding card, in Mothersill's Presidential Address, for a political approach to ageing that she understands to be crucial to social progress but that, she discerns, has limited public appeal (given entrenched convictions, and the depressing nature of much of what is to be anticipated). Progress from such a starting point is the more unlikely, she suggests (and this is her major provocation to the gerontologists) as long as a positive ageing orthodoxy holds sway. If old age is not only endurable but better than endurable for many 'successful agers,' it is, she recognizes, because the sociological and economic data, and the broad expectations drawn from them, have had little or no effect on how those who age well shape their lives; on the other hand, to turn one's gaze away from the social reality of the many is a failure of moral and political nerve. What, then, should be "our" relationship to the old people around us and among whom we may already count ourselves? She puts the point, as I read her, neutrally, though others hear some negativity here:

> even a superficial survey of the practical and political problems associated with old age suggests ambivalence and emotional conflict. We can't decide how to treat the old people in our midst, old people whose numbers are increasing and whose demands are increasingly onerous. We do not know how to feel about a future that we anticipate and that most of us hope for. How do you prepare for eventualities when prediction is, at best, based on statistics? It may be that there is no general answer. (18)

The issue is not the one familiar to most humanists (and influentially developed by Theodore Porter, Mary Poovey and others):[9] the rightness and wrongness of our trust in numbers. "Old Age" steps over that problem, in part pragmatically: the numbers may well be imperfect (some data sets are certainly better than others), and the uses to which they are put are often open to question, but statistics rightly have authority in the fields of medicine and social care, where imperfect data may be better than no data. Artefactual as they are, they allow us to generalize about "old age" and discover overall tendencies. They provide no certainties about what will happen to us as individuals but they express social realities and tendencies, and there is reason to think that they play a significant role in our expectations for ourselves. The dilemma, as Mothersill articulates it, is that we must at once live our lives in cognizance of the general picture (assisting, where we can, responsible social action) and yet maintain ... what? The determination, hope, or just habit of asserting, for as long as possible, the exceptionalism of our experience from that of the many?

Two decades on from 1999 the broad social picture has moved on somewhat, but not so substantially that the questions Mothersill asks of our individual relationship to it can be argued away. The data on solitude, frailty, ill health, depression, care burdens, income, access to work, continue to tell an outline social story of accruing "ills" and marked gender inequality in late life that appear unlikely to be eradicated in the near future. Women, in the US and UK, continue to outlive men by, on average, 5 years in the US, 3.5 in the UK (Murphy et al., see also Raleigh) – but with only a small portion of that additional time in good health. The caregivers continue to be predominantly female. British "[w]omen have a 50:50 chance of providing care by the time they are 59; compared with men who have the same chance by the time they are 75 years old" (Storey et al.; George).[10] American figures are more starkly gender-differentiated: 65 per cent of the US's 45.3m unpaid carers today are female. One in four are millennials (thirty-four or younger) ("Caregiver

[9] See, for example, Theodore M. Porter, *Trust in Numbers: The Pursuit of Objectivity in Science and Public Life* (Princeton UP, 1995); Mary Poovey, *A History of the Modern Fact: Problems of Knowledge in the Sciences of Wealth and Society* (U of Chicago P, 1998), *The Finance System in Nineteenth-Century Britain* (Oxford UP, 2003), and, with Kevin R. Brine, *Finance in America: An Unfinished Story* (U of Chicago P, 2017).

[10] See also "10 Facts about Women and Caring in the UK on International Women's Day," drawing on 2011 Census data.

Statistics"; see also Schulz and Eden). The disproportionate reliance of the system on non-white carers remains (Graham); and we could add to Mothersill's sketch some stark data on regional disparities and on the vulnerability of the old to depression (Raleigh).[11] There *have* however been significant changes in how we can interpret some of the data, notably around dementia: advances in genome-based personalized medicine have brought refinements in our ability to discern individual probabilities. If genetic screening can tell me, for example, that I am one of the "small number of people (about one person in 50) [who] inherit two copies of [the] APOE ε4 [gene]" – one from each parent – meaning that I "may be more than eight times more likely to develop Alzheimer's," I will have a significantly different relationship to the overall statistics than the person (quite possibly my brother or sister) who does not have the same inheritance. I may be less likely to rest comforted by the Alzheimer's Society's (correct) statement that "due to other contributing factors, [I] still may never develop the disease" (O'Brien).[12]

This and other developments in personalized medicine are gradually shifting understanding. Dependent on public and private investment and further technological progress, personalized medicine looks likely in the future to narrow our relation to general social tendencies, leading us to anticipate some outcomes more securely than others. Even so, it will not quite obviate the force of Mothersill's question, posed in response not to any one physiological liability but to the accumulating cluster of diminishments in biological fitness and social capacity that attend old age. The emotional problem stands: how should we feel about old age, as we look to shape our expectations for ourselves in and against what we know will be the collective tendencies? It is a question for the individual *and* for the many: a question of how each of us looks toward our own future; and a question of how to keep the social reality – the predominantly negative picture, and the social responsibilities that should flow from it – in the frame. Recent developments do not falsify her sense that "how to feel,"

---

[11] See also *Suffering in Silence: Age Inequality in Older People's Mental Health Care*, Report of the Royal College of Psychiatrists (CR221) (November 2018), www.rcpsych.ac.uk/improving-care/campaigning-for-better-mental-health-policy/college-reports/2018-college-reports/cr221, p. 2.

[12] Cultural changes are also impacting upon expectations for the future: non-binary gender identifications and mixed ethnic and racial identifications have increased rapidly of late, particularly in the sixteen to thirty-four age group; as with all social diversification trends, it will take time for the effects to work through the statistical accounts of age profiles, but at some point they will presumably impact upon the social narratives we tell about old age.

though a critical question, may not be one susceptible to clear answers; nor her conclusion that some emotional perplexity may be inevitable and even appropriate to our situation.

* * *

The emotion of a literary text is not only a matter of representation (focused on how a character or characters feel), but a property of form and content working as a whole. Karen Chase puts the point succinctly:

> No one is likely to deny that literature and emotion are deeply entangled. The difficulty begins when we try to *locate* literary emotion. Our tendency is to look to the author, to the reader, or to the individual fictional character – and this is because we incline to regard emotion as a property of individual psychologies, fictional or otherwise. But certainly one of the most telling attributes of art is the way it works as a feeling whole. … The literary work is itself an internal organization of impulse; the text itself is a structure of emotion. (Chase 2–3)

On that holistic basis, Chase goes on to describe the evocation of emotion in, for example, early Dickens: violent and disturbing verbal energy, not emanating from the central ego (which tends to be weak), but distributed across a range of personalities and communicated primarily through the working of grammar, syntax, and styles of speech (ch. 2). By contrast, Charlotte Brontë's mature fiction expresses and manages emotion by harnessing the power of space: "the self, its relations, its dreads, its possibilities exist for Brontë as so many spatial configurations. Hope is … a wide expanse seen from a protected summit. Terror is … a barrier that encloses or … too suddenly drops away" (91).

To comprehend emotion as distributed across literary form and style is to open up an approach to the question of "how to feel" about old age equipped to go beyond a structural opposition between the social data and the personal narrative, admitting more complex, deeply connected ways of relating the individual experience to the larger picture. In that vein, Alice LaPlante's *Turn of Mind* stands out from the copious body of contemporary writing about old age by its choice of a genre and a narrative style that detach us from narrow concentration on character, presenting the quality and coherence of feeling about the known (but not quite determined) proximity of death as an involving problem, not a given. Narrated primarily from the perspective of Jennifer White, a retired orthopaedic surgeon (formerly a specialist in diseases and injuries of the hand), now struggling with the effects of Alzheimer's disease, *Turn of Mind* is a detective story with a feminist undercurrent largely implicit in the depiction of close solidarities between women. The crime that necessitates 'detection' is the maiming, after death, of Jennifer's former neighbour and closest friend, Amanda O'Toole: a fatal trauma to the head, then the four fingers of her right hand expertly severed. The challenge of the narrative consists in fathoming how far a functionally impaired mind may be capable of the key requirements for 'apprehension' of criminality in others or in oneself: agency, choice, motive, and (it may be) responsibility, regret, remorse.

This is a highly-plotted novel narrated primarily from the perspective of a woman whose condition makes it impossible for her to control plot, or to perceive her own part in it except via fragments of concentrated, diminishingly lucid memory. Completion of the narrative is assisted by the device of a notebook:[13] an *aide-mémoire* for Jennifer. Its pages play host from time to time to other agents of the story, including her children (Fiona and Mark), no longer reliably known to her; her carer (Magdalena), a woman in flight from her history even as Jennifer fights to retain her own; former colleagues (among them the doctor responsible for Jennifer's medical treatment). As Jennifer's condition worsens and she is moved into institutional care, the first-person narrative perspective and the notebook device that have dominated the first two parts of this four-part novel give way to a detached second-person: the voice in Jennifer's head, watching herself at a distance, remote but not quite relinquishing connection. The role of the female detective comes gradually to the fore in these later sections. Marginal to start with (occasionally threatening, but barely impinging on Jennifer's power to recall events), Detective Luton (*luttant*: [in French] fighting, struggling) will not give up, being driven by personal history to pursue this case. Having lost her life partner to early-onset Alzheimer's at only forty-five, she has a need to know that others, by implication, might not feel as strongly. Only in the final pages of *Turn of Mind* does she discover that Jennifer is, or was (technically), the 'criminal' of the story, but that the act was instinctive, driven by love; the motives (not hers alone) were multiple, ramifying through the years. It is in the nature of the case that full 'justice' will not be possible.

Critics with an eye on etymology often remind us that 'detection' derives from the Latin "*dētegĕre*, to uncover, discover, detect."[14] It is a

---

[13]   The notebook recalls a favoured technique of Victorian sensation fiction (Wilkie Collins's *The Woman in White* (1859–60) being among the most famous examples) – another genre that plays off rational intellection against the threat of inchoate 'sensation,' but tips the balance more toward the latter.

[14]   *OED* online, detect, *v.* See Kerrigan 71; Porter.

conceptual underpinning that allows for strong parallels between narrative inquiry into crime and inquiry into the nature of dementia. By matching the attenuated cognitive capacity of an Alzheimer's sufferer to the proceduralism of detective fiction LaPlante establishes a double distance on the experience of ageing and loss of cognition that mutes what might otherwise be an emotionally depleting scenario (one with which relatively few readers would choose to engage). To a degree, Robert A. Rushing observes, detective fiction generically mutes sympathetic realism: the crimes that set its plots in motion typically frame and aestheticize the initiating act of violence, displaying it as a problem to be solved, and diminishing its reality in the process. As he puts it, "the violence in detective fiction" provides a narrative decoy from the work of remembering, or putting back together: "the reader, far from engaging in cognitive activity, is engaged in *forgetting*, forgetting real violence in favour of a spectacle manufactured for his passive enjoyment" (Rushing 126). What might, in some contexts, be a weakness of the genre thus becomes, here, a strength: the effect is to place the reader in a position akin to that of Jennifer − our diminished 'cognition' mimicking hers − though the two situations are not, of course, the same. Kept in the dark, at the mercy of the narrative release of information, we, like her, are left in perplexity and suspicion, while being spared the potential for intimate distress. We, too, are rendered largely uncertain how, rightly, to feel; which is not to say that we cannot or do not sympathize with her predicament; rather that the sympathy we feel is qualified by uncertainty about how far we should trust what we feel. And as Jennifer deteriorates, and the abuse she sustains hardens, the detective genre's preference for rational control over sympathetic identification comes into its own.

The most obvious benefit of this generic rationalization is that it relaxes the force of negative feeling when the element of contingency in ageing (that space of chance that allows us to hope our own end may be better than the statistical patterns suggest) is foreclosed. With the dementia diagnosis, the bad future signalled through the statistics is here: confirmed, worse than the average indeed, though well within the range of 'expectation' if (as in Jennifer's case) dementia runs in the family line. The game has definitely turned against one. The *Verfremdungseffekt* of sorts provided by the detective genre softens the negative distress that accompanies the first revelation, and it is assisted here by the characterization of Jennifer as a woman possessed to an unusual degree of "a rational attitude" (in Mothersill's phrasing) − "[a]lways the clinician," as her daughter puts it with love as well as acidity (229). In her recollected past, and even in her impaired present, she is forensic: temperamentally inclined, and professionally trained, to distinguish between those matters she can do something about and those she cannot. So, Amanda's death (an "ill" – as Mothersill would put it – that must be re-discovered, repeatedly, as if for the first time) is registered, like her own disease, without self-disclosing emotionality. It is in keeping with the constant invitation to substitute intellection for feeling, here, that Amanda's part in the narrative goes beyond that of 'victim' to exhibit something like a *principle* of investment in full disclosure of hidden knowledge. She had, we gradually learn, an appetite for unwanted truths (the embezzling husband; the cheating husband – and wife; the resentful child) that made her, throughout her long friendship with Jennifer's family, a dangerous "intimate": as Jennifer describes her somewhat luridly to her ex-husband, she was a "foul-weather friend," a "vulture" with a "genius [for] spotting the carcass before it has begun to rot" (185). And yet she was genuinely a friend, her intrusions forgiven by a woman who has always preferred knowledge to ignorance.

To say that *Turn of Mind* operates in a mode that validates knowledge over and above feeling is not to underestimate its capacity to open up a range of emotional perspectives on Jennifer's dementia. There is comedy here, most vividly when Jennifer escapes the care home in which she has been subject to physical and pharmaceutical control, and embarks upon a last carnival of fleeting pleasures: to drink and eat in a bar; to become an object of unsolicited attention, and too quick identification, from a self-obsessed young woman; to consort with homeless men. And at the point where Jennifer finds herself confined again, to a more secure state institution, the grammar of lost agency provides a vantage point on suffering all the more emotionally powerful for stripping away its subject – almost, not quite, entirely: "Never felt guilt. Never felt shame. Until I was brought to this place. Trussed like a chicken. Denied the right to move my bowels in private. *Purgatory* I heard one of the other residents call it. But no. That implies that heaven is within reach once you have paid" (214). This is not a novel that traffics heavily in literary allusion, but LaPlante audibly channels Beckett as much as Dante at this moment, contemplating with denotative sharpness, in lieu of eloquent pathos, the humiliation of being without the most basic physical self-determination. (Earlier, Jennifer was capable of the raging self-assertion of *King Lear* – "No daughter! No husband! No son! No encumbrances. I will pack my bags" (91) – but her condition has taken her a long way from such thespian flourishes.) Not least, *Turn of Mind*'s forensic approach to its subject provides a language and a form for an under-described experience common (one suspects) to dementia sufferers, and that may be distressing and/or perplexing in any range of degrees: "You realize, suddenly, that you have been frightening people. That thing you see in their eyes is fear. But what have they to fear from you?" (245). Second-person articulation here offers not (as some recent philosophical writing would have it) an expressive basis for ethical connection, but rather the opposite: imagining a self frighteningly adrift both from first-person identification and from the security of otherness (he, she, it, not me ...). 'You' is frighteningly close, but not securely owned.

The trajectory of Jennifer's narrative is implacable, leading deep into this destruction of identity and "rotting" of intelligence (she is defiantly materialist; the choice of metaphors is her own). In keeping with its emphatic rationalism, however, *Turn of Mind* permits its subject more than one moment of lucidity in which she and it confront the problem of "how to feel." Everyone who interacts with Jennifer has reason to want to fathom her feelings and motives. In that context a dialogue with Sarah, her former assistant at the hospital, has the value of relative neutrality (unlike most of the interrogations Jennifer undergoes, it is inconsequential for the plot). Has Jennifer ever hoped for intervention from a higher power, Sarah asks? She means, in context, 'God' or a 'saint,' but the idea of praying for a divine miracle stands in for resistance – on any terms – to what will (other things being equal) happen in the near future:

[Sarah:] *No praying for a miracle?*
[Jennifer:] None whatsoever?
　How about just plain hope?
　None of that, either.
　... I'm sorry for prying. I guess I'm just wondering. How you keep going.
　At some point we die. Except under unusual circumstances, we usually get some advance warning. Some of us know sooner than others. You're asking, how do you endure that interval between when you know you're dying and when you actually die?
　Yes, I guess so.
　... I was stymied. No one asks me such things anymore. They ask me if I want tea. If I'm cold. If I want to listen to some Bach. Avoidance of the big questions.
　My deathbed wish?
　Well, not deathbed! But do you think you'll stay as practical as time progresses? Or will you ever be tempted to ask for the impossible?
　Part of my condition is that the line between those two things is increasingly blurred. ... A dear friend of mine just died.
　Yes, I heard. I'm sorry.
　And amid the grief and the anger, I found myself feeling gratitude – gratitude that it wasn't me. So at some level I still see death as something to be put off. ... it's not yet time. Not yet. (100–1)

So sustained a conversation, between dementia sufferer and inquiring witness, on "the big questions" may seem implausible. Clinically, it is credible, Jennifer being at this point a little over two years from diagnosis (90); what strain may be felt on the reader's credulity has more to do with the sense of an address *to us*, laying out the terms of an uncertainty about how Jennifer feels that is crucial to what can and cannot be 'detected' in *Turn of Mind*. There is, she asserts (in tune with Mothersill), something genuinely 'stymying' about the emotions set running by proximity to death in late life. The difficulty of articulation may be the greater because so little is conventionally said on the subject with those whom it most concerns. Commonplace tact and concern for the feelings of the old; in the case of those with dementia, a pre-emptive judgement of incompetence; plus, perhaps, some reluctance on the part of the old themselves to depress those not yet old – all these combine to prevent such conversations from happening. Jennifer's dementia is not, as she puts it, "unusual": it is "usually" the case that "we … get some advance warning," and that general truth remains applicable to the dementia sufferer, even as the disease compresses the gap between warning and end. Hope has no place in her account of herself. "Perhaps I'm not being clear," she tells her children (unaware that she has told them many times before): "This is a death sentence. The death of the mind" (136). There is no space here for irony, of the kind Mothersill enlists in the service of, if not hope, a rationalist's openness to the possibility of being an exception from the ills that accrue with age. The strongest emotions she admits are, as throughout, prompted by Amanda who, true to character, lays them bare but also keeps them at a remove: grief for the victim of violence (for Amanda, then, but also for Jennifer herself?), anger at the fact of maiming (including the maiming of this mind?). The most intimate emotion here is also the messiest, and most fungible: the compromising of grief and anger by gratitude at being, oneself, not quite dead yet … a gratitude that reveals to Jennifer her own desire, for now, to keep going.

One subtle thought here strikes more closely than the rest at the novel's own investment in maintaining a rational distance on its subject. It is in the nature of Alzheimer's disease, Jennifer observes (it is almost the last finely rational argument of which she is capable), gradually to collapse the 'line' between practical 'endurance' (the Stoic's rational answer to the ills of life) and the desire to escape the reality our reason detects. When the distinction goes, Jennifer seems to be saying, yes she may succumb to the "tempt[ation]" to go beyond practical acceptance into terrain she can still (just) understand to be irrational: desiring to live on, somehow, anyhow, when being the subject of one's own life is no longer possible.

Irrationality so close to the end is not, apparently, a prospect that frightens her, presumably because, when it happens, she will not be herself. Her conversation with Sarah is, indeed, remarkable for the quiet consistency with which it calls the younger woman's attention to the problem of owning and remaining the possessor of one's own subjectivity, given the prospect ahead: "Yes, I guess so"; "No one asks me ... anymore"; "I found myself feeling"; "it wasn't me."

Dementia is "a very hard thing to frame," LaPlante herself has commented in an interview: the emotions it gives rise to in those obliged to witness it and (until the late stages) those who suffer it, are exceptionally 'intense.' Her own mother's dementia was, she has let it be known, of a "particularly nasty strain" – "very, very difficult, very hard." When distress threatens to be engulfing, the containing "frame" becomes almost a necessity, certainly a relief (Flood). The potential pun there may have been inadvertent, but it seems true to the core aspiration to guard all of 'us' (the author included) from a violence that would be, treated as realism, intolerable, 'heartbreaking.' Such detachment from oneself (an achievement of the novel's form, as much as of its central character) will not be a universal preference in old age, but for those, like Mothersill, to whom a rational attitude recommends itself, it may offer a bulwark against tragedy.

All the more important, then, to step back from Jennifer's detachment, as also from Mothersill's concluding preference for Epicurean Stoicism, to take in the wider textual frames in which the call to reason is articulated. In both "Old Age" and *Turn of Mind* the problem of how to feel about one's own expectations of old age, given what 'we' know, is not a problem that simply dissolves under the application of reason. It is, after all, a dual form of dilemma. Calm detachment is the rationalist's answer to the problem of 'how to feel' about the nearer proximity of the end and the amplification *toward* the end of those "ills peculiar to old age." But there is a more intractable problem here of uncertainty: of knowing much but not everything, having a general frame of expectation but no really clear sight of one's own future within it. On the first count, rationality offers a respectable answer, perhaps the best many of us can look to. On the second, there are no good, certainly no perfect answers. The best we can hope for may be a response along the lines Mothersill and LaPlante suggest: a timely articulation of quite proper forms of perplexity, ambivalence, conflict.

Works Cited

Beauvoir, Simone de. *La Vieillesse.* Gallimard, 1970.

———. *The Coming of Age,* translated by Patrick O'Brian, G.P. Putnam's Sons, 1972.

"Caregiver Statistics: Demographics." Family Care Giver Alliance, 17 April 2019, www.caregiver.org/caregiver-statistics-demographics.

Chase, Karen. *Eros and Psyche: The Representation of Personality in Charlotte Brontë, Charles Dickens, George Eliot.* Methuen, 1984.

Flood, Alison. "Alice LaPlante: 'Alzheimer's Is a Hard Thing to Frame.'" *The Guardian,* 22 November 2011, www.theguardian.com/books/2011/nov/22/alice-laplante-alzheimers-turn-of-mind.

George, Mike. "It Could Be You: A Report on the Chances of Being a Carer." Carers UK, 2001.

Graham, Rachel. "Facts about Carers: Policy Briefing August 2019." Carers UK, www.carersuk.org/images/Facts_about_Carers_2019.pdf.

Johnson, K.J., and J.E. Mutchler. "The Emergence of a Positive Gerontology: From Disengagement to Social Involvement." *Gerontologist,* vol. 54, no. 1, 2004, pp. 93–100.

Kerrigan, John. *Revenge Tragedy: Aeschylus to Armageddon.* Clarendon Press, 1991.

McGrath, Colleen. "Negotiating 'Positive Ageing' in the Presence of Age-Related Vision Loss." International Network for Critical Gerontology, 10 March 2017, criticalgerontology.com/negotiating-positive-aging/.

Mothersill, Mary. "Review." *The Journal of Philosophy,* vol. 72, no. 2, 1975, pp. 27–48.

———. "Old Age." *Proceedings and Addresses of the American Philosophical Association,* vol. 73, no. 2, 1999, pp. 9–23.

———. "Make-Believe Morality and Fictional Worlds." *Art and Morality,* edited by José Luis Bermúdez and Sebastian Gardner, Routledge, 2002, pp. 74–94.

———. "Beauty and the Critic's Judgment: Remapping Aesthetics." *The Blackwell Guide to Aesthetics,* edited by Peter Kivy, Blackwell, 2004, pp. 152–66.

———. "Art and Emotion" [review of Derek Matravers's *Art and Emotion* (Oxford UP, 1998)]. *International Studies in Philosophy,* vol. 37, no. 4, 2005, pp. 153–4.

Murphy, Sherry L., et al. "Mortality in the United States, 2017. NCHS Data Brief No. 328." National Center for Health Statistics, November 2018, www.cdc.gov/nchs/products/databriefs/db328.htm.

O'Brien, Emma. "Why Do Some People Get Dementia and Not Others?" National Institute for Health Research, https://news.joindementiaresearch.nihr.ac.uk/people-get-dementia-not-others/.

Porter, Dennis. *The Pursuit of Crime: Art and Ideology in Detective Fiction.* Yale UP, 1981.

Raleigh, Veena. "What Is Happening to Life Expectancy in the UK?" The King's Fund, 2018; updated 22 October 2019, www.kingsfund.org.uk/publications/whats-happening-life-expectancy-uk.

Rushing, Robert A. *Resisting Arrest: Detective Fiction and Popular Culture.* Other Press, 2007.

Schulz, Richard, and Jill Eden, editors. "Older Adults Who Need Caregiving and the Family Caregivers Who Help Them." *Families Caring for an Aging America*. National Academies Press, 2016, www.ncbi.nlm.nih.gov/books/ NBK396397/.

Scranton, Roy. *Learning to Die in the Anthropocene: Reflections on the End of a Civilization*. City Lights Books, 2015.

Small, Helen. *The Long Life*. Oxford UP, 2007.

Storey, Angele, et al. "Living Longer: Caring in Later Working Life." Office for National Statistics, 15 March 2019, www.ons.gov.uk/peoplepopulationandcommunity/birthsdeathsandmarriages/ageing/articles/livinglongerhowourpopulationischangingandwhyitmatters/2019-03-15.

"10 Facts about Women and Caring in the UK on International Women's Day." Carers UK, www.carersuk.org/news-and-campaigns/features/10-facts-about-women-and-caring-in-the-uk-on-international-women-s-day.

Zimmermann, Martina. *The Poetics and Politics of Alzheimer's Disease Life-Writing*. Palgrave, 2017.

3

Ageing in the Anthropocene: The View From and Beyond Margaret Drabble's The Dark Flood Rises[1]

KATHLEEN WOODWARD

> It's a losing battle, you know; the fight against the ageing process.
> – Fran thinking about her life as a seventy-some-year-old
> (Drabble, 298)
>
> If we want to learn to live in the Anthropocene, we must first learn to die.
> Roy Scranton, *Learning to Die in the Anthropocene*, stressing that we need to accept the coming death of our civilization (27)

Fran's First Thoughts

Imagine: you are a woman "well-turned seventy," white, British, living alone and independently in London.[2] You are divorced and widowed, in that order. A mother of two. You are in good health, solidly middle-class, and employed by a charitable trust that supports research on housing for the elderly. Your name is Francesca Stubbs (such a glamorous name, but you're actually known as Fran) and you are the primary fictional character in Margaret Drabble's *The Dark Flood Rises*, a novel about ageing set in England after the turn of the millennium and published in 2016. The novel opens with your point of view, offering us your frame of mind – your thoughts and feelings, your restlessness, your apprehensiveness about ageing, all delivered in a kind of stream of consciousness steadied by the author's unobtrusive omniscience.

Here you are, driving by yourself (you do many things by yourself, and you like to drive). Off to a conference outside of London. To what

[1]   My heartfelt thanks to Elizabeth Barry, Margery Vibe Skagen, Stephen Katz, Sally Chivers, Ulla Kriebernegg, Suzanne Bailey, and Jesse Oak Taylor for their inspiration and invitations.
[2]   Drabble, *The Dark Flood Rises*, 19.

do your thoughts turn? The first two paragraphs of *The Dark Flood Rises* are devoted to your musing – perhaps fixating would be a more accurate word – on the different forms your death might take. There are three. One: you imagine you're driving too fast and crash head-on into a tree. Or that the furnace in your flat, not having been properly maintained, has sparked a lethal fire in which you are engulfed. This kind of death is both brutally accidental and satisfyingly expeditious. We accord special meaning to a person's final words by virtue of their being last. What are Fran's last words? "You bloody old fool," Fran thinks, addressing herself. Or stronger, "you fucking idiot," bluntly indicting herself as the cause of her imprudent death, internalizing responsibility for what is an accident (1). Moreover, at the imaginary scene of her death, Fran pictures herself alone, speaking only to herself, not to family or friends.

In the first paragraph of *The Dark Flood Rises*, Fran is thus presented as fantasizing – and, as we will see, essentially preferring – a violent, solitary, and accidental death of her own making to one that is old age-related and connected to the life around her. What is the nature of this kind of accidental death? It is commonplace. A car accident. An accident at home. The experience of ageing itself is represented as the middle-class tragedy that Fran must confront in twenty-first-century England.[3] Best to avoid, she thinks to herself, "all the inconveniences of old age" (1).

Two: ageing-to-death. This is the second form Fran imagines her death might take. In her view, the effect, if not the very purpose of such an accidental death, is to avoid ageing-to-death with its life-threatening and ultimately mortal collateral damage, either of the slow but decisive overall weakening of the body or of a terminal disease to be suffered, a death by disease like that of her second husband being "more insidious, less violent, more cruelly protracted" than an accidental death (3). Ominously, she is feeling the signs of invading old age. For as we learn in the second paragraph from the narrator, "Fran herself is already too old to die young, and too old to avoid bunions and arthritis, moles and blebs, weakening wrists, incipient but not yet treatable cataracts, and encroaching weariness" (1).

---

[3]   Drabble closes her deft first paragraph by contrasting the ordinary middle-classness of Fran Stubbs, and her fantasized banal if brutal death, with the heroic tragedy of Antigone whose death by her own hand followed in the wake of honouring her brother's body in death. "Antigone," she concludes, "had rejoiced to die young, and in a good (if to us pointless) cause, thereby avoiding all the inconveniences of old age" (1).

These physical deficits Fran calls *inconveniences.* The almost casual vocabulary Fran chooses to describe her situation may at first seem to diminish the threat of ageing, rendering the physical accompaniments of old age as somehow prosaic, mundane, *ordinary.* But in the very contemplation of the accumulation of the inconveniences of ageing, the overwhelming effect of the mortal prospect of ageing-to-death asserts itself in the second sentence of the second paragraph of the novel: "She can see that in time (and perhaps in not a very long time) all these annoyances will become so annoying that she will be willing to embark on one of those acts of reckless folly that will bring the whole thing to a rapid, perhaps a sensational ending" (1–2).

What? As a reader, I was jolted by Fran's pre-empting the process of ageing by an act "of reckless folly"! As she imagines the physical irritations and frustrations of ageing increasing, they become a cascade, reaching a psychological tipping point.

Three: with breathtaking speed she turns to contemplating suicide. Ageing-to-death is something to be avoided at literally all costs, including the cost of her life in the embrace of suicide.[4]

Do her thoughts strike you as obsessive? As extreme? As too dark? They get darker.

If the first phase is characterized by annoyances and inconveniences, the second phase, in Fran's view, is altogether dismaying: you find yourself (if you can!) "senseless, incontinent, demented, medicated into amnesia, aphasia, indignity" (29). Thus from the very beginning of the novel, Drabble offers us an imaginative world, much like that lived by many people today in neoliberal societies, where ageing is divided into two phases, or temporalities. Drawing on the vocabulary if not the precise distinction made almost fifty years ago by social gerontologist Bernice Neugarten between the 'young-old' and the 'old-old,'[5] we might char-

---

[4]   See my essay on literary critic and writer Carolyn Heilbrun who by all accounts committed suicide in order to avoid what I am calling old ageing; for Heilbrun, "physical ageing seems to have been defined as inescapable, unremitting, and unredeemed decline" as well as a disabling illness (289). See also my essay on frailty and disability under the title "Feeling Frail and National Statistical Panic." In *The Dark Flood Rises*, one of the minor characters, an accomplished actress who lives alone in London – I take her to be in her early eighties – does in fact commit suicide. Another has in his possession "a Magic Pill" for that very purpose (108).

[5]   For Neugarten, the young-old comprised the chronological age group of fifty-five to seventy-five, individuals who are, in her words, "relatively healthy, relatively affluent, relatively free from traditional responsibilities of work and

acterize these phases as 'young ageing' and 'old ageing,'[6] categories that resonate with the pervasive use of the terms the 'third age' and the 'fourth age' but place the emphasis on process and change rather than on a state of being.[7] Distinctions between these two phases of ageing have become commonplace in contemporary culture, with the final phase contemplated by many with fear, a fear that seems altogether reasonable.

The Dark Flood Rises invites us to ask: do you – do I – think of ageing this way?

As Fran thinks to herself, "We can all expect to live longer, but it's recently been claimed that the majority of us can expect to spend the last six years of our prolonged lives suffering from a serious illness, in some form of pain and ill health." The narrator adds: "Fran found this statistic, true or false, infuriating. Longevity has fucked up our pensions, our work-life balance, our health services, our housing, our happiness. It's fucked up old age itself" (44). In Fran's view it is not social institutions or attitudes that are to blame – for example, our society's regard, or disregard, for its older members. Fran indicts longevity itself, understanding it first and foremost as a negative biological fact. The additional years of life that constitute what is in Robert Butler's wise view a revolution in longevity to be embraced are for Fran to be feared as a virtually inevi-

---

family and who are increasingly well educated and politically active" (187); for her, it was the social event of retirement that first and foremost marked the 'young-old,' not the relatively benign biological markers of ageing as envisioned by Drabble (cataracts, arthritis, etc.). People over seventy-five, the old-old, were marked largely by the status of their health; it is only "at the very end of life," Neugarten writes, that "there will be a shorter or longer period of dependency and that increased numbers of the old-old will need special care" (198).

6   In a recent opinion piece for *The New York Times* the geriatrician Louise Aronson uses the terms the 'young old' and the 'old old,' drawing on the medical procedure of vaccination as a case in point to show that members of these subgroups "don't just differ in how they look and spend their days; they also differ biologically." She suggests we use the term 'oldhood,' associating this phase with biological ageing and differentiating it from 'adulthood'; "With good luck," she writes, "some people don't move from adulthood to what we might call 'oldhood' until their 70s, and occasionally later still."

7   The unease with which critical age scholars, including myself, regard such homogenizing terms is signalled by Stephen Katz's use of scare quotes in referencing the fourth age at the same time as he acknowledges the regrettable "academic tendency to neglect older and vulnerable 'fourth age' bodies, along with general ageist assumptions in the literature that loss of physical control symbolizes a passage into status decline" (125); his point is that contradictions are inevitably at work, with people experiencing "embodiments of ageing as a fractured process of resisting, accepting, denying and recreating ageing" (126).

table catastrophe.[8] As age studies scholars, we have devoted ourselves to elaborating how ageing is not a solely physical or biological phenomenon and underscoring how the experience of ageing is inflected by multiple dimensions of our lives, including gender, race, and class. But in *The Dark Flood Rises* human ageing is presented first and foremost in terms of the biological process of growing older. And Fran devotes herself to developing strategies she hopes will deflect the second phase, keeping it at bay.[9] She walks, she swims, she drives, she texts, she keeps moving. "If you keep moving, you don't get stuck," she insists to herself (195), bringing to mind Samuel Beckett's memorable character Winnie who, in the first act of his two-act play *Happy Days*, is stuck up to her waist in sand.

Today the third age is typically associated with 'productive' ageing or 'successful' ageing, normative notions that are problematic in and of themselves. But in her portrayal of Fran, Drabble gives the third age a dark twist: Fran is trying to prevent old ageing, to outrun it as she restlessly drives to conferences and housing complexes around England, learning about new technologies to assist the elderly and inspecting care homes. She does not so much regard these years as an opportunity but as a period of incrementally increasing biological annoyances, one that foreshadows the certain catastrophe to come. Relentlessly she broods on ageing, thinking about Shakespeare's *Macbeth* and Simone de Beauvoir's *La Vieillesse*, both brilliant texts but texts that lead us into a dark vision of ageing. To compound matters, haunting the novel is a premonition of devastating climate change to come, registered by Fran as she listens to the local TV news in her hotel room and learns of earthquakes in the area, small, yes, but *unpredictable.*

I have lingered on these opening pages for several reasons, not least of which is that Fran is the central character of the novel and it is pre-

[8]   In "History of Longevity Discourses," Margaret Gullette captures perfectly the focus of contemporary popular discourses on the risks to the individual of living longer lives – that is, lives understood to be too long.

[9]   In "'Third Age' under Neoliberalism," Shir Shimoni traces the changes in England from the mid-1980s to the mid-2010s in the meaning attributed to the third age, arguing that the third age – "a temporal-normative framework for making decisions about how to live one's life" – has shifted from being associated with risks to be avoided so as to maintain one's health to being linked with an individual's cultivation of themselves as an entrepreneurial subject who embraces the possibility of life-changing adventures and flourishes in risk-taking (40). The beginning of 'young ageing' or the 'third age' varies of course, but it would be safe to say Fran is portrayed as beyond the beginning; Fran falls into the category of those who are active and avoid risks (although she does drive too fast!).

dominantly through her that Drabble introduces us to the other major characters (three of them are in their mid-seventies, and, like Fran, they regularly reflect on ageing, the central preoccupation of their lives). The opening pages also constitute the longest section in the novel, running to thirty-two pages in my edition. The rest of *The Dark Flood Rises* shifts, quasi-cinematically, from the point of view of one character to another (sometimes two at a time), with sections of much smaller length, some just a few pages long, a few as little as a paragraph. As a first-time reader of the novel, this narrative strategy created for me the illusion of a vast swath of characters, in great part because I couldn't keep them straight or rightly remember them. But looking back, in fact there aren't so many. And their stories, as they unfold over the two-month period of the novel, largely confirm – and thus amplify and intensify – the preoccupation with ageing-to-death as a senseless and inevitable bodily vulnerability that consumes Fran Stubbs.

If at first the world of *The Dark Flood Rises* appears panoramic with its cast of hundreds, it is in fact not only small, it is homogeneous. This is not the London of a Zadie Smith or a Salman Rushdie. In effect Drabble has highlighted the salience of the biological definition of ageing and old age by bracketing multiple markers of identity and meaning. All the main characters in their mid-seventies are white, and thus the experience of racism, for these characters, is not an issue. They are also sturdily – some of them even comfortably – middle-class, and therefore financial precarity is not a chief concern. With one major exception, religious faith is also not a core element of their lives. And, crucially, with the exception of a gay couple (Sir Carpenter Bennett and his long-time partner Ivor live on Lanzarote, one of the Canary Islands), all live alone in London and its environs. (Some members of the younger generation also live very much alone, with Fran's daughter Poppet being a notable case in point.) During the greater part of the novel, these characters in their seventies lead predominantly independent lives, inhabiting the phase of young ageing, related to each other by family, friendship, and chains of association (so-and-so knew so-and-so's husband), but functioning more as nodes in networks than in terms of meaningful relations of intimacy, preferring largely anonymous spaces and detached relationships with other people.

The attachments of Fran in particular are minimal, strangely so. She has, for example, developed the habit of delivering meals to her first husband who is virtually housebound, confined by a serious chronic illness to his bed in his up-scale flat. But the two of them aren't at all close. She typically doesn't even stay to eat with him. And for his part, he ungenerously appraises Fran as "withered and skinny and relentless now" (106). When Fran is travelling and finds herself stranded because of flooding, she is reluctant – seriously! – to contact her only daughter who lives in the vicinity. Fran has few cherished memories. Her parents do not constitute an important part of her psychic life; in fact, her mind turns to them only twice during the entire length of this 325-page novel, the first when she notes to herself that neither of them had suffered from dementia, providing her with genetic hope. And her grandchildren? They too do not play a valued role in her life; her son acknowledges that she has been "fairly hopeless and absent and inattentive" as a grandmother (77). As she confesses to herself toward the end of *The Dark Flood Rises*, her loneliness is "terminal" (320). When the narrator offers us a glimpse of her feeling with full force, "a grief for all things," it comes as a surprise both to her and to me as a reader:

> Fran feels a great tearfulness rising up in her, a grief for all things, a grief for her daughter and thence, from that grief, a grief for all things. She had feared that she would outlive such grief, that her heart would grow thick and cold, that grief would ebb from her as sexual hope and desire and much (though not yet all) of her social optimism had ebbed from her. … She had thought that ageing would bring calm and indifference and impersonality. (227)

Later in the novel I was grateful to learn that she felt the dull thud of knowledge in learning that one of her two close friends – but how close? not very – had died, casting in stark relief the basic superficiality of her emotional life, its essential hollowness. Her mind is busy with all matter of details and thoughts. But her life is virtually evacuated of vitality, meaningful connections to others, and a seriousness of purpose, although she does feel she is doing good work with regard to housing for the elderly (as a reader, I confess I don't find Fran's work in housing for the elderly compelling as a key aspect of her life; rather, it seems to have been chosen by Drabble as a logical choice for her character, that is, for resonating with the focus of the novel on ageing).

In *The Dark Flood Rises* Drabble makes an illuminating distinction between a *comfort*, which is heartening on a prosaic level and is predominantly a bodily sensation of a lack of anxiety as well as a feeling of low-level pleasure, and *solace*, which offers consolation and meaning on another plane altogether. What does Fran look forward to? The reassurance of the impersonal regularity and anonymity of a middle-class hotel chain; it is "safe and familiar" (319). Small pleasures. A few glasses of wine (she thinks frequently about wine). A soft-boiled egg prepared by the hotel chain precisely as she prefers it. These are her comforts. They are often experienced when she is alone, eating breakfast, for example, at her preferred middle-class hotel after "a good night, comfortable, pain-free in a big white wide premier bed" (22).

Solace, for instance, is experienced by Teresa Quinn, Fran's close friend from childhood.[10] Teresa is dying of mesothelioma. She is suffering and in pain. She is old ageing, close to death.[11] Teresa's faith – she is Catholic – and her despair lend her life meaning as does her strong love for her son Luke, who lives in Mozambique. He arrives at her bedside. Her deathbed. As they hold hands, Teresa's last words recount – for the final time – the story of his birth. It is a moving scene, resonant with meaning and a moral temporality, a striking contrast with the empty secular time in which Fran and her former husband live, one that is fundamentally devoid of higher aspirations. As the middlebrow Fran thinks, pragmatically, ironically, of herself, she "doesn't mind platitudes. A few platitudes, every now and then, are restful" (38).

This deathbed scene stands in blunt contrast to the everyday world of the novel. My point is that the world of ageing and the elderly in *The Dark Flood Rises* is populated primarily by individuals in the neoliberal sense. They are not bound together by a cohesive sense of an imagined community, whether national, religious, or otherwise. There is no collective affect of solidarity. Fran understands clearly that there are no valued social roles for the old and that the elderly are not venerable; she epitomizes the older person for whom life has largely been reduced to work (and we might add that she is lucky to have that). She equates the second phase of ageing with "uselessness" (16). Nor do there appear to be major obligations to the elderly on the part of the state. I'm reminded of Britain's Margaret Thatcher who famously said, inaugurating a neoliberal order in 1987, "there is no such thing as society. There are individual men and women and there are *families*." In the case of *The Dark Flood Rises* it is barely clear there are families.

---

[10] Solace – provided by faith and by literature – is experienced by two other characters. Ivor finds that his being is uplifted by praying, secretly and without words, in a small and empty chapel on Lanzarote; understanding that such solace may be false, he finds "there's more truth in it than in the endless discussions about doctors, diets, symptoms and medications" (75). Jo Drummond experiences "the surviving force and power" and "solace" in poems, plays, and novels (123).

[11] Close childhood friends who lost track of each other, Fran and Teresa have recently discovered they are both living in London and working in the caring professions. With Teresa, Fran is, as Drabble puts it in the opening section of the novel, "enjoying a curious last fling of intimacy. Teresa is dying, but she is dying with such style and commitment that Fran is deeply impressed and encouraged by this last passage" (21). It is telling that intimacy is something "curious" to Fran.

Indeed to me the novel underscores the Foucauldian argument that power is administered in Western societies in terms of populations, with demographic categories (the young, the sick, and the imprisoned, for example) central to managing society. Add to this that in neoliberal societies, such as Fran's, the state has progressively withdrawn from assuming responsibility for the care of its citizens, thus producing the relative isolation of ageing individuals who find themselves largely responsible for their own well-being, care, and even death (remember the ominous opening of the novel). Housing for the elderly – that is, the cordoning off of a segment of the population – is emblematic of this. Remember: Fran's job entails housing for the elderly. And in fact at dinner the night before Fran's conference on sheltered housing begins (this is the conference she is driving to as the novel opens), one of the people at Fran's table launches into a story about having recently visited a housing project where the elderly are trapped in a high rise, the building itself described as "ageing," one "which boasted (as do so many) the highest proportion of trapped and isolated old folk in Europe – the usual story, non-functioning lifts, unlit stairwells, disabilities, gangrene, graffiti: children, grandchildren and great grandchildren all in jail: gangs in the shopping precinct, carers who didn't care and didn't show or wouldn't stay more than five minutes" (18). It is a horrifying vision. As Fran notes, "cohabitation is forced upon the ill and the elderly, but more and more of the able-bodied in their mid-life choose to live alone" (3). Under these conditions, who wouldn't prefer to live alone! I hope I will not be stretching a point if, echoing anthropologist Elizabeth Povinelli's work on precarity and economies of abandonment (a key focus of her book is Australian aboriginal communities), I call the practice of cordoning off of the elderly in housing specifically for them *ordinary abandonment*. Sociality and belonging have been hollowed out in those high rises and, by extension, in other housing for the old as well. This form of abandonment is so ordinary that it recedes from view, scarcely recognizable as producing the aloneness and isolation of the elderly, a category of people in part as a very result of this process.

Ultimately how peculiar and empty and white is the vision of ageing in the novel. It may appear 'normal,' with its division of ageing into two predominantly biological phases that are presented as essentially neutral and objective – from the inconveniences of bunioned feet to the cross-to-bear that is mesothelioma. It may seem altogether familiar to many of her readers, that is to say, a commonsensical way of regarding biological ageing. Young (biological) ageing: surgery for cataracts, medication for hypertension, hip replacement, exercises for balance, endless appointments with doctors, altogether an accumulation of annoyances and inconveniences. Followed by a period of acute debility and grave health crises: old (biological) ageing. Yet for the seventy-plus-year-old characters we meet in *The Dark Flood Rises*, the distinction does seems to be a logical outgrowth of the neoliberal society in which they – and we – are immersed, one in which the subjectivities associated with health and illness are an all-consuming preoccupation, ageism is pervasive, and values that bind people together in meaningful and intimate ways are largely absent. And, we cannot forget, suffering at the hands of biological decline and ultimate death *is* an existential threat that will necessarily come, as Paul Higgs and Chris Gilleard insist.[12] It is compounded by the collapse of care on the part of the state, rendering it altogether reasonable to fear old ageing.

Ironically, the division of ageing into two phases is a result of a certain middle-class white privilege (and of course upper-class too), with the gains in longevity implicitly understood to be a birthright, even if the final years are to be feared, a 'gift' one would like to return. 'Good ageing' is succeeded by 'bad ageing.' Margaret Drabble's novel provides us with an imaginative space to think our way, feelingly, through this normative sequencing of bodily time at the end of life.[13]

The Narrator's Last Words

The opening of *The Dark Flood Rises*, which establishes Fran as its central character with ageing her preoccupation, primes us to wonder about her final words and the manner of her death. In fact, answering these questions could be said to be the very plot of the novel. Near its end Fran reflects on her experience over the past two months and is forced to acknowledge that she has

---

[12]   I agree with Higgs and Gilleard who argue that ageism is too totalizing a concept – they maintain it has risen in contemporary culture to the mistaken status of an ideology – with which to understand in particular the specific bodily experiences of old age. They endorse the vocabulary and basic distinctions of the third age and the fourth age – the third age associated with agency and self-expression, the fourth age with existential fears about ageing and decline, including frailty and the need for care, and death. "Put at the centre of analysis," they write, "this bifurcation between an 'aspirational' and a 'feared' later life avoids some of the more obvious contradictions that have beset the 'ageism as ideology' approach" (3).

[13]   At the same time, Drabble does not focus at length on characters in the second phase of ageing who suffer from extreme bodily insults over a long period of time (we learn of the stroke of Sir Bennett for instance, but not much more than that); chronicling a long-term chronic illness over a period of time in a novel presents a much more difficult challenge than portraying an acute crisis.

aged significantly. "She'd been a lot younger," she thinks, "two months ago. She'd been walking steadily on a plateau, for years, through her sixties into her seventies, but now she's suddenly taken a step down. That's what happens. She knows all about it. She's been warned many times about this downward step, the lower shelf" (319). We know that her friend Teresa has died. As the novel draws to a close we also learn that her friend Jo Drummond has passed away unexpectedly in her sleep – of cardiac arrhythmia. And Fran?

Brilliantly, Drabble withholds from us knowledge of Fran's last days, months, years. We don't learn how much time she had left and how she lived it. Nor do we know Fran's last words, a genre that had fascinated her from an early age, or the manner of her death. The final two pages of the novel are entitled "Envoi," which, as the Merriam-Webster dictionary defines it, is "the usually explanatory or commendatory concluding remarks to a poem, essay, or book." Instead of Fran's last words we are offered those of the narrator. In these two pages Fran does not even figure as a main character. We learn that Fran has died in a paragraph cast primarily from the point of view of a minor character *and* in a single sentence filled with other characters who too have died, including one whom we might only dimly recall or not even recognize: "Owen England outlived Bennett Carpenter and Fran Stubbs and Claude Stubbs and Simon Aguilera. They are all dead now." The narrator adds, deploying an annoying Olympian 'we': "We won't stand upon the order or the manner of their going" (325). I am tempted to call it a neoliberal 'we.' These people, reduced to names, are of no real importance now. If we cared deeply for Fran as a character, we might even indict the narrator for abandoning her.

As a reader I had lived through pages of Fran's thoughts and feelings and, while not captivated completely by her as a character, I had come to be curious about her fate and to enjoy her. She has a headstrong quality and gift for candour with herself that I admire. She had become a kind of intimate. But at the novel's end the narrator has surgically removed Fran from the landscape of the living as definitively as if she had been isolated in sheltered housing for the elderly, deemed 'useless' by society, receding from view – and from care. Once the central character, Fran is suddenly – and altogether impersonally – grouped with three other people, all now dead, with nothing to differentiate them but the fact that they are gone. As readers, we are thus denied the experience of mourning her, of feeling a sharp grief or the dull thud of knowledge, of contemplating what caring about her has meant to us. And we can't know whether she died instantly in a violent accident, of a slow but ultimately overwhelming cascade of biological insults, or by her own suicidal hand.

Drabble made the decision to neither confirm nor deny her character's forebodings about ageing-to-death. Drabble avoids – or, we might say, refuses – to give Fran's individual experience too much weight by showcasing it in the end, concluding – I am of course speculating – that offering us Fran's last words would have bestowed upon them far too much import. Drabble understands that while a literary portrait of an individual can illuminate and expand our understanding of the experience of others and ourselves, we can't generalize from it. This is one of the reasons, I suspect, that even in the homogeneous orbit of *The Dark Flood Rises* Drabble has given her characters vastly different experiences of young ageing and old ageing.[14] But the way Drabble has structured her novel assures that Fran's fears – and the categorizing of ageing into 'young ageing' and 'old ageing' – carry the weight of the narrative. What emerges in *The Dark Flood Rises* as 'normal' in terms of ageing in relation to the human life course is a phase of benign ageing in the form of the accumulation of *inconveniences* followed by a phase of pain and ill health. At the same time, this normative view of ageing – its emphasis on the neoliberal individual's biological experience of ageing as divided into two phases – is in fact decidedly singular. For as I have stressed, the world of the characters in *The Dark Flood Rises* is small and homogeneous, a network of white middle-class English citizens who, in addition, share intellectual interests.

Ageing in the Anthropocene

Ageing in Drabble's novel is circumscribed by the constricting values of neoliberal society. Ageing in England is haunted by another prospect too, one that is planetary in nature. The ominous title of the novel, we remember, is *The Dark Flood Rises*. One of its singular achievements is the dramatic juxtaposition of the temporality of human ageing, as experienced in the small and homogeneous world of its characters, and the long duration of geological time.[15] It surprises me to realize that in addition to Fran's fate as a character, what I remember most vividly from the novel is not the everyday travails of the main characters as they live into ageing but rather the increasing threat of apocalyptic flooding, catastrophic earthquakes,

[14]   We also see this embodied in exceptions that prove the rule. Fran, for instance, considers Dorothy, a woman who has suffered from dementia for years and lives in a group home, as "truly old," although she is in fact Fran's chronological age (44).

[15]   Wayne Hope reserves the term 'temporality' for human existence: temporality for him "is the ground for thinking about the relationalities that connect past, present and future. Temporality thus involves memory, expectation and attention to the present" (22).

and volcanic eruptions, threats that seem at several points in the novel to be imminent, only to recede. I found the most powerful effect – an affect, really – of the novel to be the fearful feeling of the recognition of the impersonal and explosive force to come of tectonic planetary shifts, the earth cracking, the human species to be extinguished perhaps in the process. I was worried for Fran when she became stranded on a flooded highway, wondering if this was to be a titanic catastrophe. Would she be killed in tumultuous floods?[16] A few pages later Drabble returns to the thread of Fran's story as if nothing had happened. I was afraid for Bennett and Ivor on the island of Lanzarote as a cascade of small earthquakes nearby appeared to be radiating outward, coming closer to their home. Would the two of them be lost?

With the exception of Fran's daughter Poppet, the characters are virtually oblivious to the import of these threats on the planetary level. In her mid-forties, allergic to multiple substances, living alone, and working from her cottage in the countryside (she does statistical work), Poppet cares deeply about the planet and tracks extreme weather events through the internet website Climate Crisis (she can follow tornadoes in Texas, forest fires in Sumatra, earthquakes in the Canary Islands). But if the other characters are not concerned with climate change, we as readers, along with the author and the narrator, can fathom and feel with fear what they can't. Midway through the novel the omniscient narrator tells us that the crack in the earth beneath the Atlantic Ocean and near the Canary Islands is widening, creating an atmosphere for the reader of imminent catastrophe (174). And here Fran proves prescient in an ironic sense. I have neglected to mention until now that in the first thirty-two pages of the novel (remember, they are devoted to her point of view), she imagines a fourth way she might die – in a cataclysm of earthquakes, an extraordinary event, not an ordinary accident.[17] Planetary apocalypse haunts her psyche but seldom rises to the surface.

[16]   The extreme flooding that England experienced in November 2000 was associated with climate change.

[17]   The narrator takes care to insist that Fran has in fact always been interested in earthquakes – a planetary event – albeit in a manic posthuman way: in the opening pages of the novel we learn that Fran "has often thought it would be fun to be in at the end, and no blame attached. One wouldn't want to be *responsible* for the end, but one might like to be there and know it was all over, the whole bang stupid pointless unnecessarily painful experiment. An asteroid could do it, or an earthquake, or any other impartial inhuman violent act of the earth or the universe. She can't understand the human race's desire to perpetuate itself, to go on living at all costs" (10).

The well-known Indian author Amitav Ghosh has indicted novelists for not engaging with the urgent and momentous problem of climate change.[18] He argues suggestively that the aesthetic form of the modern novel itself, embedded as it is in the regularity of the ordinary and the small scale of the mundane, militates against it, given that climate change is characterized by wild, outsized, and unpredictable events. For me the triumph of *The Dark Flood Rises* is precisely that Drabble imagines the collision of ordinary human time experienced in terms of the orderly expectations of middle-class life regarding longevity (as phobic as the fourth age might be regarded), with the *longue durée* of geological time, time punctuated by inevitable if unpredictable large-scale catastrophe. Drabble renders this *longue durée* of geological time palpable without having to borrow from the genres of science fiction and fantasy, genres that Ghosh argues are more conducive to representing the dangers of climate change. If Drabble does not share with us the final days, or months, or years of Fran's life, whether it takes the form of steady incremental decline or acute deterioration and disease (or both, in that order), Drabble does write climate change into her novel. Ostensibly serving as a kind of background in *The Dark Flood Rises*, planetary-scale phenomena rise to the surface.

Indeed, as I worried for several of the characters threatened by floods and earthquakes as individuals, my mind turned to the coming potential consequences of climate change on the level of the collective human species. A dark truth about the future hit me with the thud of understanding. Through *The Dark Flood Rises* we glimpse the momentous transition in which we find ourselves in regard to ageing and longevity: we are moving from a century characterized by unprecedented gains in longevity, a kind of golden age of ageing, albeit only for certain people, and entering an era that will, I have no doubt, be characterized by losses in longevity. The scientists Simon Lewis and Mark Maslin assert in the very third sentence of *The Human Planet: How We Created the Anthropocene*, the "Earth now supports 7.5 billion people living, on average, longer and physically healthier lives than at any time in our history" (3). How could living longer and physically healthier lives ever be sustained into the ever-coming-closer future characterized by climate change? Imagine: fears regarding ageing such as

---

[18]   See Stephanie LeMenager's essay on climate change and genre in which she identifies "the weather section of *The New York Times*" as presenting us with a new Anthropocene genre, an anti-obituary that brings news of "de-individualized bodies arrayed amid story-fallen trees and flooded streets," "news without the therapeutic structuring of plot, the obituary denied the familiar arc of an individual life" (221).

those Fran experiences as she visualizes ageing into her eighties could well be regarded as quaint in the future. In his recent book *Down to Earth: Politics in the New Climatic Regime* the French philosopher Bruno Latour argues that rising inequality, increasing migration, and climate change constitute a single global phenomenon, "*one and the same threat*" (9). Margaret Drabble too understands climate change as a threat-multiplier, driving this point home with a subplot about present and imminent waves of immigration from Africa and the Middle East, people fleeing famine as well as war, possibly casualties of climate change. If Foucault understood the work of the modern state as managing populations, now the prospect is the crashing of populations from other countries on the shore.

Methodologically, I began this essay focusing on the opening pages of Drabble's novel and then pivoted to consider the concluding pages, tying the two together. Attention to first and last words, close reading: it is a time-honoured mode of literary criticism, one I especially love because it anchors us to the imaginative world of the text. But *The Dark Flood Rises* has also spun me surprisingly loose from the text, inviting me – as one of its readers – to open up the question of the relationship between ageing and the Anthropocene, or more pointedly, about ageing *in* the Anthropocene. As I have already suggested, scales of time are central to thinking about the Anthropocene. We might refer to the ground-breaking work of the historian Dipesh Chakrabarty, for instance, who helpfully distinguishes among three different timescales – geological time, the time of the evolution of life on the planet, and the time of world history or human history (with the history of capitalism a prime narrative). He argues that our epoch is distinguished by the imbrication – the entanglement – of these three timescales for the first time.[19] To these timescales I want to add a composite fourth, the smallest of the four: human life expectancy and human lifespan.

How can we bring together the fields of critical age studies and humanistic studies of climate change, fields that to my knowledge have not been in conversation with each other?[20] Assemble two piles of recent books

[19]   In "The Human Condition in the Anthropocene," Chakrabarty, drawing on the phenomenology of Heidegger, begins to develop the idea of how the experience of the affect of falling (he calls it a mood in the ontological, not psychological sense), of falling into deep time, discloses to us in a flash of understanding the crisis that is climate change – and that is our radical decentring.

[20]   I'm inspired not only by Drabble's novel but also by recent essays focused on the relationship between critical age studies and postcolonial studies. See Rüdiger Kunow and Silke van Dyke.

intended for an educated general reading public for each of them: you
will find no entries in the indexes of either pile that refer to the other.[21]
What lines of inquiry might we follow? What might we do? Here are some
questions we might pose:

- How do imaginative worlds and works – in literature, theatre, cinema
  and new media – disclose to us multiple dimensions of the possible
  relationships between ageing and climate change?
- Drawing on what has come to be called the new materialism as well as
  other fields, how might we design research projects to study the differing concepts of ageing, longevity, death, and extinction throughout human history and across objects (a planet, for example), species,
  and organisms of different scales and times?[22]
- Considering that the complex matter of climate justice is often raised
  on behalf of the poor and people of colour, as well as primarily in
  terms of uneven impacts on nations (so-called developed nations and
  their others, including India and China), how might we pose questions of climate justice – and climate refugees – in relation to ageing
  and the elderly?[23]

[21]   Consider the recently published books on climate change intended for an
educated public audience by Naomi Klein, Elizabeth Kolbert, Simon Lewis and
Mark Maslin, and David Wallace-Wells (see Works Cited for further details);
in the indexes you will find no references to ageing. Similarly, in the recently
published books on ageing intended for an educated public readership by Robert
Butler, Margaret Gullette, Ashton Applewhite, and Louise Aronson (see Works
Cited), there are no entries in the indexes for climate change or global warming.
The only publication I have found that addresses this conjunction is a special
issue of *Generations* on ageing and the environment (climate change is specifically mentioned), edited by Kathy Sykes and Karl Pillemer; they name climate
change as "the biggest global health threat of the twenty-first century" (7) and
point out that research in public health "suggests that environmental problems
disproportionally compromise the health of the older population" (8). For more
informal work on disaster and ageing, see the four postings on the blog of the
Association for Anthropology, Gerontology, and the Life Course under the title
of "Aging in an Age of Climate Change": https://anthropologyandgerontology.
com/aging-in-an-age-of-climate-change-part-1/.
[22]   We might consider, for instance, the evocation of "forest time" in Richard
Powers's magnificent novel *The Overstory* (255).
[23]   In the literature on climate change, the demographic and geographical categories generally evoked are the poor, people of colour, and the Global South,
not the elderly. More unusual is a reference to a particular person. See Stephanie
LeMenager's essay "Climate Change and the Struggle for Genre"; as she notes,
Ta-Nehisi Coates concludes his eloquent memoir, written as a letter to his son

- What core principles should guide our inquiries? Collaboration among disciplines? Consultation across sectors? A respect for long spans of time as embodied in the subjects and objects of inquiry?

- What do elders in indigenous nations, societies, and cultures have to teach others about how they have conceptualized and lived their relationship to the Earth and to each other, and how do they understand their place in the world today, especially in connection with climate change?[24]

- Is there a way to draw on the potential power of the old to resist the denial of climate change and to advocate for social practices at all levels – local, regional, national, and global – to combat climate change? Would this require imagining a new role for the old (or some of the old) that recognizes their – our – unique place in world history as demographically the largest old age cohort that has ever existed and at a time of catastrophic threat to the human species?[25]

- And finally, how can we deploy the categories of young and old, and the heuristic of generational time with its affective power, to deepen our understanding of the gravity of climate change and the peril we – and others in the biosphere – face?

---

about the danger of being black in America, on the note of climate change. In terms of ageing, Ghosh, in *The Great Derangement*, briefly relates the story of his elderly mother's inviolable attachment to her family home in Kolkata – to place – notwithstanding the extreme risk she faces from climate change (53).

[24] In "Cli-fi, Petroculture, and the Environmental Humanities," Stephanie LeMenager reminds us that given the history of settler colonialism, the domains of environmental humanities and indigenous studies are difficult to reconcile; she counsels care in not appropriating or simplifying indigenous ideas, pointing out that it needs to be recognized "that some aspects of the post-human thought which has been so revelatory for those of us coming from a settler perspective only begins to approach the never-humanist thought systems of indigenous philosophers" (162).

[25] As reported in *The New York Times* by Sharon Jayson, the number of grandparents as a percentage of the population in the United States has soared, reaching 69.5 million in 2014, an increase of 24 per cent since 2001. See historian Gerald Gruman's far-reaching essay on "The Cultural Origins of Present-Day 'Age-ism'" in which he argues that the development of an older demographic – or what is called population ageing – is a salutary mark of modernity and that, contrary to an ageist prejudice that sees old people as having no future, *"the ageing population does have a future, as it becomes re-engaged at the frontier of modern cultural adaptation and realization through historical time"* (380). If Gruman were to write his essay today he might well consider such engagement as related to climate change. Elders Climate Action is the name of an organization devoted to the issue of climate change.

Allow me to pursue briefly the latter question, one that in great part has to do with the rhetoric of persuasion regarding climate change, and one that will return us to *The Dark Flood Rises*.

In discussions of climate change it is common to encounter the assertion that it is impossible for human beings to grasp the magnitude of the scale of geological time. Why? Because, it is argued, we are constitutionally incapable of stretching our imagination beyond two or three or four generations, a critical constraint that, when compounded by the thickets of political processes, renders it virtually impossible to address the coming catastrophe of climate change. As Chakrabarty writes in "Anthropocene Time," "if we do not take into account Earth-history processes that outscale our very human sense of time, we do not quite see the depth of the predicament that confronts humans today" (6). In *The Long Thaw: How Humans Are Changing the Next 100,000 Years of Earth's Climate*, computational ocean chemist David Archer lays out the science of climate change in matter-of-fact prose, explaining events in the planet's geological past and rehearsing scenarios for the future in terms of carbon cycle feedbacks. "Looking forward, a century is about how far I can really imagine," he acknowledges, thinking in terms of generations. "Sixty years is grandchildren. One hundred is great grandchildren or great, great grandchildren" (5). He does not, however, pursue the interweaving of the two – climate change and generational thinking, or, perhaps better, generational imagination. And as the narrator of *The Dark Flood Rises* comments toward the end of the book, referring to global warming, "Although it's a hot topic, paradoxically, it simultaneously lacks urgency. People can't get their minds around the time spans involved" (299).

I want to suggest, on the contrary, that we can draw on what I am calling generational time as a strength or capacity of imagination rather than a crippling constraint, embracing it rather than considering it a limitation to press home the urgency presented by climate change. Importantly, generational time involves us affectively as well as cognitively.[26] Entailing two, three, and four generations, perhaps even more, generational time is our singular way of understanding future time, linking us in altogether meaningful ways to others whose futures we care about deeply. I am convinced in fact that the most influential way to frame the dangers of climate change is precisely in terms of the future of generations who are our intimates or whom we *feel* to be our intimates – our children and our grandchildren, and by extension,

[26]   See Kyle Bladow and Jennifer Ladino's collection of original essays on affect theory and ecocriticism.

children and grandchildren around the globe.[27] Invoking children is a familiar rhetorical strategy in arguments for policy change in virtually all domains.[28] It can be a cynical and manipulative strategy. But it certainly need not be. Our children are profoundly important to us. But my stipulation – it is a hope – is this: we need to take care to represent generational time in terms of entire lives. We need to imagine not just children as young children but as adults living into old age – that is, *growing up and growing old* in a world defined by climate change to come. We need to envision the members of the generations who will follow us living out the full measure of their days and lives, with the crucial timescale being human life expectancy and the lifespan.[29] We need to write old people – elders – into arguments and narratives about climate change, valuing them – and our own future – as we value children, and insisting on the worth of longevity as a human good.[30] I have long been taken with the psychoanalyst D.W. Winnicott's understanding – so deftly put – that there is no such thing as a baby, meaning that a baby cannot exist in isolation but depends upon the love and care of a parental figure to thrive, as elders depend on those younger. We need to embrace interdependencies across the life course, understanding that whole lives and generational reciprocity are at stake.

---

[27]   Some may object that this understanding of generations – with a focus on generational continuity – privileges and protects the idea of the family; it does. At this point in time, when the survival of the human species is at stake, we need to imagine a future in terms of biological reproduction. I agree with Ian Baucom who argues that "the function of engaged critique must pivot from one focused on infra-human concerns for the struggle of freedom to one focused on the trans-human category of species" (3–4). In this essay I am unable to consider the important matter of the lives of non-human animals.

[28]   See, for example, Sarah Ensor's "Terminal Regions: Queer Ecocriticism at the End." "Children," she points out, "traditionally serve as the trump card in the pocket of mainstream environmental thought" (53).

[29]   Here we might consider the arguments – specifically their rhetorical posture in relation to generations, youth and age, and the full course of human life – in *Juliana v. United States* (2015), a landmark lawsuit against the United States on behalf of children who are aggrieved by the concrete effects of climate change as well as by its future threats. "By 2100, these Youth Plaintiffs (many of whom should still be alive), and future generations, would live in a climate system that is no longer conducive to their survival," the lawsuit states, calling attention, albeit briefly, to the consequences of climate change on the ability to enjoy long lives (36).

[30]   In *Restoring the Quality of Our Environment*, a US White House Report issued by the Environmental Pollution Panel in 1956, longevity was specifically mentioned as being threatened by anthropogenic pollutants, including carbon dioxide. See https://babel.hathitrust.org/cgi/pt?id=ucl.b4116127;view=1up;seq=9.

The philosopher Samuel Scheffler, addressing generational questions in relation to climate change, calls attention to what he terms our worrisome 'temporal parochialism.' Even as we have become more cosmopolitan geographically, with interdependencies proliferating around the globe, we have become, he argues, more parochial in relation to those who came before us and will come after us. As he writes, "our sense of the connections among different human generations has become increasingly impoverished, as compared, say, with more traditional societies, which often had rich and vivid conceptions of the importance of *ancestors* and *descendants* and of the continuity of the generations" (3). It strikes me that Fran exemplifies this poverty of generational imagination.[31]

Consider, for example, the recently published book *The Uninhabitable Earth: Life after Warming* by the American writer David Wallace-Wells. He is unsparing in terms of what he foresees as catastrophic climate change. He also tells us in passing – it is a very important remark – that in 2018 he and his wife had a baby girl while he was writing his book. When the twenty-first century comes to an end, he says, his daughter will be old. As a reader, I couldn't help but calculate precisely how old his young daughter would be in 2100 and I found myself struggling to imagine the bleak if not horrific environment in which this old woman, today a child, would find herself. In *The Uninhabitable Earth*, Wallace-Wells holds in tension the virtually certain experience of "climate suffering" in the too-near future (153) and "the ready optimism" that a child represents (135). Reading his book, I register the urgency of climate change today. As Wallace-Wells says elsewhere, "Climate change isn't a reason not to have kids. Kids are a reason to stop climate change" (Twitter, 20 December 2018, 10:40 am).

We might consider as well the altogether wise book on climate change by psychiatrist Robert Jay Lifton. Writing after he had turned ninety, Lifton concludes his meditation on the affective twin threats to the human

---

[31]   In his moving and intelligent memoir *My Father's Keeper: The Story of a Gay Son and His Aging Parents*, Jonathan Silin tells us he has come to understand that his parents, so absorbed by their incapacities and the demands of everyday life in their old age, are unable to attach themselves in meaningful ways to the past or the future, suggesting to me that psychic connections to the past and the future or, as I've called it, generational imagination, may very well be lost to us in periods of deep biological distress compounded by everyday stress. He writes, "Caring for my parents, I see what it is like to be locked in the moment, devoid of all connections backward or forward. They can only think from day to day, their calendar marked by visits to the various doctors and visits from other healthcare personnel … They don't look forward … The future is filled with anxiety" (27). Elsewhere he writes, "the unyielding demands of the body imprison my parents in the present" (50).

species of annihilation from nuclear war and climate change by invoking generational time – or what we might call generational attachment. I quote his last words, the inspiring last paragraph of his book:

> Why does this all matter to a ninety-year-old man who will not himself experience the worst climate disasters that might await our species? For me it is simply a matter of that larger human connectedness. Whatever our age, we are part of a bond much greater than ourselves, part of a flow of endless generations that include forbears as well as children and grand-children. The bond is not only biological but is related to all we do and experience in the world. This principle of the great chain of being – and I speak as a secular person – takes on special importance as we approach the end of individual life. The human chain has never been more aware of the mind's capacity for attending to our species by renewing and enhanc-ing our habitat. Of course it is very late in the game, but at the same time far from too late. (*The Climate Swerve: Reflections on Mind, Hope, and Survival*, 155–6)

I take his words as my own: whatever our age, we are part of a bond much greater than ourselves, part of a flow of endless generations that include forebears as well as children and grandchildren. But are we part of a flow of endless generations?

On the level of everyday life, closer to my own home, literally, I can point to one of my neighbours, a woman my age. She wakes up in the middle of the night fearing for her children (she has two) and grandchildren (she has three) because of the horrific prospects of climate change (she wants her son to move away from New York's coast). What is she doing besides worrying? She has campaigned for Jay Inslee, Washington State's governor and in 2019 a candidate for president of the United States; his primary political issue was climate change. (I contributed to his campaign.) It bothers me that Fran in *The Dark Flood Rises* isn't worrying for her daughter – and her daughter *studies* climate change. I find myself wishing she had a capacity for generational attachment.

Finally, I am convinced that it is completely unnecessary to fully comprehend the scale of geological time in order to wake up to the threat of climate change. In fact, the future could be said to be here, now, in embryo. As Ursula Heise writes in *Imagining Extinction: The Cultural Meanings of Endangered Species*, the very power of the concept of the word 'Anthropocene,' "resides not in its scientific definition of a geological epoch, but in its capacity to cast the present as a future that has already arrived" (67). As Roy Scranton astutely writes in his book *Learning to Die in the Anthropocene*, by which he means learning to accept that civilization as we know it will necessarily change, *"Everybody already knows"* (68). If we have associated climate change in the past with geological time, the *longue durée*, and small incremental differences, recent events – the floods, the cyclones, the earthquakes – have transformed our relationship to the time of climate change. The future has moved into the present. As Ghosh has written in *The Great Derangement*, "we have entered a time when the wild is the norm" (8).

A Final Portrait

Rhetorically, books on global warming, climate change, and the Anthropocene close on a note of hope. And interestingly, toward the very end of *The Dark Flood Rises*, Drabble offers a measure of hope to Fran, alleviating, at least for the moment, her anxieties about old ageing-to-death. The scene is a closing party reminiscent of those found in novels by Virginia Woolf, a reception following the memorial for Jo Drummond. Quite by accident Fran meets an old woman nearing ninety in the powder room. It turns out they had met before. Here is the final paragraph of this section of the novel:

> There is something extraordinarily gallant and moving about Betty, the survivor, the noble atheist of the left. She is nearing ninety, and yet she shines with an undiminished, with an increasing radiance … Fran could not have said, will not be able to say, what it is that speaks to her through Betty Figueroa, who has travelled the oceans of the wide world and come home to Cambridge to rest. It is a light from another world, from another shore, from a distant mountain … for a while, sitting amidst the chatter and the crumbs and the growing debris with Betty, in the same haven, she is almost at peace. (313)

Whatever you may think about the prose of this passage (I find the tone overly sentimental), the import is clear: simply being with this lovely woman who is a generation older provides solace to Fran. Betty also represents for Fran an ideal old woman, a "self-contained, undemanding, fortifying" woman who has lived an adventurous and inspiring life and whose aura is magnetic and enigmatic (122). In this novel devoted to ageing, she embodies a good old age, having remained in good health and, so far at least, escaped what Shir Shimoni calls the 'temporal-normative framework' of ageing that has guided Fran's life as an older woman, ageing divided into young ageing and old ageing. She represents the ardent desire to live to an old age characterized by a long health span, a large number of years when one is illness-free, avoiding the misery of being "incontinent, demented, and medicated into amnesia" (29).[32] This is not the first time Drabble has deployed the narrative strategy of staging a meeting between women of different generations. Her novel *A Natural Curiosity*, published in 1989, also concludes by offering a positive model for older women. At its end, three middle-class white women in their mid-fifties set off to see an older woman, a woman of wealth and wit whom I imagine to be in her mid-seventies. Like *The Dark Flood Rises*, *A Natural Curiosity* is quite long and introduces us to a panoramic world of characters of many ages. It concludes by giving this older woman the closing paragraphs, the last word, the final line of the narrative, one that promises a meeting of generations in a mode of "pleasurable anticipation" (309). I take the ending of *A Natural Curiosity* as a warm invitation to women to invent ways of being older – positively – given the virtual absence of compelling models for older women at the time it was published. I also take the ending of the novel as an invitation to middle-aged women to take time with older women, developing a strong sense of generational time and establishing attachments across generations at the farther end of age. I am drawn to the idea of creating connections between generations in the service of modelling ageing in a positive vein for older women. In truth, to me it is more than an idea, it is an *ideal*.

But what are the implications for ageing – and future generations – in the epoch of the Anthropocene? As a thought experiment, we might ask an impolite question, drawing on the knowledge that Drabble was seventy-seven when *The Dark Flood Rises* was published (she was born in 1939). Can we imagine Drabble writing, twenty years from now, a novel that concludes with a near one-hundred year-old woman visiting a woman a generation older? The answer is assuredly no. If the longevity revolution has increased life expectancy for many over the course of the last century, climate change will take an enormous and sobering toll on what has come to seem for many a birthright – living into one's nineties and beyond. Life expectancy will diminish, perhaps plummet. Perhaps the human lifespan itself will shrink.[33] Thus as the human population

---

[32]   Early in the novel Drabble offers her readers a glimpse of an ideal figure of an old man; he is indigenous to Lanzarote, tending a garden: "A stocky old man, naked, his broad back and shoulders towards them, was trundling a wheelbarrow full of weeds towards a small smoking bonfire. His back was the burned red brown of red clay, he was Adam, he was the first and last man in Paradise. The red sun was setting, tingeing his solid elderly ruddy flesh with its radiance" (56).

[33]   The important distinction between life expectancy and the lifespan is often

grows more vulnerable in the epoch of the Anthropocene, one of the losses we may very well have to anticipate and bear is the loss of years as older adults – of age. In fact, life expectancy has recently decreased for the first time in the history of modern Britain. It has also decreased in the United States.[34] Today our challenge is not to invent role models of older women, as it was in great part twenty years ago. In the face of climate change, that seems trivial.[35] We need to turn our face to a future longer than that of our individual lives. I want to say to Fran: stop obsessing about ageing, there is work to do!

The Posthuman and Dieback

I return briefly to the immense frame of geological time. If we think about human life expectancy and the lifespan not in relation to previous and future generations but in relation to the cataclysmic cracking of the earth, the scale of human life expectancy and the lifespan shrinks even further in the epoch of the Anthropocene – not just literally in terms of the count of human years, but in terms of significance in the large order of the universe. The import of human life expectancy in Drabble's England is diminished as the measure of things in the enormity of the face and frame of the non-human. What this allows us to glimpse is that as age studies scholars we have understood the coming of old age – existentially and socially – as limned by historical conditions, with the historical implicitly conceptualized as the history of the human. As Tobias Menely and Jesse Oak Taylor write in *Anthropocene Reading*, "In the Anthropocene all scholars are called upon to become Earth system humanists, which involves thinking about how these systems interrelate with, internalize, and destabilize one another" (4).

misunderstood. The human lifespan refers to the upper limit of years of life of the human species, generally understood to be 115 years. Life expectancy, on the other hand, is dependent upon many factors, including biological insults, such as serious disease and a toxic environment. Lewis and Maslin make this mistake when they observe that there has been "impressive recent progress in human lifespans" (369).

[34]   Stephen Castle in *The New York Times.*

[35]   Twenty years ago we did not have a capacious living archive of models of vital old women. What we did have – it was an auspicious moment historically – was a developing feminist consciousness of older women as a group, what I called in "Inventing Generational Models" a *generational consciousness* of older women. I argued then that we need to think beyond the Freudian familial model of two generations to three generations and that we needed ourselves to create models of old women attached to other generations, models that do not necessarily depend on identification. Here I am arguing that we think in terms of three to four generations (or more) but for another reason altogether – climate change.

For me *The Dark Flood Rises* opened up a space of reflection about climate change, attesting to the power of the literary imagination. The scholarly world, with its conferences and the editing of books, gave me deadlines to articulate my thoughts. I've attended scholarly colloquia and conferences about the Anthropocene and have read widely about climate change (unlike close reading, this is what I would call ordinary reading). But it was *The Dark Flood Rises* that led me to climate change through critical age studies and in the process disclosed to me – and I hope to others – a facet of how a posthuman age studies might begin to take shape. It led me to consider the relevance of the catastrophic event of forest dieback – recently in the news because of fires in the Amazon rain forest – to the possible future fate of the human species. Once a tipping point has been reached because of the consequences of climate change, a forest can self-destruct. That may well be the fate of the human species intertwined as we are with the lives and deaths of other species.

Envoi

I want to close on the last scene in *The Dark Flood Rises* that features Fran and is told from her point of view. We find her in her favoured middle-class hotel resolving to soldier on, to put one foot in front of the other, even as she registers her "despair" and "terminal loneliness" (320). The very last we see of her she is having dinner (curry and merlot), alone. This hotel and this meal: they offer her comfort. But we also see her taking a moment of pleasure in the grandmother with her four-year-old grandson at a table nearby. "It's a small moment," comments the narrator, reminding us of the stake we have in generational attachment, "but it will see her more cheerfully on her way, in the morning, to the unknown destination. Seeing it through, that's the best she can do" (323).[36] If this small moment doesn't rise to the level of solace, it does take her out of the sphere of her solitude. I like to think that perhaps, even at this late date, Francesca Stubbs is practising generational thinking, stretching her capacity to imagine generational time into the future.

---

[36] I commented earlier on my use of close reading as a methodology as well as what I call invitational reading and ordinary reading. Here, methodologically, I am mirroring the structure of the text as a way of giving my commentary form that takes inspiration from the art of the novel itself.

Works Cited

Applewhite, Ashton. *This Chair Rocks: A Manifesto Against Ageism.* Macmillan, 2019.

Archer, David. *The Long Thaw: How Humans Are Changing the Next 100,000 Years of Earth's Climate.* Princeton UP, 2009.

Aronson, Louise. "Stop Treating 70- and 90-Year Olds the Same." *The New York Times,* 11 August 2017. https://nyti.ms/2vpTYj1.

———. *Elderhood: Redefining Aging, Transforming Medicine, Reimagining Life.* Bloomsbury, 2019.

Baucom, Ian. "History 4: Postcolonial Method and Anthropocene Time." *Cambridge Journal of Postcolonial Literary Inquiry,* vol. 1, no. 1, 2018, pp. 123–42.

Bladow, Kyle, and Jennifer Ladino, editors. *Affective Ecocriticism: Emotion, Embodiment Environment.* U of Nebraska P, 2019.

Butler, Robert N. *The Longevity Revolution: The Benefits and Challenges of Living a Long Life.* PublicAffairs, 2008.

Castle, Stephen. "Shortchanged: Why British Life Expectancy Has Stalled." *The New York Times,* 30 August 2019. https://nyti.ms/2Lcq1uY.

Chakrabarty, Dipesh. "The Human Condition in the Anthropocene." 2015, p. 181. The Tanner Lectures. https://tannerlectures.utah.edu/Chakrabarty%20manuscript.pdf.

———. "Anthropocene Time." *History and Theory,* vol. 57, no. 1, 2018, pp. 5–32.

Drabble, Margaret. *A Natural Curiosity.* Viking, 1989.

———. *The Dark Flood Rises.* Farrar, Straus, and Giroux, 2016.

Ensor, Sarah. "Terminal Regions: Queer Ecocriticism at the End." *Against Life,* edited by Alastair Hunt and Stephanie Youngblood, Northwestern UP, 2016, pp. 41–55.

Ghosh, Amitav. *The Great Derangement: Climate Change and the Unthinkable.* U of Chicago P, 2016.

———. "Writing the Unimaginable." *The American Scholar,* Autumn 2016, pp. 42–53.

Gruman, Gerald. "The Cultural Origins of Present-Day 'Age-ism': The Modernization of the Life Cycle." *Ageing and the Elderly: Humanistic Perspectives in Gerontology,* edited by Stuart F. Spicker, Kathleen Woodward, and David D. Van Tassel, Humanities P, 1978, pp. 359–87.

Gullette, Margaret Morganroth. *Ending Ageism, or How Not to Shoot Old People.* Rutgers UP, 2017.

———. "History of Longevity Discourses." *Encyclopedia of Gerontology and Population Aging,* edited by Danan Gu and Matthew E. Dupre, Springer, 2019. https://link.springer.com/referencework/10.1007/978-3-319-69892-2.

Heise, Ursula. *Imagining Extinction: The Cultural Meanings of Endangered Species.* U of Chicago P, 2016.

Higgs, Paul, and Chris Gilleard. "The Ideology of Ageism *versus* the Social Imaginary of the Fourth Age: Two Differing Approaches to the Negative Contexts of Old Age." *Ageing and Society,* vol. 19, 2019, pp. 1–14.

Hope, Wayne. *Time, Communication and Global Capitalism.* Palgrave Macmillan, 2016.

Jayson, Sharon. "More Grandparents Than Ever." *The New York Times,* 20 March 2017. https://nyti.ms/2nsBPy6.

Katz, Stephen. "Part Two: Introduction." *Ageing in Everyday Life: Materialities and Embodiments*, edited by Stephen Katz. Policy P, 2018, pp. 125–6.

Klein, Naomi. *This Changes Everything: Capitalism vs. the Climate*. Simon and Schuster, 2014.

Kolbert, Elizabeth. *The Sixth Extinction: An Unnatural History*. Henry Holt, 2014.

Kunow, Rüdiger. "Postcolonial Theory and Old Age: An Explorative Essay." *Journal of Aging Studies*, vol. 39, 2016, pp. 101–8.

Latour, Bruno. *Down to Earth: Politics in the New Climatic Regime* [2017]. Translated by Catherine Porter. Polity P, 2018.

LeMenager, Stephanie. "Climate Change and the Struggle for Genre." *Anthropocene Reading: Literary History in Geologic Times*, edited by Tobias Menely and Jesse Oak Taylor. Pennsylvania State UP, 2017, pp. 220–38.

———. An interview conducted by River Ramuglia. "Cli-fi, Petroculture, and the Environmental Humanities." *Studies in the Novel*, vol. 50, no. 1, 2018, pp. 154–64.

Lewis, Simon L., and Mark A. Maslin. *The Human Planet: How We Created the Anthropocene*. Yale UP, 2018.

Lifton, Robert Jay. *The Climate Swerve: Reflections on Mind, Hope, and Survival*. New Press, 2017.

Menely, Tobias and Jesse Oak Taylor, editors. "Introduction." *Anthropocene Reading: Literary History in Geologic Times*. Pennsylvania State UP, 2017, pp. 1–24.

Neugarten, Bernice L. "Age Groups in American Society and the Rise of the Young-Old." *Annals of the American Academy of Political and Social Science*, vol. 415, 1974, pp. 187–98.

Povinelli, Elizabeth. *Economies of Abandonment: Social Belonging and Endurance in Late Liberalism*. Duke UP, 2011.

Powers, Richard. *The Overstory*. W.W. Norton, 2018.

Scheffler, Samuel. *Why Worry about Future Generations?* Oxford UP, 2018.

Shimoni, Shir. "'Third Age' under Neoliberalism: From Risky Subject to Human Capital." *Journal of Aging Studies*, vol. 47, 2018, pp. 39–48.

Silin, Jonathan G. *My Father's Keeper: The Story of a Gay Son and His Aging Parents*. Beacon P, 2006.

Sykes, Kathy, and Karl Pillemer, editors. "The Intersection of Aging and the Environment." *Generations*, vol. 33, no. 4, 2009–10.

Thatcher, Margaret. "Interview: 'Aids, Education, and the Year 2000!'" with Douglas Keay for *Woman's Own*, 31 October 1987, pp. 8–10.

Van Dyke, Silke. "The Othering of Old Age: Insights from Postcolonial Studies." *Journal of Aging Studies*, vol. 39, 2016, pp. 109–20.

Wallace-Wells, David. *The Uninhabitable Earth: Life after Warming*. Penguin Random House, 2019.

Woodward, Kathleen. "Inventing Generational Models: Psychoanalysis, Feminism, Literature." *Figuring Age: Psychoanalysis, Bodies, Generations*, edited by Woodward. Indiana UP, 1999, pp. 149–68.

———. "The Legacy of Carolyn Heilbrun." *Tulsa Studies in Women's Literature*, vol. 24, no. 2, 2005, pp. 283–90.

———. "Feeling Frail and National Statistical Panic: Joan Didion in *Blue Nights* and the American Economy at Risk." *Age, Culture, Humanities*, no. 2, 2015, pp. 347–67.

4

Age and Anachronism in Contemporary Dystopian Fiction

SARAH FALCUS

Dystopian novels of the late twentieth and early twenty-first centuries are inherently concerned with the exploration of lateness in the form of what Frank Kermode calls 'the sense of an ending,' an expression of apocalyptic thinking through writing and reading. It is, as many have pointed out, no surprise that in the time of mediatization, consumerism, globalization, ecological devastation and rapid technological change, writers have increasingly turned to the dystopian imagination. Many of these texts take the form of what Raffaella Baccolini and Tom Moylan call critical dystopias, texts which "maintain a utopian impulse" (7) in their critical exploration of our contemporary moment. Through their dystopian visions, critical dystopias force us to confront our present and so hold out the possibility of change, of a different future. Dystopian fiction exploits a feeling of species precarity and lateness, whether this is due to war, technological overreaching, illness/plague, ecological devastation and/or a combination of these factors and others. It evokes species (and often planetary) vulnerability, as Tom Moylan has argued in his *Scraps of the Untainted Sky*, at the same time as it warns the reader that such a future *may* be avoided.

Central to many of these dystopian visions is a form of generational anachronism, or disorder. In these worlds, apocalyptic environmental and social collapse frequently results in, and is often tied to, societies where the life course, progress and the promise of the future are all disrupted by threats to generational continuity. These may take the form of mass infertility, the danger of longevity, uncontrolled population growth or decline, and/or technological changes to the nature of the human. Underlying these events may be globalization and migration, war and violence, technological development, or illness and plague. They may remain unexplained. Nevertheless, the anachronism that then results is both reflective of science and speculative fiction's central concern with time and the future, and specifically a temporal anxiety that brings together a sense of individual, species and planetary lateness. Threats to the future, and by extension therefore our ways of imagining the future, are both inextricably linked to and metonymically represented by generational disorder and by figures of ageing. Our sense of an ending therefore depends upon and foregrounds narratives of ageing and generational identity, making ageing itself fundamental to dystopian writing.

Generational order is, of course, important to much fiction. Generational success and security are aligned to the reproduction of social norms and structures: reproduction therefore ensures the future as the past. Central to this figuration of time – in fiction and in broader cultural understanding – is the child. Drawing on Carolyn Steedman's *Strange Dislocations*, Rebekah Sheldon considers the link between the child and the future that develops through the long nineteenth century, arguing that:

> The link forged between the child and the species helped to shape eugenic historiography, focalized reproduction as a matter of concern for racial nationalism, and made the child a mode of timekeeping. Through a developmental model that linked embryonic growth to the succession of evolutionary forms, the child came to summarize the deep biological past of the species. At the same time, the child's own reproductive potential subsumed her individual growth within the broader story of generational succession and lineage. Thus the child became legible not only as a record of the past but as a recipient of a specific biological inheritance freighted with consequence for the future. (3)

Into the twentieth century psychoanalysis and psychology are brought to bear on the image of the child to make her "cipher for the future of the adult and … cipher for the future of the species" (4). In this study of the child as a figure of the future in American culture, Sheldon is building on Lee Edelman's polemic critique of what he terms 'reproductive futurism' in *No Future: Queer Theory and the Death Drive*. As John Brenkman summarizes Edelman's position: "the appeal of these figures of the child lies in their power to awaken our nostalgic identification with the innocent and fulfillable child … and then link the child's promised fulfilment and identity to a better future, which inevitably turns out to be the present social and cultural order purged of its troubling and threatening elements" (175). For Edelman, in the image of the child as the future, reproductive futurism "impose[s] an ideological limit on political discourse as such, preserving in the process the absolute privilege of heteronormativity by rendering unthinkable, by casting outside the political domain, the possibility of a queer resistance to this organizing principle of communal relation" (2). The figure of the child therefore promises a (heteronormative) future that is nevertheless simply an extension of the same, minus anything that currently disturbs the body politic.

Sara Ahmed nevertheless offers us another way to consider the role of the child in her discussion of dystopian film: "Given that all of us face no future as finite beings, the thought of the future might be the thought of the human, or the thought of what Marx calls 'species being.' Without there being a species, individual being, by implication, becomes pointless" (183). She acknowledges that this humanist turn to the next generation takes us back to Edelman's reproductive futurism, but insists that children here signify the future that we need in order to persist in the present:

> It is not that 'no children' simply means 'no future' but that 'no children' signifies the loss of a fantasy of the future as that which can compensate me for my suffering; it is the very fantasy that there is something or somebody who I suffer for that is threatened. If what it is for is what comes after, in this survival logic of deferral, then the loss of 'the after' is experienced as the loss of 'the for.' (Ahmed 183)

Accepting that this does not mean we should leave unquestioned the implications of the signifier of the child as the future, she nevertheless insists that what the child shows us is the "anxiety of hope" (Ahmed 184) central to thinking about the future.

This focus on the child as the figure of futurity, whether this is an inevitable "survival logic of deferral" or a heteronormative suppression of the queer, may blind us to its shadow side: the figure of the old person and the spectre of ageing itself. Though the child is indeed the "cipher of the adult" (Sheldon 4) and representative of a "broader story of generational succession and lineage" (Sheldon 3), her efficacy as symbol of the future paradoxically depends upon her as a child, stuck in a stasis that resolutely ignores the potential lifespan and the possibility of ageing. The child promises the future, but only ever as a continuation of the same. And this promise, despite its inherent replication, is nevertheless premised on leaving behind those who represent the past: the old.

Cynthia Port, like Sheldon, draws on Edelman's use of queer theory to interrogate the heteronormative temporality of reproductive futurism, but links this specifically to ageing studies and the devaluation of age itself in contemporary (specifically American) culture:

> No longer employed, not reproducing, perhaps technologically illiterate, and frequently without disposable income, the old are often, like queers, figured by the cultural imagination as being outside mainstream temporali-

ties and standing in the way of, rather than contributing to, the promise of the future … And like queers, the old have projected onto their bodies that which normative culture fears and represses within itself: the knowledge of eventual bodily failure and mortality. (3)

This reading of time, progress and ageing is not new. As Mary Russo pointed out in her essay on anachronism in 1990 (also referenced by Port), "progressivism still dominates the commonsensical notions of a life course, generational difference, and social change. Hope, desire, understanding, and optimism seem ineluctably joined against the forces of the past, the backward, the unenlightened, the old" (21). Underpinning the future as imagined in and signified by the figure of the child, therefore, is the image of the old as the past, as redundant and as an obstacle to that future.

Critiquing futurity and the progress model, Russo advocates the celebration of anachronism and risk: "Anachronism means literally 'against time.' More, generally, however, it refers to an historical misplacement … Thus, as I understand it, anachronism is a mistake in the normative systematization of time. As such one *risks* anachronism" (21). My use of anachronism in this article adopts this very broad reading of it as a mistake in the 'normative systematization' – or generational organization – of time. What follows is an analysis of two dystopian novels that depict the risks of generational anachronism in their representations of future societies afflicted by problems with reproduction. P.D. James's *The Children of Men* (1992) imagines an England in which there is mass, unexplained infertility, something that results in acquiescence to a totalitarian ruler. Yoko Tawada's *The Last Children of Tokyo* (2018) depicts an isolationist Japan struggling with ecological disaster, opaque governance, and a reversal of generational order as children are born weak and frail, and the older generation thrive and remain healthy. Both novels can be considered as 'demodystopias': "Dystopias that are brought about by demographic change or that make population matters a salient concern" (Domingo 725). Though he sees the roots of this type of dystopia in classic works such as George Orwell's *Nineteen Eighty-Four* (1949), Aldous Huxley's *Brave New World* (1932) and Yevgeny Zamyatin's *We* (1924), all of which show some concern with the pronatalist and eugenic ideas of their twentieth-century times, Andreu Domingo identifies the emergence of the 'demodystopia' after World War Two. In particular, Domingo notes the influence of gerontophobic ideas in novels of more recent decades, coinciding with ageing populations in many countries in the Global North (733). In *The Children of Men* and *The Last Children of Tokyo* generational disorder, or anachronism, threatens the future of the individual, the species and, in the case of Tawada, is linked to planetary destruction. Futures based on childlessness or frail children raise the spectre of ageing populations and anxieties about ageing as decline contribute to the sense of 'lateness' in the narratives. *The Children of Men* then follows the promise of the child in a thriller narrative of reproductive futurity that relies on its shadow side: the figure of the hysterical/useless old person. *The Last Children of Tokyo* rejects the closed promise of reproductive futurism in favour of the disordering of time itself. This novel reimagines both childhood and ageing to suggest that anachronism may be embraced as a form of risk that cannot be avoided, as, in Russo's words, "a condition of possibility" (27). This vision of the risk of anachronism offers a way of thinking beyond reproductive futurism and the possibility of reconceptualizing generational relationships.

The Children of Men

Edelman offers *The Children of Men* as a paradigmatic example of the functioning of the figure of the child in cultural discourse, where "we are no more able to conceive of a politics without a fantasy of the future than we are able to conceive of a future without the figure of the Child" (11). The novel is also an example of what Sheldon calls the "sterility apocalypse," in which mass fertility problems affect whole populations and threaten humanity as a species (151).[1] In England in 2021, scientifically inexplicable infertility has resulted in an ageing society ruled by the Warden, Xan Lyppiatt. In a classic narrative of dystopian totalitarianism, the current punitive measures (compulsory fertility examinations, restricted emigration, coercive relocation to cities, deportation to penal colonies and forced 'suicide' of older people) are defended through a discourse of freedom: "What we guarantee is freedom from fear, freedom from want, freedom from boredom. The other freedoms are pointless without freedom from fear" (James 95). As Soo Darcy argues, "Under Xan's regime, the body is disciplined through a series of systems and controls that echo Foucault's description of a drive towards both increased usefulness – through, it is hoped, the discovery of a fertile human – and docility that allows the population to be ruled without disorder" (98).

---

[1]   Darcy points out that the novel *The Children of Men* is often overlooked by critics, with far more attention paid to the film, in part because the latter engages more overtly with issues of race and migration (88). For example, Sheldon and Ahmed analyse the film and not the novel.

The novel then relates a thriller narrative as a group of rebels attempt to protect Julian, a miraculously pregnant woman (bearing the first child for twenty-five years), with the aid of jaded Oxford historian, Theo. The plot of the novel is therefore driven by and propelled towards the figure of the child as the future.

As Darcy explains, *The Children of Men* is part of a renewed interest in dystopian writing that explores reproduction in the context of emerging reproductive technologies in the late 1980s and early 1990s (91). Julian represents the opposition to the (bio)power exercised by the Warden and her fertility takes on the quality of "mysticism" that Sheldon argues is found in sterility narratives: "Women sit in the place of life-itself, coordinating its translation from élan vital to species-being, and so women's fertility is invested with all of the mysticism of that which eludes control" (151). Julian is consistently described in Mary-like terms (shrouded in a cloak, looking on peacefully as others argue, fully committed to her Christian faith). The birth itself takes place in a basic woodshed surrounded by the natural world and provides the culmination of journey, plot and a novel in which Julian has consistently served as a patient, passive and pregnant (in all senses) symbol of the future, in just the way Sheldon suggests the fertile woman functions in sterility narratives: "Infertility is the conceit, but restoration is the point ... the single fertile woman appears out of nowhere, her pregnant body promising the return of a calculable future guided by human sovereignty over Earth's abundance" (151–2). The sense of loss and anxiety that infertility brings is articulated by Theo in terms of a generational imagination: "our minds reach back through centuries for the reassurance of our ancestry and, without the hope of posterity, for our race if not for ourselves, without the assurance that we being dead yet live, all pleasures of the mind and senses sometimes seem to me no more than pathetic and crumbling defences shored up against our ruins" (James 9). The promise of the reproductive woman and her child is then the promise of our own generational succession and therefore of the future of the species, based on the security of past generational identity.

In her analysis of the adaptation of the novel, Ahmed argues that the film is about Theo's conversion from hopelessness and isolation to hope and relationality, and that his anxious care for the pregnant woman encapsulates the film's vision of futurity, "where the future is embodied in the fragility of an object whose persistence matters" (186). The novel foregrounds Theo's development in its two-part structure ("Omega" and "Alpha," comprised of Theo's diary entries and a third-person narrative focalized through him). Theo learns to care for Julian (and for the child to come), to the point at which he feels himself merging with her during childbirth (James 225) in a way that exemplifies Ahmed's description of care as "not about letting an object go but holding on to an object by letting oneself go, giving oneself over to something that is not one's own" (Ahmed 186). Nevertheless, as Ahmed points out in relation to the film, the fact that Theo's care culminates in a reassertion of patrimony closes down possible alternative futures. The novel makes clearer and more troubling the power of patriarchal and generational structures. In "Omega," Theo admits that he is like Xan, solitary and emotionally disconnected (James 16). He also demonstrates generational disregard, admitting to a lack of love for his mother and to being horrified by his dying father (James 26–7). Of course, whilst this depiction of Theo prepares the ground for his steady transformation in part two of the novel, it at the same time warns us that Theo's conversion will take a very particular shape and perhaps suggests that we should be wary of a narrative dominated by his perspective. Theo's hope in "Alpha" is all very clearly founded on the heterosexual order and on a specific form of masculinity (man as provider and protector), undoubtedly echoing Xan's own quest for male power and (biopolitical) control. Theo adopts the role of protector, saving Julian and her child from both Xan and Rolf (Julian's husband) as both try to exploit the promise of the child. The culmination of Theo's newly sentimental and masculinized role nevertheless positions him as the threat to Julian and her child: after killing Xan, Theo takes the coronation ring from the Warden and puts it on his own finger, acknowledging the "shadow in [Julian's] eyes" when she sees it (James 239). In its image of Theo as Xan's replacement, the novel suggests that the hope of happiness, and the future in which that can be realized, are ultimately determined by, and a return to, past structures of gender, generation and power. That makes more ambiguous, but does not necessarily undo, the promise of the child as the figure of the future, for, as Sheldon points out, the figure of the child is at its most potent when under threat. In its depiction of Theo's increasing dominance and final assumption of power, the novel represents the alignment of reproductive futurity with the patriarchal status quo.

If Theo's care for another and the location of the future in the figure of a child are central to the articulation of hope in this novel, then much of the anxiety that Ahmed identifies as essential to dystopian thinking (anxiety about what may become if nothing is done) is located in the figure of the old person. Ahmed suggests that there is "an intimacy between anxiety and hope. In having hope we become anxious, because hope involves wanting something that might or might not happen. Hope is about desiring the 'might,' which is only 'might' if it keeps open the possibility of the 'might not'" (183). The threat of the might not – the threat in *The Children of Men* of no children and the end of the species – is inextricably linked to and metonymically represented by the threat of ageing itself and the burden of an ageing population. The link between Omega (the end of reproduction) and ageing is indicated on the first page of the novel as Theo begins his diary on the day of the death of the last human whose birth was recorded, also the day of Theo's fiftieth birthday and, ironically, given its connotations of newness and fresh starts, the 1st of January. Omega is specifically imagined as the burden of an ageing population throughout the novel. As one of Theo's early diary entries explains:

> The world didn't give up hope until the generation born in 1995 reached sexual maturity. But when the testing was complete and not one of them could produce fertile sperm, we knew that this was indeed the end of *Homo sapiens*. It was in that year, 2008, that the suicides increased. Not mainly among the old, but among my generation, the middle-aged, the generation who would have to bear the brunt of an ageing and decaying society's humiliating but insistent needs. (James 8)

Theo's articulation of species lateness as a decline narrative of ageing (Gullette) and the burden of care underpins the vision of the child as the symbol of the future. The middle-aged and old are a source of anxiety, representing the future that will be if things do not change.

The state's response to the burden of an ageing population is a series of strategies designed to maximize the productivity of the population and minimize dependency. Longevity, which is a feature of this dystopian world, is supported by state-sponsored care and therapies, such as massage and sports like golf, in order to help people to "retain the illusion, if not of youth, of vigorous middle age" (7). Immigrants are sent back when they reach the age of sixty (or if they become incapacitated or ill). And, most strikingly of all, the old are encouraged to partake of group suicide when they become dependent or otherwise unproductive. As Nancee Reeves points out, speculative literature has long explored euthanasia as a means of population control (103). Sara D. Schotland's analysis of Thomas Middleton's *Old Law* (1618–19), about the forced execution of men at the age of eighty and women at the age of sixty, provides evidence of this. Reeves notes the great increase in this theme in speculative works of the nineteenth century and into the early twentieth, related to the development of Darwinian evolution and eugenics (Reeves points to texts that take very different positions on euthanasia, such as H.G. Wells's *When the Sleeper Wakes* (1899) and E.M. Forster's "The Machine Stops" (1909)). Some speculative fiction explicitly explores age-related killing, where enforced suicide and murder are related to the spectre of decline and the burden of an ageing population, seen in Anthony Trollope's *The Fixed Period* (1881–82, analysed by Reeves) and in diverse forms in William F. Nolan and George Clayton Johnson's *Logan's Run* (1967), Ally Condie's young adult novel *Matched* (2011), and Margaret Atwood's short story "Torching the Dusties" (2014). The "Quietus" (group drownings) in *The Children of Men* are, therefore, part of a long tradition of speculative writing about ageing and enforced death.

The depiction of the Quietus attended by Theo in the first part of the novel is horrific, making clear the inhumanity of the practice and the lack of consent involved. The scene sees the brutal murder of Hilda, wife of Theo's old university mentor, Jasper. When Theo visits Jasper and Hilda earlier in the novel, he is shocked to find Jasper physically aged and Hilda unkempt and unresponsive. Jasper's assertion that the previously strong-willed and intelligent Hilda had talked about the Quietus (by implication that she had considered volunteering for this) seems unlikely to Theo (James 46). Jasper's praise for the government's provision of financial compensation to relatives of Quietus participants implies that he may have a motive for Hilda's death, adding to the sense that the Quietus is a morally abhorrent practice. The Quietus is therefore part of the evidence of the totalitarian and violent nature of the Warden's regime provided by the rebels. It is also the impetus for Theo's decision to help them.

At the same time, the depiction of the Quietus, and specifically the representation of Hilda, unsettles the moral indignation that the practice is meant to produce. Significantly, the Quietus in question involves only female participants. Theo's description stresses the parodic nature of the event, as old women enter beach huts that "for so many decades had echoed with the laughter of children," dress in white robes "like a bevy of dishevelled bridesmaids" and "sway ... to the music, holding out their white skirts and clumsily pirouetting" (James 71–2). The anachronistic disjunction of youth and aged bodies has the effect of distancing both Theo and the reader from the women and turning them into spectacles. This is then emphasized by the description of Hilda's attempt to escape from the boat:

> She was only about twenty yards from him now and he could see her plainly, the wild white hair, the nightdress sticking to her body, the swinging, pendulous breasts, the arms with their weals of crêpy skin. A crashing wave tore the nightdress from her left shoulder and he saw the breast swaying obscenely like a giant jellyfish. She was still screaming, a high, piercing whistle like a tortured animal. (73)

The grotesque description of Hilda emphasizes her aged and specifically female body, the very body that is now unable to offer the reproductive labour that the society seeks as a way to halt its own decline into extinction. Hilda's body has projected onto it fears about mortality and the end of reproductivity, the things the society in this novel is most fearful about. This aged body is diametrically opposed to the vision of Julian's fecund body before which Theo kneels later in the novel.

Other depictions of ageing characters emphasize the sense that the figure of the child as the future depends upon its shadow: the figure of the hysterical and/or useless old person. For example, Theo encounters an eccentric, paranoid old priest when he visits St Margaret's church to meet with the rebels, describing the man in ghoulish terms: "Theo thought that he had never seen anyone so old, the skull stretching the paper-thin, mottled skin of his face as if death couldn't wait to claim him" (James 52). The anxiety about ageing and mortality emerges again when Theo imagines the custodian at the Pitt Rivers Museum – an ageing Classics don – entombed in the building, "the frail body mummified or rotting at last under the marble gaze of those blank unseeing eyes" (James 83). The figure of the embodied old woman returns later in the novel when Theo steals from an old couple in order to provide supplies for the flight with the rebels. The man and woman are frightened and submissive and the woman, in particular, is described as frail and dependent. Accepting that he needs to untie her so that she can use the toilet, Theo describes her as "stinking with fear, lying in rigid embarrassment, unable to meet his eyes" (James 203). The couple's physical limitations and vulnerability make them obstacles to Theo's pursuit of the future in the form of Julian's child. When it is later revealed that the woman has died, Theo's guilt causes him to round on Julian: "How many other lives will your child cost before she gets herself born? And to what purpose?" (James 216). These questions articulate the guilt and anxiety that underlie the figure of the child as the future. At moments like this, the novel draws attention to its own reliance on reproductive futurism and ageing as decline. The hysterical and deeply embodied old woman, and the decrepit and redundant old man, come to haunt this text as a reminder that the future as articulated in the promise and hope represented by the child depends upon the anxiety generated by the old. *The Children of Men* is an example of the ways in which the dystopic imagination depends upon figures of ageing and narratives of anachronism in order to generate the combination of anxiety and hope necessary to dystopic visions of the future, even as, at key moments, the novel seems to foreground that very dependence.

The Last Children of Tokyo

Early in Yoko Tawada's prize-winning *The Last Children of Tokyo*,[2] the one-hundred-year-old Yoshiro reflects on the nature of time: "The years are recorded in rings inside the trunk of a tree, but how was time recorded in his own body? Time didn't just spread out gradually, ring after ring, nor was it lined up neatly in a row; could it just be a disorderly pile, like the inside of a drawer no one ever bothers to straighten?" (6). As this quotation indicates, linear time – symbolized by generations – is undone in this novel as it depicts an ageing society in which generational dependency is radically altered. The novel must be situated in relation to Japan's ageing population and declining birth rate. It was also written in the wake of the 2011 Tōhoku earthquake and tsunami, which resulted in the Fukushima Daiichi nuclear disaster.[3] The sense of apocalyptic ending inherent in rapid demographic change (heightened by the 'statistical panic' generated by media and cultural responses – see Woodward) and large-scale natural disasters provides the context for a novel that nevertheless comes to interrogate the linear model of time that relies upon the child as the promise of the future and the old as redundant representatives of the past. Generational succession and ageing are, therefore, key concerns in *The Last Children of Tokyo*, but unlike *The Children of Men*, the novel presents a complex vision of these things that is more akin to anachronism as a form of risk-taking than anachronism as a problem to be solved in order to secure reproductive futurity.

Japan's demographic change is significant, both in statistical and cultural terms. The National Institute of Population and Social Security Research "Population Predictions for Japan: 2016 to 2065" suggest that the percentage of over sixty-fives will increase from 26.6 per cent in 2015 to 38.4 per cent in 2065 (based on the medium-fertility projection). The old-age dependency ratio is predicted to increase from 43.8 in 2015 (an average of 2.3 working-age people for each person over sixty-five) to 74.6 (an average of 1.3 working-age people for each person over sixty-five) by 2065 (3–4). The profound changes caused by the ageing of the population have created a sense of what we might describe as lateness within Japanese society, as the future itself is called into question:

---

[2]   This novel was originally published as *Kentoshi* in Japanese (2014). It was translated and published as *The Emissary* in the United States and as *The Last Children of Tokyo* in the UK. It won the prestigious National Book Award for Translated Literature in 2018 in the US.

[3]   Tawada visited Fukushima and spoke to those affected before writing the novel (Tawada and Campbell).

For a growing number of older adults, their future – and perhaps the future of Japan as a whole – is shadowed by a rapidly ageing (and dying) population. In a country where one in four are over the age of 65, and a third of those require assistance in daily tasks due to frailty, dementia, or other chronic health issues that accompany advanced age (Naikakuchō 2015), the consequences of an ageing society are increasingly evident. In cities, old vacant homes fall into disrepair, as their elderly occupants no longer have children willing to inherit them. In the countryside, villages that have existed for centuries have been reduced to a few dozen elderly residents, all conscious of the reality that they will be the last. (Danely 14–15)

In addition to concerns about the burden of the ageing population, Japan's declining birth rate has contributed to a popular discourse about children being over-protected and lacking in physical resilience. And both of these things find their way into *The Last Children of Tokyo*. The novel shares with *The Children of Men* features of the "sterility apocalypse" (Sheldon): the threat of degeneration and loss of species. Here, though, reproduction does still occur. The children born, however, are weak and frail, failing flagbearers of the future. At the heart of this novel is, therefore, a reversal of generations: children will remain dependent on adults, with their lives bound to a form of premature senescence, and adults will outlive them as they experience extreme longevity. Children tend not to be looked after by their parents, but by older generations. So Mumei, the child in this novel, is cared for by his great-grandfather, Yoshiro. The reversal of generations (weakness–strength, progress–decline) and confusion of age/youth are exacerbated by this care structure, making anachronism central to the novel.

The significant temporal and generational gap between Mumei and Yoshiro is used to explore the impact of apocalyptic political, social and environmental change. Unlike *The Children of Men*, this novel is not driven by a thriller or quest narrative, where both reader and protagonist seek the fulfilment of the child/future/end. Instead, it is concerned with the everyday life and experiences of Yoshiro and Mumei, interspersed with Yoshiro's memories. Through these experiences and memories, the dystopic nature of the world is revealed in fragments. There is wholesale contamination; wild animals have disappeared; weather and light are unpredictable; and genetic mutations are rife. Tokyo's centrality within Japan is also subverted as it relies on Okinawa for food and has experienced significant depopulation, a scenario which reflects the current post-Fukushima context as some people moved out of Tokyo to be further away from the contaminated areas. In *The Last Children of Tokyo*, Japan is ruled by an opaque system that has strong totalitarian elements, despite the persistence of elections.[4] The government and police force have been privatized. Technological development has regressed – for example, electronic goods are largely rejected and there is no internet. Self-surveillance ensures conformity amongst the population. The country has enforced an isolationist policy so strict that foreign words are no longer used – leading to word play that, as translator Margaret Mitsutani acknowledges, is not always translatable within the novel. She gives the example of the way that the new isolationist policy in *The Last Children of Tokyo* produces terms that were formerly written in kakatana script, such as the replacement of "jogging" with "*kakeochi*":

> 'Kakeochi' in its new sense is supposed to mean 'if you *kakeru* (run) your blood pressure will *ochiru* (go down).' In English, that became 'eloping down,' which sounds odd. In the Japanese, it simply says that Mumei's generation don't know about the connection between kakeochi and romantic love, but I had to add a somewhat longer explanation that would suggest 'elope' – a young woman climbing down a ladder in the middle of the night to meet her lover. (Kittaka)

Within the novel, attention is drawn to language's role in shaping cultural life through satirical descriptions of new Japanese national holidays: 'Encouragement for the Aged Day' and 'Apologise to the Children Day' are satirical versions of real Japanese holidays such as 'Respect for the Aged Day.' Word play like this and the creation of terms such as 'young-elderly' are reminiscent of the long tradition of attention to the power of language in shaping the social imaginary in speculative fiction (from *Nineteen Eighty-Four* to Atwood's *Oryx and Crake* (2003); see Baccolini and Moylan 5). Yoshiro is a novelist and his linguistic pedantry and knowledge of now redundant words cement his sense that he is out of time and apart from the generation represented by Mumei. Yoshiro thus experiences a form of something seen in many of Tawada's characters: exophony. In *The Last Children of Tokyo*, however, this is a form of temporal exophony that makes the mother tongue into a different language over time, forcing Yoshiro to continually monitor his expressions. Tawada emphasizes this sense of linguistic strangeness by incorporating some Japanese signs into the prose and having Yoshiro reflect on the

---

[4] The novel may be responding here to fears of a return to a more hardline nationalism in the government of Shinzō Abe (see Nilsson-Wright and Fujiwara).

ways in which they translate into meaning.[5] Foregrounding translation in
these ways, Tawada reminds the reader of the refusal of language itself to
function as a closed system. As Susan C. Anderson argues, "By making
visible the instability of language and its referents, Tawada's texts provoke
her readers to probe the constraints grounding conventional perceptions
and identities and open themselves up to the plurality of possibilities and
subjectivities such linguistic instability can provide" (360; see also Maehl;
Arslan; Yildiz). Language itself draws attention to the sense of instability
inherent in subjectivity and therefore in social and temporal systems.

The gap between Yoshiro and Mumei is linguistic, generational and
embodied (in terms of health and illness), but it is also one of the before
and after (Berger) that characterizes apocalyptic fiction. Yoshiro remembers
meeting people from other countries, using electronic devices and living
in a busy, polluted Tokyo. His memories equate roughly to the present of
the reader. Mumei, of course, remembers none of this and finds some of
his great-grandfather's language and reactions confusing. There are echoes
here of the Man and the Boy from Cormac McCarthy's *The Road* (2006)
and undoubtedly Tawada is exploiting the symbolism of the child to generate what Ahmed calls "the anxiety of hope" (184). The Boy, like Mumei,
accepts the apocalyptic 'after' as all that there is; both are creatures of
and in their present moments. The Man and Yoshiro experience great
grief for what has gone and guilt for the damage done to the world, but
the children are entirely accepting of the present situation. Significantly,
however, and unlike in *The Road*, in this novel we are increasingly given
access to Mumei's point of view. This access to the child's perspective casts
the world in new ways, capturing Mumei's fleeting, fragmented thoughts
and the way he understands and accommodates his bodily restrictions. For
example, though Yoshiro frets about Mumei's difficulties in dressing, the
child turns these into a fantastic imaginary:

> He wanted to take off his pajamas, but with two legs he couldn't decide
> which to start with, and while he was puzzling over this problem he
> remembered the octopus. Maybe he had eight legs, too, and it just looked
> like two because each one was a bundle of four, tied tightly together …
> There was an octopus inside him: *Octopus, get out of there!* (Tawada 97)

Mumei's point of view offers a counterpoint to that of Yoshiro: instead
of grief and guilt, we see acceptance and accommodation, and every-

---

[5]   Tawada writes in both German and Japanese and her work is often concerned with issues of translation and relocation/migration (see Adelson 158–60).

day joy and pleasure. Significantly, Mumei recognizes the redundancy of much of Yoshiro's language (Tawada 114–15) and does not understand why he retains it and teaches it to his great-grandson, only to advise Mumei not to use the words (98). Mumei's thoughts suggest that Yoshiro's in some ways nostalgic insistence on language that has been lost (and, implicitly, on a world that has gone) holds him back from the possibilities of creating new meaning and new possibilities. The novel, then, does rely upon the figure of the child and the elucidation of generational time and identity in order to explore its dystopian before and after. Nevertheless, Mumei cannot signify hope and the future in the ways in which children function in novels such as *The Children of Men* and *The Road*, because his premature ageing, Yoshiro's longevity and their relationship confuse easy expectations about ageing, youth and the life course. Mumei cannot be "a cipher for the future of the adult" or a "cipher for the future of the species" (Sheldon 4), just as Yoshiro is not redundant and declining. Instead, *The Last Children of Tokyo* draws on the symbolism of the child as malleable and flexible in order to suggest that hope lies not in a return to the same – a resolution of generational disorder – but in a more fundamental openness to the future itself, for both child and older adult.

If this novel balances its depiction of generational guilt and responsibility for the harm caused to species and planet with an openness to the future, then its approach to gender contributes to its sense of instability and possibility. Remembering a visit to her family home with her young daughter, Yoshiro's wife, Marika, imagines the brutal and even murderous actions of previous generations, expressing her fear of generational inheritance: "The umbilical cord binding the generations of a respectable old family is also a rope round the neck" (Tawada 87). Explicitly rejecting gendered Japanese familial structures (described by the Japanese term *ie*), Marika's response to the weight of the familial past is to leave home and run a school for "children with no-one to look after them" (Tawada 69). If reproductive futurity and the promise of the child are based firmly in the dominance of the heterosexual order, then *The Last Children of Tokyo* rejects this completely. Though Mumei and Yoshiro are identified as great-grandson and great-grandfather, we become aware that sexual and gender differences are weakening and changing in this new world. Single-sex toilets in schools have disappeared as "the difference between the sexes became less and less clear" (Tawada 115). Stages such as the menopause now affect large numbers of men (Tawada 110). And, in echoes of Virginia Woolf's *Orlando*, people may change sex during a lifetime, something that appears to happen to Mumei near the end of the narrative.

The disordering of gender and generations depicted in the novel leads to a disordering of time itself, a recognition of the open nature of the future. Yoshiro can no longer imagine the future and, for him, this is a matter of terrible grief because it is related to the loss of Mumei and with that the loss of his expectations of generationally based futurity (Tawada 36). Yoshiro's sense of anxiety and even hopelessness reminds us of Ahmed's point that "'no children' signifies the loss of a fantasy of the future as that which can compensate me for my suffering" (183). This sense of future loss is related tangentially to Yoshiro's occupation as a writer: he chooses to write picture postcards to his family because there is little space to fill and "[b]eing able to see the end of anything gave him a tremendous sense of relief" (Tawada 55). Yoshiro has tried writing for children, but cannot because a realist treatment of the world "would only end in frustration at the absence of solutions, making it impossible to arrive at a place one could only reach in books" and "reading about an ideal world wouldn't help the boy change the world around him any time soon" (Tawada 16). Yoshiro expresses here the difficulties inherent in the utopian/dystopian genre: its relationship to change. In the case of *The Last Children of Tokyo*, hope lies in the acceptance of instability, what Sheldon calls the open nature of systems, and the problematization of, rather than prescription for, the future. In this sense, the novel accepts rather than tries to ameliorate the risk of anachronism.

The illness of the children in this novel is presented as a failure of evolution, the degeneration of individuals and therefore species, a form of biological lateness. Mumei, for example, is assessed for "cellular destruction" (Tawada 19) by the doctor. Nevertheless, the narrative of degeneration which characterizes the reversal of generational order in this novel is complicated by the depiction of the children as adaptive creatures. The teacher, Yonatani, watches his pupils' physical play, in which they find ways to manage their environments, and in this process find pleasure. Yonatani is "sure they had evolved far beyond his own generation" and in teaching them he must embrace uncertainty: "All he could do was feel his way forward, unsure of the way, thinking carefully about each new thing he encountered, turning every doubt into words to give to his pupils" (Tawada 119). Yoshiro also tries to teach future generations, but he comes to the realization that the norms and standards by which he lives have changed beyond measure. Like Yonatani, Yoshiro realizes the need to stand in a different relation to the past and to generational power:

> Assuming he had knowledge and wealth to leave to his descendants was mere arrogance, Yoshiro now realized. This life with his great-grandson

was about all he could manage. And for that he needed to be flexible, in mind and body, with the courage to doubt what he had believed for over a century ... He was not really an 'old man,' but a man who, after living for a century, had become a new species of human being. (40–1)

The novel remakes both the child and the old person as adaptive, posthuman creatures that must accept the instability of both the present and the future. Care is central to this articulation of the future in the novel, as it is in *The Children of Men*. It is in caring for Mumei that Yoshiro comes to feel anxiety for the future and in that feeling to articulate the sense of a future at all. Unlike *The Children of Men*, however, this novel does not turn to "the social forms in which hopes for happiness have already been deposited" (Ahmed 187), but instead offers a more radical reimagining of hope that is not prescriptive.

The novel exploits the possibility of opening up space for different kinds of stories, adopting the kind of freedom encouraged by Port: "A rejection of reproductive futurist ideology not only might open up the kinds of stories that could be told about the life course but also could validate lives that do not cohere into a recognizable narrative" (6). As Tara Beaney argues, the insistence on "narrative possibility" is at the heart of Tawada's work as her "surrealist poetics generate narrative possibility by paying attention to the agency of language and matter, allowing randomness to act as poetic principle" (96). The adoption of randomness and contingency are seen in Yoshiro and Yonatani, as they accept a form of posthuman identity that depends upon openness and not the replication of the same that is ensured by reproductive futurity. The final section of the novel brings randomness and contingency into the structure of the narrative itself, as it more explicitly adopts the surrealism many note in Tawada's other writing. This begins as Mumei experiences an ironically presented "time slip" (Tawada 125) and becomes fifteen years old, seemingly undergoing a gender transition, and now unable to walk or to talk without the aid of an electronic device (Tawada 126–7). His increasing physical disability is accompanied by explicit signs of ageing, such as the greying of his hair, further emphasizing premature senescence and prompting close comparisons between Yoshiro and his great-grandson, again complicating generational and life course models. Notably, however, Mumei's response to the changes in his body is remarkably accepting; he is not surprised by his increased debility and even finds his new, mechanically produced voice "warm, bright and full of life" (127). This form of very rapid ageing – and the anticipation of further physical decline – is not a matter of grief for Mumei. Instead, grief is felt by the chronologically older generations, whose bodies remain active and healthy. Again, the novel exploits the child as a figure of hope, but complicates the closure and generational order of reproductive futurism in the depiction of this aged, gender-fluid, physically declining boy.

As Mumei's time slip and rapid ageing suggest, time itself becomes uncertain in this final part of the novel. The emissary plot that provides the title for the Japanese and US editions of the novel returns here, as Mumei finds a ticket for an ocean liner in his pocket and 'remembers' a future in which he has been chosen to travel to India in order that his body may be studied to provide data about Japanese children's health and potentially to help other countries. This plot is a challenge to the totalitarian regime, something imagined in terms of both time and space: "It was clearly necessary to think of the future along the curved lines of our round earth. The isolation policy that looked so invulnerable was actually nothing but a sand castle" (Tawada 130). As "wisps of memory come back from the future" (Tawada 128) and the environment becomes more and more estranging (with glass roads covering caverns in the contaminated earth), the reader is directed not to a future resolution, but to a concentration upon the intimacy of Mumei's increasingly surreal experiences, meaning that the novel rejects the movement towards closure that propels reproductive futurity.

The novel ends with Mumei lying on the beach with his ex-neighbour Suiren, feeling himself turn into a woman and finally unable to speak or move. Suiren's face becomes lungs, broad beans and finally the faces of Yonatani and Yoshiro as 'darkness' again comes for Mumei: "darkness, wearing a glove, reached for the back of his head to take hold of his brains, and Mumei fell into the pitch-black depths of the strait" (Tawada 138). As Beaney points out, this ending has been read as a reference to the 2011 tsunami, but, more significantly, it is an image that emphasizes the openness of the future: "The ending foregrounds the intra-action of agencies, with Mumei's free association and then the dark water itself taking charge of the narrative, in an act of randomness that draws attention to the uncertainty of the future" (96). The fragmented, temporally disjointed and surrealist nature of this final part of the book makes reading this as an 'ending,' as closure and prediction for the future, impossible. Instead, we are left with contingency, instability and openness, and the possibility of futures which are not configured as the purview of children alone. Like *The Children of Men*, *The Last Children of Tokyo* is a novel of generational disorder, where the threat to the next generation – and in this case the longevity of the older generation – generate the hope and anxiety necessary to the dystopian world vision. Nevertheless, *The Last Children of Tokyo* rejects the binary of youth and age that underlies reproductive futurism in a narrative that in both form and content insists upon the necessity of contingency and change.

Conclusion

The rise in and popularity of (critical) dystopian fiction in recent decades should not blind us to the long tradition of utopian and dystopian writing in which these latest trends must be located. Nevertheless, the sense of lateness and individual, species and planetary vulnerability that emerges in dystopian fictions of the late twentieth and early twenty-first centuries undoubtedly tells us much about the fears and hopes of our globalized, mediatized and damaged world, and our sense of ourselves as a species within a technologically-mediated human existence. Dystopian fiction attempts to generate anxiety for the loss of the future and in that way puts forward the possibility that there is hope and that the future might be different from the terrible dystopian imaginary (see Ahmed). To articulate its threats, dystopian fiction relies on generational disorder and anachronism, and figures of ageing. Frequently foregrounding the figure of the child as the future, these novels nevertheless depend on ageing itself and often explicitly on the figure of the old person. Together the child and the old generate the combination of hope and anxiety necessary to dystopian projects. This can lead to futures simply imagined as the self-same – Sheldon's closed systems and Ahmed's description of the turn to existing social forms as sources of happiness (187), as seen in *The Children of Men*. But in texts like *The Last Children of Tokyo*, these figures of ageing are repurposed in ways that are fundamentally more open and challenging, and that offer a future based on contingency and instability, where hope is bound inextricably to fear and anxiety. What *The Children of Men* and *The Last Children of Tokyo* demonstrate is that we need figures of ageing and generational anachronism to realize our fears and hopes, to realize our futures. Ageing is central to the dystopic imagination.

Works Cited

Adelson, Leslie A. "'The Future of Futurity: Alexander Kluge and Yoko Tawada.'" *The Germanic Review: Literature, Culture, Theory*, vol. 86, no. 3, 2011, pp. 153–84.

Ahmed, Sara. *The Promise of Happiness*. Duke UP, 2010.

Anderson, Susan C. "Water under the Bridge: Unsettling the Concept of Bridging Cultures in Yoko Tawada's Writing." *Pacific Coast Philology*, vol. 50, no. 1, 2015, pp. 44–63.

Arslan, Gizem. "Orientation, Encounter, and Synaesthesia in Paul Celan and Yoko Tawada." *The Future of Text and Image: Collected Essays on Literary and Visual Conjunctures*, edited by Ofra Amihay and Lauren Walsh. Cambridge Scholars, 2012, pp. 199–230.

Atwood, Margaret. *Oryx and Crake*. Virago, 2009.

———. "Torching the Dusties." *Stone Mattress: Nine Wicked Tales*. Virago, 2014, pp. 259–308.

Baccolini, Raffaella, and Tom Moylan, editors. *Dark Horizons: Science Fiction and the Dystopian Imagination*. Routledge, 2003.

Beaney, Tara. "Confronting 'Unforeseen' Disasters: Yōko Tawada's Surrealist and Animistic Poetics." *Ecozon@*, vol. 10, no. 1, 2019, pp. 81–98.

Berger, John. *After the End: Representations of Post-Apocalypse*. U of Minnesota P, 1999.

Brenkman, John. "Queer Post-Politics." *Narrative*, vol. 10, no. 2, 2002, pp. 174–80.

Condie, Ally. *Matched*. Penguin, 2011.

Danely, Jason. "Hope in an Ageing Japan: Transience and Transcendence." *Contemporary Japan*, vol. 28, no. 1, 2016, pp. 13–31.

Darcy, Soo. "Power, Surveillance and Reproductive Technology in P.D. James' *The Children of Men*." *Women's Utopian and Dystopian Fiction*, edited by Sharon R. Wilson. Cambridge Scholars, 2013, pp. 88–111.

Domingo, Andreu. "'Demodystopias': Prospects of Demographic Hell." *Population and Development Review*, vol. 34, no. 4, 2008, pp. 725–745.

Edelman, Lee. *No Future: Queer Theory and the Death Drive*. Duke UP, 2004.

Forster, E.M. "The Machine Stops." *Selected Short Stories*, edited by David Leavitt and Mark Mitchell. Penguin, 2001, pp. 91–123.

Gullette, Margaret Morganroth. *Declining to Decline: Cultural Combat and the Politics of the Midlife*. UP of Virginia, 1997.

Huxley, Aldous. *Brave New World*. Vintage, 2007.

James, P.D. *The Children of Men*. Faber, 1993.

Kermode, Frank. *The Sense of an Ending: Studies in the Theory of Fiction*. Oxford UP, 2000.

Kittaka, Louise George. "*The Emissary*: Power, Poison, Pain and Joy inside Its DNA." *The Japan Times*, 4 August 2018, www.japantimes.co.jp/culture/2018/08/04/books/emissary-power-poison-pain-joy-inside-dna/.

Maehl, Silja. "Canned Foreign: Transnational Estrangement in Yoko Tawada." *Alien Imaginations: Science Fiction and Tales of Transnationalism*, edited by Ulrikw Küchler et al. Bloomsbury, 2015, pp. 73–91.

McCarthy, Cormac. *The Road*. Picador, 2010.

Moylan, Tom. *Scraps of the Untainted Sky: Science Fiction, Utopia, Dystopia.* Routledge, 2018.

Nilsson-Wright, John, and Kiichi Fujiwara. "Japan's Abe Administration: Steering a Course between Pragmatism and Extremism." Chatham House, The Royal Institute of International Affairs, 2015, https://www.chathamhouse.org/sites/default/files/publications/research/20150914JapanAbeAdministrationNilsson WrightFujiwara.pdf.

Nolan, William F. and George Clayton Johnson. *Logan's Run.* Buccaneer Books, 1967.

Orwell, George. *Nineteen Eighty-Four.* Penguin, 2008.

"Population Projections for Japan: 2016 to 2065." National Institute of Population and Social Security Research (IPSS), 2017, www.ipss.go.jp/pp-zenkoku/e/zenkoku_e2017/pp_zenkoku2017e_gaiyou.html.

Port, Cynthia. "No Future? Aging, Temporality, History, and Reverse Chronologies." *Occasion: Interdisciplinary Studies in the Humanities,* vol. 4, 2012, arcade.stanford.edu/sites/default/files/article_pdfs/OCCASION_v04_Port_053112_0.pdf.

Reeves, Nancee. "Euthanasia and (D)Evolution in Speculative Fiction." *Victorian Literature and Culture,* vol. 45, 2017, pp. 95–117.

Russo, Mary. "Aging and the Scandal of Anachronism." *Figuring Age: Women, Bodies, Generations,* edited by Kathleen Woodward. Indiana UP, 1999, pp. 20–33.

Schotland, Sara D. "Forced Execution of the Elderly: *Old Law,* Dystopia, and the Utilitarian Argument." *Humanities,* vol. 2, 2013, pp. 160–75.

Sheldon, Rebekah. *The Child to Come: Life after the Human Catastrophe.* U of Minnesota P, 2016.

Tawada, Yoko. *The Last Children of Tokyo,* translated by Margaret Mitsutani. Granta, 2018.

Tawada, Yoko, and Robert Campbell. "Yoko Tawada: The Fascination of Exophonic Literature." *NHK World,* 28 April 2019, www3.nhk.or.jp/nhkworld/en/ondemand/video/2043047/.

Trollope, Anthony. *The Fixed Period.* Phantasmo Press, 2015.

Wells, H.G. *When the Sleeper Wakes.* Phoenix, 1994.

Woodward, Kathleen. *Statistical Panic: Cultural Politics and the Poetics of the Emotions.* Duke UP, 2009.

Woolf, Virginia. *Orlando,* edited by Rachel Bowlby. Oxford UP, 1998.

Yildiz, Yasemin. *Beyond the Mother Tongue: The Postmonolingual Condition.* Fordham UP, 2012.

Zamyatin, Yevgeny. *We.* Penguin, 1993.

5

Grandpaternalism:
Kipling's Imperial Care Narrative

JACOB JEWUSIAK

"[B]ut who can argue with a grandmother?" quips the exasperated servant to the Widow of Kulu in Rudyard Kipling's 1901 novel *Kim*, critiquing the woman's penchant for charms and pills to cure her grandson's "most lamentable windy colic" rather than merely cutting back on the boy's prodigious consumption of unripe mangoes (218, 216). The widow claims confidently that "None but a grandmother should ever oversee a child. Mothers are only fit for bearing" (217). When the lama refers to Kim as a son, the widow responds: "Say grandson, rather. Mothers have not the wisdom of our years. If a child cries they say the heavens are falling. Now a grandmother is far enough separated from the pain of bearing and the pleasure of giving the breast to consider whether a cry is wickedness pure or the wind" (275). For the widow, the relationship between parent and child brings the two positions too close together – the mother's temporal proximity to the child, her inability to distance herself from the affectively charged events of childbirth and breastfeeding, causes her to overreact. The grandmother, on the other hand, coolly applies the knowledge of her long years to the intractable problems of child rearing, correctly diagnosing the gaseous nature of the boy's cry. Adopting the widow's terminology, the lama replies that Kim "is in the spirit my very 'grandson' to me" (275). In *Kim*, it is the temporal distance that intervenes between grandparent and grandchild that serves as a means of mutual understanding between the two positions. Rather than frame empire as the paternalistic relation between father and son, Kipling substitutes the grandparent/grandchild dyad: a structure that makes power appear more rooted in affective bonds than disciplinary ones, a matter of choice rather than coercion. As I will go on to argue, the grandpaternalism of empire that Kipling sketches in *Kim* serves as an affective manifestation of colonial policy after the Indian Uprising of 1857, using the representation of age to narrativize the successful transition from the liberal project of reform to indirect rule. To do so, Kipling revises the position of the colonized within the imperial imagination: away from an impressionable and unruly child in need of instruction to an already developed and innocuous older person deserving of care.

The significance of old age in Kipling's work has gone largely unacknowledged by critics who attend to the many youthful protagonists who sail, hunt, and explore their way across the plots of Kipling's fiction. His memorable heroes – Harvey Cheyne sailing the Atlantic, Mowgli dashing through the jungle, and Stalky and Co. terrorizing their teachers – reveal Kipling's investment in the Bildungsroman and its focus on youth for shaping the author's political and aesthetic imagination. His work reflects the pervasive belief in the youthful wellspring of empire, while at the same time reinforcing a vision of imperialism as virile and rejuvenating.[1] For this reason, many critics provide accounts of youth's significance in Kipling's work, ranging from Gayatri Spivak's claim that it "is Kipling's genius to stage the imperialist as child" to Jed Esty's contention that "*Kim* represents colonial India in terms of endless youth" (51, 11). For Don Randall, Kim "demonstrates that the imperial progress is a youthful procession, in all its moments. ... He represents an empire always vital and burgeoning, never yet at its apogee, and certainly not ever at the beginning of its decline" ("Imperial Boy" 43). Obscured by the long shadow cast by youth in Kipling's work, his older characters refashion the colonial relation along different generational lines – away from the patriarchal relationship between father and son, and toward the dyad of grandfather and grandson. The reciprocity, rather than competition, between grandparents and grandchildren symbolically reconciles the seemingly insurmountable ideological differences between the English and Indian people. Age serves as the catalyst for imaginatively removing those markers of difference coded onto the skin and manners of others.

Many postcolonial critics assert that European colonization founds itself upon the construction of the colonizer/colonized relationship as a patriarchal binary between a father and child. Frantz Fanon writes in *Black Skin, White Masks* that "A white man talking to a person of color behaves exactly like a grown-up with a kid, simpering, murmuring, fussing, and coddling" (14). This attitude, he argues, pervades the institutions that surround the colonized individual – such as doctors, police, and employers – reinforcing the inferiority of the Other. The asymmetrical power relations

---

[1]   In *Dandies and Desert Saints*, James Eli Adams writes that "middle-class manhood" was characterized by a "widespread preoccupation with a comprehensive discipline that linked the rule of empire to an exacting regimen of self-control" (115). Catherine Hall avers that "In the second half of the nineteenth century, a particular kind of white colonial identity became increasingly distinctive across these areas of white settlement. This was a culture of sturdy manhood and domesticated femininity, of respectability, and of racial exclusion" (70–1).

that inhere in the Manichean allegory between parent and child provide the discursive framework for justifying the metropole's authority and constructing a subject responsive to power. As Anne McClintock writes,

> Projecting the family image onto national and imperial progress enabled what was often murderously violent change to be legitimized as the progressive unfolding of natural decree. Imperial intervention could thus be figured as a linear, nonrevolutionary progression that naturally contained hierarchy within unity: *paternal fathers ruling benignly over immature children*. The trope of the organic family became invaluable in its capacity to give state and imperial intervention the alibi of nature. (45, emphasis added)

By naturalizing the patriarchal asymmetry of power, the colonies provided an arena that reinvented fatherhood on a global scale, supporting a pathological creed of generational responsibility along racial lines.[2] In "the name of universal progress," Duncan Bell writes of colonial rhetoric, "it was legitimate, and even necessary, to aid the 'immature' peoples of the world reach 'maturity'" (867).

While Kipling endorsed empire along the normatively patriarchal line – in "The White Man's Burden" he infamously describes the colonized as "Half-devil and half-child" and entreats the colonizer to "Have done with childish days" and "search your manhood" – his representation of the relationship between Teshoo Lama and Kim provides an alternative to this restrictive paradigm (8, 50, 56). Opposed to the diachronic asymmetry in power between father and son – where one obtains power merely by arriving before the other – *Kim* revises the colonial relationship into a synchronic playing field between grandparent and grandchild. For Simone de Beauvoir, the father becomes increasingly aligned with disciplinary power over the course of the eighteenth and nineteenth centuries, while the grandfather becomes associated with the reparative values of playfulness and mutual understanding: "the grandfather, no longer being the head of the family, became the children's abettor over their parents' heads, while for their part the children found in him an amused and indulgent companion" (200).[3] In a colonial context, grandpaternalism results in

---

[2]   The critical application of the father/son relation to *Kim* takes many forms. For example, Jeremy Krikler argues that the "autobiographical elements in *Kim* reveal the impact of master-servant relations on the British in India and the way in which these coiled about the parent-child relationship of whites in the Raj" (24).
[3]   Lynne Segal corroborates Beauvoir's view: "As many have noticed, infantile pleasures can resurface, for instance, in the special affinity grandparents often exhibit playing with their grandchildren, perhaps in ways they never managed

a more playful relation that mitigates the didactic tension at the heart of the 'civilizing' mission of liberal imperialism. By expanding the perimeter of the family beyond the father/son nucleus, Kipling also modifies the way affect radiates between what he imagines as the Indian 'periphery' and the metropolitan 'centre.'[4]

Kim follows the development of its eponymous protagonist, who begins the narrative as an Irish orphan on the streets of Lahore, through his education and eventual employment in the British secret service as a spy. Early on, he meets a lama who serves as a mentor and spiritual counterpoint to the colonial regime: the two narratives intertwine by the end of the novel, as the lama's search for the sacred "River of the Arrow" overlaps with an official mission to disrupt a Russian plot to destabilize British hegemony. *Kim*'s combination of the indigenous and colonial plot has resulted in a perennial critical ambivalence regarding the novel's celebration of Indian diversity and its reinforcement of a naturalized racist hierarchy. Abdul JanMohamed writes, for example, that Kim provides "a positive, detailed, nonstereotypic portrait of the colonized that is unique in colonialist literature" (78). And Phillip Wegner avers that Kipling "produces a utopian figure of India – an India where conflict, disorder, and finally historical change have been eliminated" (143). Even Edward Said, acknowledging the novel's emphasis on "surveillance and control over India," also asserts Kipling's "love for and fascinated attention to its every detail" ("Introduction" 330). In contrast to this critical tradition, John Kucich contends that rather "than eroding social hierarchy, Kipling's multivalent imperialism absolutely depended on it" (138). He finds a darker strain in Kipling's work, affirming "middle-class ideological principles" as "'classless' through the fluid dynamics of sadomasochism" (193). *Kim*'s appreciation of "happy Asiatic disorder" – far from disabling a racial hierarchy – works to obscure the material effects of such socially entrenched inequities (66). This essay argues that *Kim* deploys age inversions to further engrain a model of racial difference as innocuous and natural as growing older. The patriarchal model of empire posits the father as European and the child as Native – in this vertical relation, power flows

---

with their own children, when responsible adulthood was a status they were still struggling hard to achieve" (31).

[4]   In the idiosyncratic relationship between Kim and his elderly interlocutors, Kipling redefines the limits of colonial power by experimenting with new models of familial organization. Noel Annan writes that for "Kipling, as for nearly all Victorians, the greatest of all involuntary in-groups is the family, the great protector against the world's hostility and the inculcator of love and decency" (332).

down as a means of controlling subject populations. Yet in *Kim*, a Tibetan lama occupies the position of elder, while an Irish boy fills that of youth. This inversion of the ordering of age and race attests to a larger rethinking of the networks of dependence between the metropole and the colony, representing a shift away from disciplinary performances of power to more indirect modes. In his retrospective account of Indian life after the Uprising of 1857–58, Kipling demonstrates the effectiveness of indirect rule by framing it as the playful relationship between a grandparent and grandchild – a narrative strategy that relies upon age to performatively defuse the ideological tension of contexts such as race, class, and gender.

Though the Indian Uprising took place over forty years before the publication of *Kim* and over twenty years before the events of the novel begin, it pervades the atmosphere of Kipling's happily content and pluralistic Indian society. Bloody anecdotes about the slaughter of English women and children at Cawnpore entrenched the Uprising in the English imagination as an unprecedented act of violence that required a strong response by the military: Rudrangshu Mukherjee writes that "British rule in India, as an autocracy, had meticulously constructed a monopoly of violence. The revolt of 1857 shattered that monopoly by matching an official, alien violence by an indigenous violence of the colonized" (93). The British military response "destroyed entire villages … hanged Muslims with pork stuffed into their mouths and … blew mutineer-rebels from guns" (Bender 4). It was a testament to the discursive flexibility of empire that it justified such violence by drawing on the ideology of the Victorian family.[5] As Edward Said argues, the British response to the Uprising was filtered through "the world of imperialist polemic, in which the native is naturally a delinquent, the white man a stern but moral parent and judge" ("Introduction" 311). The British represented the Uprising as a misfiring of the relationship between father and son, processing racial and cultural difference as the otherness of age, as a misbehaving child in need of correction. As Jed Esty writes, "imperialism generally casts its subject peoples not as radically different, but as an underdeveloped or youthful version of their rulers, not quite ready for self-government" (16).[6] Similarly, while

---

[5]   Radha Achar asserts that the novel marks a change in the metaphors used to describe the colonial relation: "In *Kim* we see the concept of savage as 'noble and uncorrupt' as vestigial and its being replaced by a new one that validates Paternalism and Trusteeship of European races towards 'natives' now seen as 'children'" (49).

[6]   Benedict Anderson writes that in the aftermath of civil war, historians often represent the event as a fraternal conflict between brothers rather than a war

the Uprising inspired widespread changes to the administration of the
empire – not least the disestablishment of the East India Company – the
government remained invested in cultivating the appearance of family ties
between metropole and colony.[7]

British historians writing after the Uprising drew deeply on familial
metaphors to describe the relations between the colony and the metropole,
even as they deployed a racist arsenal of adjectives to describe the 'muti-
neers.' Charles Ball, in his 1860 *The History of the Indian Mutiny*, relates an
anecdote about native officers for the 70th regiment who desired to be sent
to Delhi to fight the uprising. Pleased by the news, the Governor-General
responded to the petition of the sepoys with an edifying letter: "Trust
your officers. Look to your colonel as your friend and guide. *Look to the
government as children look to their father.* Let me hear that you have done
your duty, and I shall know how to mark with distinction the zeal and
faithfulness of the 70th" (160–1, emphasis added). The Governor-General's
response, far from inspiring a sense of filial responsibility, roused instead an
Oedipal backlash: "intelligence was shortly afterwards received … that the
fidelity of the 70th regiment could not be depended upon … substituting
for the honourable word they were to have borne as a distinctive mark
upon their colours, the ignominious and recreant epithet of 'Traitors'"
(161). John Kaye's 1880 *A History of the Sepoy War in India* also provides
evidence of the short-circuiting of the father/son relationship. When the
British government reprimanded King Wajid Ali Shah of Oude for mis-
managing his kingdom, Kaye writes that,

> Nervous and excitable at all times, and greatly affected by these words, the
> King essayed to speak; but the power of utterance had gone from him. So
> he took a sheet of paper and wrote upon it, that he thanked the Governor-
> General, and would regard his counsels as though they had been addressed by
> a father to his son. There are no counsels so habitually disregarded … (132)

---

between two sovereign nations, thus emphasizing the underlying connections that
transcend the schism (205–7).

[7]   In the eighteenth century, William Jones posited a form of family connection by analysing the shared linguistic structures between Eastern and Western
languages: "The *Sanscrit* language, whatever be its antiquity, is of a wonderful
structure; more perfect than the *Greek*, more copious than the *Latin*, and more
exquisitely refined than either, yet bearing to both of them a stronger affinity, both
in the roots of verbs and the forms of grammar, than could possibly have been
produced by accident; so strong indeed, that no philologer could examine them all
three, without believing them to have sprung from some common source, which,
perhaps, no longer exists" (28).

Immediately after the departure of the Governor-General, the King returns to his "childish" ways: "with an understanding emasculated to the point of childishness, he turned to the more harmless delights of dancing, and drumming, and drawing, and manufacturing small rhymes" (132). While these British historians register the failure of the filial relationship as giving rise to colonial disobedience, their accounts contain Indian subjects who deploy childhood strategically as a means of resistance to a patronizing imperial regime.[8] Both Ball and Kaye are unwilling to recognize what they view as childish disobedience as a form of conscious opposition. Even as histories of the Indian Uprising demonstrated the flaws in the paternal structure of empire, their accounts were blinkered by an inability to understand the colonial relation as determined by anything other than patronizing distance between father and son.

The paternalistic relationship between father and son provided a narrative structure for supporting the project of liberal imperialism, which morally justified empire by bringing the 'light of civilization' to what it viewed as backward societies. The Uprising, however, called this project into question: as Karuna Mantena writes in *Alibis of Empire*, after 1857 the liberal attempt to reform Indians to be more like the British became viewed as a cause for resentment and rebellion (4–5). Shifting away from moral justifications of empire to "sociological and anthropological theories of native society" marked the transition to indirect rule, the belief that "the imperial order would be best preserved by the insinuation of imperial power in the customary order of native society rather than through its repudiation and transformation" (Mantena 22, 150). In its more decentralized approach to governance, the policy of indirect rule invested power in native institutions as a way of mitigating the kind of generational antagonism that emerged from a metropole intent on shaping the colony in its image. While writers such as George Henry Maine provided the epistemological groundwork for this shift in policy, it was Kipling who gave it a narrative form, filling in the affective void left behind by the failure of empire's 'civilizing' mission. In *Kim*, Kipling frames empire as the playful relation between grandparent and grandchild – replacing the didactic project of colonial transformation with a regime of preservation and care.

---

[8]   While Kaye writes approvingly of the patriarchal relation, his description strains credulity: "The Sepoy looked to his officer as to one who had both the power and the will to dispense ample justice to him. In every battalion, indeed, the men turned to their commandant as the depository of all their griefs, and the redresser of all their wrongs. They called him their father, and he rejoiced to describe them as his 'babalogue' – his babes" (258).

Kim recounts the history of the Uprising – called "the Black Year" – through a conversation between the lama and an older, native soldier (54). Early in the novel, Kim and the lama encounter "an old, withered man, who had served the Government in the days of the Mutiny as a native officer in a newly raised cavalry regiment" (48). When the old soldier guides them to the Grand Trunk Road, the lama asks why he carries a sword by his side. The soldier, "as abashed as a child interrupted in his game of make-believe," replies, "'that was a fancy of mine – an old man's fancy. Truly the police orders are that no man must bear weapons throughout Hind, but' – he cheered up and slapped the hilt – 'all the constabeels hereabout know me'" (54). Fearing another outbreak of violence after the Uprising, the British prohibited native inhabitants of India from bearing arms. The old soldier's allegiance to the empire during the upheaval of 1857 grants him the exception to carry arms in a land where they have been forbidden. However, this right also derives from the soldier's age – the perception that his "withered" frame presents less of a threat than a young soldier (48). The "plague" and "madness" that caused the sepoys to turn "against their officers" arises from a dysfunction in the patriarchal relation, sending shockwaves throughout the familial networks of India: "My people, my friends, my brothers fell from me" (54, 55). The soldier's "game of make-believe" and his "old man's fancy" serve as strategies for exercising power in place of the inflexible and unsuccessful relation between father and son. The old soldier positions the Indian subject as a grandparent – not as a child in need of correction, but as an older person who has the freedom to engage in non-threatening play.[9]

Different forms of play radiate throughout *Kim*: in the competitions between characters from different races and castes, in its fictionalization of the geopolitical conflict between Russia and England, and in the form

---

[9]   See also Kipling's "On the City Wall," in which the elderly revolutionary Khem Singh is interned under light security in Lahore. When he escapes during an episode of religious violence, he discovers that life has changed since his younger days: "He fled to those who knew him in the old days, but many of them were dead and more were changed, and all knew something of the Wrath of the Government. He went to the young men, but the glamour of his name had passed away" (242). In addition, the narrator observes, "Khem Singh was old, and anise-seed brandy was scarce," and so the great revolutionary decides "I will go back to Fort Amara of my own free will and gain honour" (242). The treatment of Khem Singh by the British government and his desire to experience the simple pleasures of his captivity reflect a similar treatment to that of the old soldier in *Kim*, contributing to a larger pattern of the position of the elderly native in Kipling's social hierarchy.

of the novel itself, which eschews a conventionally linear teleology for an aleatory, episodic structure. In Matthew Kaiser's account, play pervades all aspects of Victorian modernity: "a world truly in play, by the modern conviction that we are trapped in the infinite regress of ludic representation, in a game that never ends, in the illusion's reflection" (4). While critics often celebrate play as a liberating force, it "can absorb," Kaiser writes, "the most horrific and depressing Victorian phenomena: wars of imperial expansion, or the dehumanizing conditions of crime- and disease-infested slums" (16). In *Kim*, for example, "child play" "masks ideology while downplaying geopolitical violence and imperial espionage" (Kaiser 16). But the novel complicates an easy connection between child's play and the passive absorption of ideology. Kim's games take place in the high-stakes world of imperial espionage while the old soldier's play retains the razor-sharp edge of his cavalry sabre. This suggests that it is not merely play itself that mitigates the effects of ideology, but its connection with the mystifying effects of performing age in an unconventional manner.

Before he becomes involved in games of political intrigue, the young Kim "loved … the game for its own sake – the stealthy prowl through the dark gullies and lanes, the crawl up a water-pipe, the sights and sounds of the women's world on the flat roofs" (5). When he learns – through eavesdropping – about an imminent British attack in the north, Kim uses this knowledge to impress his audience: warming "to the game … he was playing for larger things – the sheer excitement and the sense of power" (49). Hannah Arendt writes that it is the autotelic quality of Kim's play – playing for the sake of the game itself – that creates such a strong resemblance to life, which must also be "lived and loved for its own sake" (217). Ostensibly stripped of any ideological motivation, Kim's pure play leaves only life itself "in a fantastically intensified purity, when man has cut himself off from all ordinary social ties, family, regular occupation, a definite goal, ambitions, and the guarded place in a community to which he belongs by birth" (Arendt 217). If Kim's play demonstrates the provisionality of ideological markers relating to race, caste, and religion, it does so in service to a colonial fantasy that enables the master of these codes vast social power and mobility. His many disguises – as "a low-caste Hindu boy" or the "inconspicuous dress of *chela*" – demonstrate Kim's fluidity of identity, registered by the boy's bewildered question to himself: "Who is Kim?" (139, 183, 120). Mahbub's answer cannot fully account for the possibilities opened by Kim's play, and he allows his sentence to remain open rather than conclude with an essential identity that subtends all the others: "'Among Sahibs, never forgetting thou art a Sahib; among the folk of Hind, always remembering thou art – ' He paused, with a puzzled smile" (145). In *Kim*'s imagination of the colony as a playground of identity that has been mastered by a white child, the resolution of existential crises maps onto the epistemological knowledge related to governing the empire.

Kim's ability to slip between different identities is linked to a deeper fluidity of age: for Kim's child play, we learn, is part and parcel of the adult world of the Great Game.[10] The "Great Game that never ceases day and night," as Lurgan describes it, refers to the contest between England and Russia for influence in Central Asia (177–8). According to Malcolm Yapp, the term originated from Captain Arthur Conolly, who wrote in 1840 to a new appointee in Qandahar: "You've a great game, a noble game before you" (quoted in Yapp 181). While Conolly's original use of the "great game" arose from the 'civilizing mission' of liberal imperialism, the military historian J.W. Kaye recontextualized the term around the defence of British India from what he viewed as external and internal threats (Yapp 184). Kipling's fictionalization of the Great Game in *Kim* is not attuned to the historical reality: Gerald Morgan writes, for example, "that there never was a centrally organized intelligence network in Central Asia as suggested by Kipling and alleged by Soviet historians" (62). But the novel also manipulates the ideological dimensions of the Great Game by filing down its hard edges – both its 'civilizing' thrust and its explicit violence – into a playful drama about Kim's age, poised between youthful zeal and the mature task of imperial espionage. Kim's ambiguous maturity becomes most apparent in his sexuality. When Kim claims to be a priest, the Widow of Kulu responds by challenging his virility, "'We priests! Thou art not yet old enough to – ' She checked the joke with another laugh" (71).[11] Later in the novel, when the now adolescent Kim

---

[10]   Kim's ability to code switch at will exists in tension with the rigidly stratified Indian society. Tim Christensen argues that this represents a fundamental asymmetry between race and identity in the novel: "the internal rupture is claimed as a source of freedom that only whites have the capacity to enjoy, while static boundaries define all other Indian ethnicities. Whiteness stands apart because it names freedom from the ideal of the self as a totality, while other Indian ethnicities are largely bound by such an ideal" (22–3). Don Randall, on the other hand, suggests that Kim's youth (rather than his whiteness) plays the larger role in scrubbing away ideological markers: "The child or, as in the present case, the boy of imperial fictions, therefore is presumed to have an intuitive, unmediated, 'natural' relation with his world. The boyish presence thus de-historicizes, depoliticizes. The boy provides an alibi of disinterestedness" ("Ethnography" 87).

[11]   Young and yet wise for his "little years," Kim provides an imaginative answer to one of the generational tensions at the heart of the Great Game: Shareen Brysac and Karl Meyer write that "The young were driven by both ambition and belief

encounters the Woman of Shamlegh, he refuses her advances and complains, "How can a man follow the Way or the Great Game when he is always pestered by woman?" (258). Sexually desirable and yet celibate, Kim places the Game before the imperatives of heteronormative sexuality and reproduction – leaving him, as Esty writes, "eternally adolescent, always developing but never developed enough" (22). In *Kim*, the Game comes before sex and the conventions of marriage.

Beyond (or before) the sexual norms relating to the marriage plot and the family, Kim falls into a pattern of Kiplingesque characters who must search outside the nuclear family for personal fulfilment. Like most of Kipling's heroes, who are either orphaned or abandoned by their parents to languish in boarding school, Kim must search for sources of affection and instruction beyond the biological father and mother. In "Baa Baa Black Sheep," a fictionalized version of Kipling's own traumatic childhood, the narrator's parents send their son and daughter to live with the evangelical Aunty Rosa for five years while they live in Bombay. In contrast to Aunty Rosa's emotional and physical abuse, "the grey man" Uncle Harry serves as the "great hope and stand-by" for the eponymous black sheep because he takes the young boy on walks and discourses about the navy (178). Serving as an emotional crutch in an otherwise lonely childhood, the grandfather figure takes the side of the child when the forces of the world appear arrayed against him. The Head of the school in *Stalky and Co.* and the elderly Baloo in *The Jungle Books* fulfil similar roles by intervening between the children and the adult world that threatens them, empowering and respecting the youth that fathers and surrogate-fathers often demean. In many of Kipling's works, the parental figure's condescending use of power is linked to the arbitrariness of age. The creation of intimacy across generational lines attests to the possibility for more equitable relations outside of the parent/child dyad, in elective relationships that contest a view of age as manifesting a natural, patronizing gap.

Linked by a shared contrast with the adult years of professional drudgery, youth and old age demonstrate a similarly ludic structure that underwrites the otherwise very different realms of Kim's work in the Great Game and the lama's following of the Way. When Kim reflects on the Great Game he observes that "'it runs like a shuttle throughout all Hind. And my share and my joy' – he smiled into the darkness – 'I owe to the lama here. Also to Mahbub Ali – also to Creighton Sahib, but chiefly to the Holy One'" (226). Of course, of the three men it is only the lama –

---

in the rightness of their cause; their elders were often possessed by half-examined ideas and a determination not to appear weak" (*Kim* 94; *Tournament* xxxvi).

the one privileged by Kim – who remains ignorant of the Great Game
or its workings. Instead, the lama contributes to Kim's understanding of
the Game through the philosophy of the Middle Way, which proscribes
"the fire of any desire or attachment, for that is all Illusion" (94). When
Kim protests that he has unique responsibilities relating to his whiteness,
the lama replies: "I am an old man – pleased with shows as are children.
To those who follow the Way there is neither black nor white, Hind
nor Bhotiyal" (214). The lama's injunction to strip away all markers of
identity goes deeper than the disguises provided by Lurgan Sahib, which
only transform one's outside appearance. The Way provides Kim with a
structure for locating his sense of self amidst the different roles that he
performs – from Friend of All the World, to chela, to schoolboy, to lower-
caste Hindu, and so on.

The lama likens his own old age to the experience of a child at play to
underline the way difference results from the projection of ideology rather
than anything essential to the individual him- or herself. "Surely old folk
are as children," the lama says, "They desire a matter – behold, it must
be done at once, or they fret and weep! Many times when I was upon the
Road I have been ready to stamp with my feet at hindrance of an ox-cart
in the way, or a mere cloud of dust" (196). When Kim avers that "thou art
indeed old, Holy One," the lama replies that "A Cause was put out into
the world, and, old or young, sick or sound, knowing or unknowing, who
can rein in the effect of that cause? Does the Wheel hang still if a child
spin it – or a drunkard?" (196). Reflecting on his own great age provides
a way for the lama to address what he views as equally illusory markers
of difference that underwrite the individual's entrapment on the Wheel.
Like the lama, Kim thinks,

> I am very old … Every month I become a year more old. I was very young,
> and a fool to boot, when I took Mahbub's message to Umballa. Even when
> I was with that white Regiment I was very young and small and had no
> wisdom. But now I learn every day, and in three years the Colonel will …
> let me go upon the Road. (139)

Excited by the prospect of setting out on the road, Kim imaginatively accel-
erates his ageing to anticipate the pleasures of his future adventures. Both the
lama and Kim manipulate the conventions that delimit identity by filtering
them through what they perceive as the more innocuous category of age.

The lama draws together the states of old age and youth at the beginning of the novel, downplaying his own knowledge to talk with children
at a level of equality: "We be followers of the Middle Way, living in peace

in our lamaseries, and I go to see the Four Holy Places before I die. Now do you, who are children, know as much as I do who am old" (7). In one moment, the lama lectures to an awe-struck audience, peppering his speech with arcane Chinese quotations; yet he treats even these examples of scholarship "simply as a child engrossed with a new game" (241). The narrator continually references the lama's childishness: "Simply as a child the old man handed [Kim] the bowl" and the "lama had waked and, simply as a child bewildered in a strange bed, called for Kim" (15, 72). Such behaviour by the man with the "thousand-wrinkled face" does not register as a senile reversion to a less developed state of life – a second childhood – but indicates the way childhood and old age unashamedly draw out the networks of dependence and play immanent in all social life (12). The lama realizes, after gaining strength hiking through his beloved mountains, that "I became strong to do evil and to forget" (260). He laments that the hills "strengthened me to do evil, to forget my Search. I delighted in life and the lust of life. I desired strong slopes to climb. I cast about to find them. I measured the strength of my body, which is evil, against the high hills" (261). In openly rejecting strength, *Kim* uses the lama's youthful old age to present dependence as enabling the play that connects individuals of different races and castes – the model of empire Kipling implicitly endorses in the novel – while the adult strives to create an exclusive, professional image of self-reliant importance.

While the lama encourages play – for example, allowing the "children of the house [to tug] unrebuked at his rosary" – the middle-aged men in the special services take events much more seriously (41). The Great Game, far from taking on the ludic qualities that characterize Kim's enjoyment, takes on life-or-death consequences for characters like Colonel Creighton, Lurgan Sahib, and Mahbub Ali. For these characters, the Great Game has become a profession that does not provoke Kim's exhilaration in play or the lama's wonder in his quest. Matthew Fellion writes that "He [Kim] is playing. The men, meanwhile, are undertaking a mastering of children through adult knowledge that operates on similar assumptions and through similar mechanisms to the mastering of 'the Orient' by means of European knowledge" (900–1). Marked by the twinned discourses of youth and old age, Kim and the lama have an immediate ability to take pleasure in the Game. Lurgan, on the contrary, creates games for others to play, initiating new recruits into the Great Game through hazing rituals that verge on emotional and psychological abuse. Mahbub also takes his responsibility to the state and to Kim seriously, establishing himself as a father to the boy and giving him advice about how to best conduct his future. Mahbub's desire to be taken seriously prompts him to dye his beard "scarlet with lime (for he was elderly and did not wish his grey hairs to show)" (19). The rejection of old age – Mahbub's desire to appear within the bounds of a virile adulthood – marks his exclusion from the vectors of play that connect the poles of the grandfather/grandchild dyad.[12]

One of the anxieties regarding Kim throughout the novel relates to the fear that he will mature into an adult too quickly and lose the childishness that gives him such zest for the Game. When Kim arrives at the Gates of Learning for his education, "His quickness would have delighted an English master; but at St. Xavier's they know the first rush of minds developed by sun and surroundings, as they know the half-collapse that sets in at twenty-two or twenty-three" (126). "He ripens too quickly – as Sahibs reckon," Mahbub observes as he argues to enrol Kim under the auspices of Lurgan's instruction (131). The Game privileges the stage before adult enervation, and the accession to maturity comes at the cost of the pleasure that animates the many performances of the successful agent. Yet, in addition to this pleasure – or because of it – the agent gains some special access to the culture that he is meant to infiltrate: "A very few white people, but many Asiatics, can throw themselves into amazement as it were by repeating their own names over and over again to themselves, letting the mind go free upon speculation as to what is called personal identity. When one grows older, the power, usually, departs" (187). To become an adult, that is, serves as shorthand for the acquisition of masculine, middle-class, Western values: a stable identity. However, these values do not translate fully to the project of espionage, as growing older atrophies identification with and the ability to enter imaginatively into other cultures. Kim's unparalleled success at the Great Game occurs while his identity remains unmoored, before his epiphany at the end of the novel when everything clicks into place: "'I am Kim. I am Kim. And what is Kim?' His soul repeated it again and again. … with an almost audible click he felt the wheels of his being lock up anew on the world without" (283). While the reader will never know about his future in the secret service, the evidence in the novel suggests that the newly centred Kim will have more difficulty navigating the play of identity demanded by the Great Game.

---

[12]   Hurree Chunder Mukherjee represents an exception to the connection between play and age. He creates puns, disguises himself as a pharmacist to trick Kim, and plays a parting joke on the Russian spies. But Hurree also remains invested in a strict professional hierarchy that characters like Kim and the lama eschew, reminding Kim of departmental seniority and desiring ethnographic and professional renown.

In the wider geopolitical conflict of *Kim*, the play of childhood and old age animate the contest between empires for influence over the Punjab. The Russian and French spies fail in their mission to usurp British hegemony precisely because they adopt the patriarchal stance of the father to the son. When they encounter Hurree Chunder Mukherjee, the spies immediately lapse into the patronizing rhetoric of the disciplinarian: "'He represents in little India in transition – the monstrous hybridism of East and West,' the Russian replied. 'It is *we* who can deal with Orientals'" (240). Criticizing the laxity of the British empire, the Russian endorses a more strictly delineated hierarchy between colonizer and colonized. Observing the lama's poise, the Russian explodes: "'But look at the folds of the drapery. Look at his eyes – how insolent! Why does this make one feel that we are so young a people?' The speaker struck passionately at a tall weed. 'We have nowhere left our mark yet. Nowhere! *That*, do you understand, is what disquiets me'" (241). The Russian's sense of racial superiority crumbles when confronted with the lama, who embodies an ancient tradition that bewilders the spy's understanding of national hierarchy: the roles reverse, and the Russian begins acting like a petulant child rather than the stern father. In his aggressive attempt to appropriate the paternal role, the Russian repeats the failures of the British regime before 1857 that attempted to shape India into its own image – and suffers a similarly painful bout of violence. The relationship between Kim and the lama counters this example of failed policy because they are linked in play and mutual dependence: in Kipling's conciliatory imagination, their bonds represent the power of governance that is based on consent rather than coercion. However, fractures appear in Kipling's benign account of indirect rule. The fact that the lama consents in ignorance of Kim's true motives suggests that the truth behind indirect rule – of the racial or ethnic identity of the agents directing power for the sake of governance – matters less than the ability of the policy to craft an efficacious narrative of playful relation.

As the Russian's disciplinary paternalism is met with failure and violence, the relationship of Kim and the lama survives through the reparative values of care and preservation. After being struck in the face by the spy, the lama contracts an illness that makes his departure from the hills difficult. The Woman of Shamlegh provides men to help transport him, but Kim eventually takes up most of the burden: "It was never more than a couple of miles a day now, and Kim's shoulders bore all the weight of it – the burden of an old man, the burden of the heavy food-bag with the locked books, the load of the writings on his heart, and the details of the daily routine" (271). After the high-stakes conflict of the Great Game, this scene draws Kim – and the reader – back down to the simplest needs of the human being: away from geopolitical aggression and toward the circuits of care that link one individual to another. Such care, Kipling implies, takes a greater toll than the professional world of espionage. Both the lama and the Widow of Kulu describe Kim's eventual capitulation to the illness that afflicted the lama as a kind of cannibalism: "It is true that the old eat the young daily," the widow observes, and the lama claims that "I have stolen strength from thee" and "lived on thy strength till the young branch bowed and nigh broke" (274, 273, 288). Yet Kim's sacrifice also comes with compensation, as he acknowledges to the lama that "Thou leanest on me in the body, Holy One, but I lean on thee for some other things" (273). Though the terms of their exchange differ – Kim offers bodily aid, the lama spiritual or moral – the two provide mutual care for one another. And though separated by a large gulf of time, Kim's youth and the lama's old age meet on a horizontal plane as equals, the same planar structure – a game board, so to speak – upon which the many actors carry out their moves and counter-moves in Kipling's fictionaliza-tion of the Great Game.

When Kipling deploys the grandparent/grandchild dyad in *Kim*, he draws on Western conventions related to grandparents and grandchildren as a way of giving narrative shape to the colonial relationship between Britain and India. The dyad informs the way Kim plays the Great Game and how he navigates through the many layers of a stratified society further riven by British imperialism. In the India that Kipling represents, the violence of imperialism resides in a past that has been overcome. He critiques the paternalistic rhetoric of the disciplinarian father as ignit-ing the hostilities that resulted in the Uprising and turns to what I have called grandpaternalism to imagine a contented 'now' that extends across India's geographical expanse. This representational strategy both supports and draws inspiration from the policy of indirect rule: far from the child in need of instruction, the colonized emerges as an older person resistant to development but deserving of care. Where liberal imperialism treated the markers of racial and cultural difference as problems to be resolved through Anglicization, indirect rule promoted a form of cosmopolitan pluralism that, in theory, preserved diversity. In *Kim*, Kipling disguises the structural violence of imperialism by grafting the playful relationship between grandparent and grandchild onto other forms of meaningful dif-ference, using this seemingly innocuous relation as a heuristic for develop-ing more disturbingly efficient modes of social knowledge and control.

Works Cited

Achar, Radha. "The Child in Kipling's Fiction: An Analysis." *The Literary Criterion*, vol. 22, no. 4, 1987, pp. 46–53.

Adams, James Eli. *Dandies and Desert Saints: Styles of Victorian Masculinity*. Cornell UP, 1995.

Anderson, Benedict. *Imagined Communities: Reflections on the Origin and Spread of Nationalism*. Verso, 2006.

Annan, Noel. "Kipling's Place in the History of Ideas." *Victorian Studies*, vol. 3, no. 4, 1960, pp. 323–48.

Arendt, Hannah. *The Origins of Totalitarianism*. Meridian, 1962.

Ball, Charles. *The History of the Indian Mutiny*. London, 1860.

Beauvoir, Simone de. *The Coming of Age*, translated by Patrick O'Brian. Norton, 1996.

Bell, Duncan. "Empire and Imperialism." *The Cambridge History of Nineteenth-Century Political Thought*, edited by Gareth Stedman Jones and Gregory Claeys. Cambridge UP, 2011, pp. 864–92.

Bender, Jill. *The 1857 Indian Uprising and the British Empire*. Cambridge UP, 2016.

Brysac, Shareen, and Karl Meyer. *Tournament of Shadows: The Great Game and the Race for Empire in Central Asia*. Abacus, 1999.

Christensen, Tim. "The Unbearable Whiteness of Being: Misrecognition, Pleasure, and White Identity in Kipling's *Kim*." *College English*, vol. 39, no. 2, 2012, pp. 9–30.

Esty, Jed. *Unseasonable Youth: Modernism, Colonialism, and the Fiction of Development*. Oxford UP, 2012.

Fanon, Frantz. *Black Skin, White Masks*, translated by Richard Philcox. Grove, 2008.

Fellion, Matthew. "Knowing Kim, Knowing in *Kim*." *SEL: Studies in English Literature, 1500–1900*, vol. 53, no. 4, 2013, pp. 897–912.

Hall, Catherine. "Of Gender and Empire: Reflections on the Nineteenth Century." *Gender and Empire*, edited by Philippa Levine. Oxford UP, 2004, pp. 46–76.

JanMohamed, Abdul. "The Economy of Manichean Allegory: The Function of Racial Difference in Colonialist Literature." *Critical Inquiry*, vol. 12, no. 1, 1985, pp. 59–87.

Jones, William. *Discourses Delivered Before the Asiatic Society and Miscellaneous Papers, on the Religion, Poetry, Literature, Etc. of the Nations of India*, edited by James Elmes, vol. 1. London, 1824.

Kaiser, Matthew. *The World in Play: Portraits of a Victorian Concept*. Stanford UP, 2012.

Kaye, John William. *A History of the Sepoy War in India, 1857–1858*, vol. 1. London, 1880.

Kipling, Rudyard. "Baa Baa Black Sheep." *The Man Who Would Be King and Other Stories*. Oxford UP, 2008, pp. 170–97.

——. *The Complete Stalky and Co.* Oxford UP, 2009.

——. *The Jungle Books*. Oxford UP, 2008.

——. *Kim*. Penguin, 2011.

——. "On the City Wall." *The Man Who Would Be King and Other Stories*.

Oxford UP, 2008, pp. 221–43.

——. "White Man's Burden." *Complete Verse*. Anchor, 1989, pp. 321–3.

Krikler, Jeremy. "The Historical Significance of Autobiographical Elements in *Kim*." *Kipling Journal*, vol. 87, 2013, pp. 24–44.

Kucich, John. *Imperial Masochism: British Fiction, Fantasy, and Social Class*. Princeton UP, 2007.

Mantena, Karuna. *Alibis of Empire: Henry Maine and the Ends of Liberal Imperialism*. Princeton UP, 2010.

McClintock, Anne. *Imperial Leather: Race, Gender, and Sexuality in the Colonial Contest*. Routledge, 1995.

Morgan, Gerald. "Myth and Reality in the Great Game." *Asian Affairs*, vol. 4, no. 1, 1973, pp. 55–65.

Mukherjee, Rudrangshu. "'Satan Let Loose upon Earth': The Kanpur Massacres in India in the Revolt of 1857." *Past and Present*, vol. 128, 1990, pp. 92–116.

Randall, Don. "Ethnography and the Hybrid Boy in Rudyard Kipling's *Kim*." *Ariel: A Review of International English Literature*, vol. 27, no. 3, 1996, pp. 79–104.

——. "The Imperial Boy as Prosthesis." *Victorian Review*, vol. 32, no. 2, 2009, pp. 41–4.

Said, Edward. "Introduction to *Kim*." *Kim*. Penguin, 2011, pp. 291–331.

Segal, Lynne. *Out of Time: The Pleasures and Perils of Ageing*. Verso, 2014.

Spivak, Gayatri. "Resident Alien?" *Relocating Postcolonialism*, edited by David Theo Goldberg and Ato Quayson. Blackwell, 2002, pp. 47–65.

Wegner, Phillip. "'Life as He Would Have It': The Invention of India in Kipling's *Kim*." *Cultural Critique*, vol. 26, 1993–94, pp. 129–59.

Yapp, Malcolm. "The Legend of the Great Game." *Proceedings of the British Academy*, vol. 111, 2001, pp. 179–98.

6

"I Could Turn Viper Tomorrow": Challenging Reproductive Futurism in Merle Collins's The Colour of Forgetting[1]

EMILY KATE TIMMS

Grenadian author Merle Collins has talked in an interview about the collective optimism felt about the future after the Grenadian Revolution of 1979, when the Grenada United Labour Party government was overthrown by the New Jewel Movement (NJM), a Black Power organization that turned into a Marxist political party. This event was seen as a turning point, cementing Grenada's status as an independent postcolonial country after Britain relinquished the territory in 1974. Collins describes the affection felt for the new Prime Minister, a young revolutionary called Maurice Bishop, in terms of his rapport across generations of ordinary Grenadians, epitomized by a famous photograph of an older woman touching the young Premier's face (Scott, "Fragility of Memory" 105).[2] The image symbolizes the confection of youth and old age as a postcolonial political stratagem wherein a beneficent grandmother figure nurtures the hope that revolutionary black youth represents.

Collins reflects on the popular perception that Bishop was an approachable and sympathetic agent of change: "'De boy nice, he nice, all behind he head nice!' [Everything is nice, good or attractive about him] Dah's ting you hear. So you think about the body, and how people view the man, the individual" (Scott, "Fragility of Memory" 105). Collins draws on her memories of collective utterance to link revolutionary legitimacy and masculine youthfulness. Bishop is called a 'boy' – instead of the British university-educated, Marxist activist he was – implying that his political appeal was accentuated by his youthfulness. Throughout the rest of the interview Collins repeatedly references how young people and stu-

[1] This work was supported by the Arts and Humanities Research Council and the White Rose College of the Arts and Humanities.
[2] The photograph is reproduced in George Brizan and Kwamina Brizan, *Grenada: Fortitude and the Human Condition* (121).

dents were at the forefront of the NJM movement in resistance to the former Prime Minister Eric Gairy's *ancien régime*, which was characterized by longstanding incumbents, corruption, and violent suppression of opposition both before and after Grenada was granted independence (Scott, "Fragility of Memory" 99, 102; also see Meeks 138–48). According to Collins's testimony, Bishop's youth and masculine vigour propelled the New Jewel Movement's popularity. He seems to embody the NJM's motto, devised by the Grenadian Carnival calypsonian Lord Melody, of "forward ever and backward never."[3] The interview subtly delineates a distinction between gendered and aged bodies within Grenada's postcolonial politics.

The hope for the future symbolized by Bishop's youth was crushed when a protracted period of political tension between Bishop and his Deputy Prime Minister erupted into violence. Bishop and several prominent party figures and students were killed by the People's Revolutionary Army, the military wing of the government, and in November 1985 the United States of America invaded the country to quash the potential civil war and protect American 'interests' in the Caribbean basin (Meeks 165). In this essay, I prise apart the strategic connection between youth and old age in Grenada's revolutionary politics to elucidate how Collins's fiction fosters new intergenerational relationships without simply venerating youth and youthful male bodies – and the political violence with which they became tragically associated in retrospect.

The relationship between race, gender, and embodied ageing at stake here is the central concern of my reading of Collins's second novel *The Colour of Forgetting* (1995). Collins worked in the NJM administration as Head of Research on Latin America and the Caribbean, writing speeches for Bishop, and acting as a translator for diplomatic meetings. The Prime Minister's assassination, the Grenadian Revolution's implosion, and subsequent American invasion preoccupies her critical and creative writing (see Collins, *Grenada*; Collins, "Understanding through Poetry"). *The Colour of Forgetting* is set on the fictional island Paz, a thinly veiled allusion to the real Grenada. The novel is experimental in structure and genre, as Collins interweaves various chronologies and intergenerational histories

---

[3]   The chorus for the Calypso became the official motto of the NJM:
Grenada is moving fast
We reaching somewhere at last
Our motto we must remember
'Forward ever and backward never!' (cited in Searle 102)

together, with passing references to major political events. As such, *The Colour of Forgetting* describes Paz, but speaks allegorically to Grenada's colonial inheritance as well as its contemporary revolutionary history. The novel dramatizes how older women operating in the shadow of the 'black matriarch,' a Caribbean social stereotype characterized by households managed by a paradoxically domineering yet selfless black woman (Senior 100–2), are central figures who attempt to negotiate the traumatic legacies of Paz's white patrilineal colonial governance and a postcolonial revolutionary present.

My reading of this figure of age in Collins's work begins by drawing on ageing studies research on 'reproductive futurism' – a term that I will explain shortly – to consider how Collins challenges the collective belief that children can guarantee Paz's cultural and economic fortunes. Next, I analyse how Collins's aesthetics draw on the conventions of the Caribbean trickster to show how older women expand received notions of intergenerational care in the novel, which are problematically predicated on expectations that the ageing matriarch can 'heal' inherited postcolonial traumas through simply relating genealogical knowledges (Cooper 187–8). Finally, I read Collins's novel as deploying the repeated aesthetic trope of the crossroads, often associated with tricksters, to show how an intergenerational community of women use their trickster-like bodies and modes of sensory perception to negotiate Paz's (and by extension Grenada's) intergenerational postcolonial trauma and develop a more inclusive future.

"Forward Ever, Backward Never":
The Reproductive Futurism of Postcolonial Paz

The Colour of Forgetting follows generations of seer women, each named Carib, and the creole Malheureuse family. The novel opens with the most recent, and final, Carib wandering away from Leapers' hill, a site where Paz's indigenous Amerindian population committed suicide by jumping into the ocean rather than resign themselves to colonial rule (Collins 1–2).[4] Carib repeats a prophecy of "Blood in the north, blood to come in the south, and the blue crying red in between" (3). The novel depicts Carib's unfolding prophecy through tracing the fortunes of generations of the Malheureuse family, particularly the centenarian Mamag, her adopted great-niece Willive, and great-grandnephew Thunder. The generational storytelling occurs in

---

[4]   The site is the exact match of Grenada's Sauteurs where, as a last resort, the indigenous Kalinago killed themselves in resistance to colonial rule by jumping into the ocean.

response to Thunder hearing ancestral spirits and voices as a child, which frequently upset or incapacitate him and cause a crippling fear of his meteorological namesake. Carib recommends that telling the Malheureuse story will help quieten the spirits as he comes to understand his ancestral history (14). The source of intergenerational conflict in *The Colour of Forgetting* centres on the issue of land ownership. The narrative recounts ever-widening cycles of intergenerational dispossession and violence over land, fuelled by colonization and Paz's incorporation into a global economy. It gradually traces back the generations of Malheureuses to the time of plantation slavery, when the white plantation owner Malheureuse beat his African slave John Bull to death (35–6). In the narrative present the Malheureuse family genealogy includes both white European and African ancestry. Mamag's brother, Uncle Son-Son, harbours avaricious ambitions for land left to his siblings and their children and claims that his position as the 'legitimate' son – meaning born within wedlock – of a white European ancestor entitles him to the land (25–6). Echoing the behaviour of the ancestral Malheureuse, Son-Son arranges for his nephew Ti-Moun to be beaten, claims the land, and evicts Ti-Moun's wife Cassandra and the infant Willive. Land disputes are repeated in the next generation when the new postcolonial revolutionary government tries to forbid peasants from buying small agricultural plots of under five acres, arguing that Paz would be economically uncompetitive. These reforms pitch young revolutionary adults such as Thunder against their older parents, including Willive, who wish to buy land, but under the reforms cannot afford to do so (156–7). The government calls a town meeting which ends in a riot with many leaping to their deaths from a fort like the indigenous Caribs centuries before. Eventually, a "Great Power," a proxy for the USA, intervenes with an economic reform plan (173). The failed Revolution is one event among a repeated cycle of intergenerational hostility, economic dispossession, and gendered and racialized violence, beginning with colonial conquest and finishing with neo-colonial economic subjugation.

Critics have analysed Collins's use of time and chronology in the novel to discuss Grenadian cultural wounding after the brutal ending of the revolutionary government and subsequent American invasion. Alison Donnell (78), Susan Meltzer (85), and David Scott (*Omens of Adversity* 75) each argue that a linear chronology associated with the new revolutionary government is juxtaposed with a 'mythopoetic' model of cyclical time of spirits and ancestors.[5] But their readings underestimate the extent

---

[5]   I hesitate to deploy the term 'mythopoetic' or 'magical realism' to describe the palpable presence of spirits on Paz as to do so underestimates how these

to which these models of time are racialized and gendered to create a hierarchy of knowledges. Such readings espouse the aforementioned 'reproductive futurism,' a concept originating in queer theory (Edelman 1–2), and used by ageing studies scholar Cynthia Port to describe the questionable rhetorical association of children or childhood with a collective future that excludes other age groups. Port argues that reproductive futurist readings fetishize the future with the effect of bypassing the need for action in the present and devaluing the contribution that ageing people may make in their community (18–19). I develop Port's theorization to explore how critical interpretations of the fictionalized depiction of Grenadian history and its revolution in *The Colour of Forgetting* threaten to sustain a distinctly postcolonial iteration of reproductive futurism, a problematic hope that the advent of a new generation alone can bring about the meaningful emancipation from the racialized and capitalist economies of Paz's colonial order. Rather, I argue that Collins critiques collective convictions that children will rescue the island from an ongoing cycle of colonial and postcolonial trauma and violence by showing how a future-oriented youthful culture of 'progress' maintains pernicious colonial hierarchies and damages younger generations' well-being.

Scott argues that Paz's revolutionary government pursues an ideological commitment to time as linear progress, indicated by its project of agricultural and economic modernization (*Omens of Adversity* 94–5). As one government supporter in the novel summarizes: "this idea of federation and Caricom and all thing. ... We have to come together to go forward!" (Collins 167).[6] The notion of collective progress is enshrined in the need to move "forward," echoing the NJM's revolutionary motto "forward ever, backward never." Yet recursive – cyclical or repeated – modes of time in *The Colour of Forgetting* conflict with the forward-looking 'progress' narrative peddled by the revolutionary government. Scott interprets the representation of such models in the fictional Paz as part of Collins's allegorical purpose, showing that the Grenadian Revolution is "merely one significant episode in a larger story of generations of conflict in what is now imagined and represented as the cyclical pattern of a general history whose generative logic is catastrophic" (*Omens of Adversity* 74–5). The Amerindians' mass suicide, John Bull's murder, the Malheureuse land dis-

---

presences inform the cosmological worldview of many people living in Grenada, and the Caribbean more generally.

6   Collins references CARICOM (the Caribbean Community), an organization of Caribbean states dedicated to regional integration and economic development, which came into being in 1973.

putes, and the marketplace riot collectively constitute repeating moments of violence within Paz's "catastrophic" circular history (*Omens of Adversity* 88). The symbolic function of time as repetition in the novel repudiates the promise of forward-looking postcolonial politics for the island.

However, Scott's analysis misses the way in which Collins links the linear 'forward ever' thinking of the revolutionary government with colonial racialized and gendered laws and policies. The postcolonial revolutionary administration ironically replicates the inequalities of plantation slavery and post-emancipation *metayage* to perpetuate intergenerational violence.[7] Decades before the Revolution takes place Son-Son reads codified forms of knowledge in accordance with European laws on lawful matrimony: "according to the will, you know, as the son read and interpret it careful careful, only lawful children and their descendants should inherit of this land. The unlawful had no place. No rights" (Collins 25). He uses the law to uphold privileges associated with claimed European bloodlines to evict fellow Malheureuse from familial land, as previously mentioned, and form a larger plot to own and cultivate as a 'right.' Mamag recognizes that Son-Son's respect for written law is tied to his belief in his own racialized superiority: "is like you feel white blood bastard more respectable than straight black blood bastard?" (50). She exposes Son-Son's claim to racialized purity as a fantasy, but he remains undeterred in his conviction that "law is law" (51). While collective knowledge and memory indicate that Son-Son is illegitimate though ancestral miscegenation, such knowledge does not unseat the priority afforded to Paz's colonial legal processes. The colonial system of racialized patrilineal inheritance also privileges the 'young' and shuns the experiential knowledge of older generations. For example, Son-Son intermixes the law's rhetorical focus on 'children' as the inheritors of land and property with his conviction that he is a 'legitimate' white bastard. Son-Son positions himself as the rightful 'white' heir (the Child) over his chronometrically younger nephew Ti-Moun, who objects to being removed on the grounds of old 'black' labour having cultivated the ground: "even after the old people work so hard on the land?" (52–3). A similar pattern of economic dispossession is threatened by the revolutionary government's proposed land reforms – something true of Grenada as well as Paz. By banning the sale of 'uneconomic' plots and encouraging older black rural smallholders to merge their land into large cooperative farms, the reforms are interpreted as disproportionately benefiting the

---

[7]   *Metayage* refers to the system whereby after the abolition of slavery in Grenada, former slaves were allowed to stay on estates provided that they gave owners a share of their crop yield (Meeks 134).

younger generations of wealthy 'high-browns and whites' of the country (142), whose ancestors under the colonial plantation system owned the land. The law is twisted again to fit the logic of reproductive futurism and ironically maintains the status quo of colonial *metayage*. The past and the 'ancestral' are shunned in favour of the future and men who can lay claim, at least rhetorically, to being white and youthful (even when technically older than their dispossessed relatives).

DeLoughrey is more hopeful than Scott in her reading of the novel, arguing that the interweaving narrative strands in Collins's novel constitute a 'spiral' model of time which "creates a dialogue between the haunting nature of the past and the promising capacity for change which is attributed to the future" (254). This reading of spiral time applauds a logic wherein 'progress' or the 'future' is repeatedly pushed onto black children, which enables Thunder's revolutionary generation to bypass their responsibilities for Paz's post-revolutionary predicament. For DeLoughrey, Paz is in "transition … to the Africanised future" which depends on "women to physically and imaginatively reproduce the nation's past and future" (265).[8] After the disagreements over the land reforms lead to a riot in Paz City's marketplace and the Great Power intervenes, Thunder, now an adult, concludes that his daughter Nehanda and her generation are "out front" and "will write the names we ignore all the time" (Collins 201). Young girls, in other words, must now carry the burden of Paz's postcolonial fortunes. Thunder's conviction begins another cycle of Paz's history as he echoes beliefs held by Willive and the women of the local Nutmeg Pool that their children will elevate the island's condition. They tell the young Thunder that "you is all of we future. All-you young people, you is this country future. All of us future" (Collins 101). DeLoughrey inadvertently reads the novel through the lens of a racialized and gendered reproductive futurism as (female) children are ultimately interpreted as the new key to finding a new course for Paz after the Revolution fails, and women are there to produce children and encourage collective beliefs that children can change the island's fortunes.

Yet Collins is sceptical of the premise that children and young people represent Paz's salvation. Indeed, the promise of either linear progress or spiral time prioritizes pedagogic systems either rooted in colonial punishment or diasporic black radicalism. Both methods have physical and psychological implications for children's health and well-being. Adult women including Willive encourage children to 'write' the country's future through mastering book-learning and passing exams (Collins 100). Thunder endures regular beatings at school, however, at the hands of a patriarchal headmaster. Willive demands that Thunder sit at the headmaster's desk and endure the beatings, as "the beating is only for a time. Is the future that important" (105). Obtaining a secondary school scholarship and ostensibly fulfilling his promise comes at the cost of Thunder bearing the strap, a punishing colonial education that, given his familial history, echoes the merciless beating of the ancestral John Bull by Malheureuse. If the colonial education at home is rooted in physical punishment, Thunder's subsequent education in the colonial metropole has deleterious effects on his psychological well-being. After earning a university scholarship to study in London, he is subjected to systemic racial abuse. As a result:

> England drove him further inside himself, listening only to the thunder in his head, too depressed to write home, his head too full of noise to allow enough silence to participate … He left the country the day after the course was finished, returning, with a deeper silence and a degree in Accountancy. (153)

His experiences in London expose the promise of colonial education; far from offering the 'expansion of the mind' it promises for its colonial subjects, it isolates him and so amplifies the ancestral spirits inside him with damaging effects on his well-being. Collins acknowledges the conspicuous continuities between educational 'progress,' patrilineal book-learning, racial hierarchies and physical and psychological subjugation in both Paz's colonial education system and study in the metropole.

In the first instance, this subjugation appears to be countered by the younger students' demonstrations on Paz, influenced by the Black Power movement and left-wing Marxist-Leninist ideological thought. In interviews Collins has discussed the centrality of the Caribbean Black Power movement, built on the American movements of the 1960s and 1970s, as a way to discuss, for the first time, "what being black meant" in Grenada's postcolonial politics (Scott, "Fragility of Memory" 98). I would suggest that *The Colour of Forgetting* marks a strategic troubling of the revolutionary legacy of Black Power in Grenada. Reading Collins's fictionalized revolutionary youth activism alongside Grenada's historical context reveals further continuities between the reproductive and racialized intellectual inheritance of colonialism and the newer youth-led Black Power movement, which became the new revolutionary government in 1979. In the novel, participating in Black Power gatherings has detrimental consequences for Thunder's wellbeing. When he joined the rallies "because he started to link the Black Power idea with all he knew about Da [his paternal grandmother] and Mamag and his grandfather" it aggravates the noises in Thunder's head ("the demonstration made him hear thunder roaring inside his head") and he has to withdraw (136). There is no therapeutic link between radically black and left-wing thought and activism and postcolonial Paz's economic and cultural history. The students' emphasis on the abstracted socioeconomic politics of 'blackness' is observed with bemusement by older residents: "young people were talking so much about being black. As if, Willive said sometimes, they just discover" (114). Regarding Paz as a parallel for Grenada, such bemusement serves as a pointed indictment of the revolutionary government's investment in elitist articulations of Marxist-Leninist ideology that were divorced from the realities of everyday life. Consequently, the land reforms appear to Willive to be an academic exercise rather than grounded in lived reality: "Practical! Practical is word in book. I telling you about practical life we go through" (166). For older generations, the youth-led revolutionary movement may be founded upon the promise of black empowerment, but the Marxist-Revolutionary frameworks underpinning the government will see a return to the black poor being, in practice, dispossessed from land they worked hard to obtain as their small plots become merged into cooperatives.

Not only are such ideas divorced from Paz's local context and histories of racialized struggle, but they also seem symbolically ill-fated. After the disagreements over the land reforms lead to a riot in Paz City's marketplace and the Great Power intervenes, Thunder concludes that it will be his infant daughter's generation which will right the wrongs of Paz's predicament (201). Thunder names his daughter after Nehanda Charwe Nyakasikana, the Shona revolutionary spiritual leader in colonial Rhodesia and claimed by Zimbabwean nationalists as an icon of anti-colonial resistance (Kuba 166). The effect is to displace responsibility for solving Paz's issues onto another younger generation, continuing the cycle of reproductive futurist tendencies, which absolves the current, youthful and male-led revolutionary administration from taking further remedial action. Yet the fact that Nehanda is part of the Malheureuse story – the surname in French meaning unlucky, unfortunate and miserable – undermines the hopefulness of the Black Power movement as a whole. Collins criticizes the association of children with a Black Power-led future as equally suspect in practice as the pre-revolutionary colonial education system. To 'read' and 'write' the future via book-learning and student activism endangers Thunder's well-being, reinforces mechanisms of patriarchal colonial control, or defers hope onto black female futurism.

The novel's epilogue exposes how belief in the redemptive power of children alone is a fallacy. The chapter takes place on the *Huddersfield*, a boat taking Carib, locals, and tourists from Paz to Eden. The boat passes by Kick-em-Ginny, an underwater volcano and the name of a water spirit dwelling in the sea.[9] A "young body" is sceptical of the volcano's existence, and mocks "an old body" who warns the captain when the boat goes near the water spirit (Collins 205). In this case Kick-em-Ginny erupts and rocks the boat, causing a baby to die by choking on vomit (213). The symbol of the sea claiming the baby's life demonstrates that children are just as vulnerable as adults to Paz's traumatic cycle of disaster. The baby's fate contrasts with a sleeping older man who survives. He communes with his dead wife to reassure the bewildered passengers: "he explains that Miss Mae say is not so bad, really. That it's twenty years to the day since his wife, Miss Mae, went to meet her Maker" (211). Collins suggests that older people possess uncodified, embodied forms of knowledge that are overlooked by younger people, and such knowledges can be the key to survival: "sometimes an old body might tense with the habit [of passing over the volcano …]. The older heads return to dust … And by-and-by Kick-em-Ginny disappears" (205). That an "old body might tense with the habit" implies a corporeal way of knowing which would not satisfy the young body's demand for precise information. Old bodies and embodied knowledges are here symbolically connected to the land and sea. As older bodies age and return to the earth as dust, Kick-em-Ginny becomes metaphorically buried in the sea and collective memory. Bodily signifiers such as smiles, glances, and tensed limbs indicate how older people may 'read' the dangers of the landscape and spirits, but such gestures remain undecipherable to younger people. That the old man should wake up to deliver an explanation while the crying baby is silenced seems to be a knowing provocation. Instead of placing children, codified knowledge, and linear progress at the crux of the novel's future, older people's embodied knowledges and ways of reading the landscape have the capacity, it seems, to bypass the reproductive futurism of revolutionary 'progress' and cycles of traumatic disaster.

Trickster Aesthetics as Postcolonial Intergenerational Care

Collins uses the Malheureuse family story to explore the potential of older women's embodied knowledge as a means of shaping intergenerational caring relationships and healing Paz's traumatic postcolonial lega-

---

[9]   The name is adapted from Kick 'em Jenny, an underwater volcano offshore from Grenada.

cies. These embodied epistemologies contrast with book knowledge and Marxist ideas. For Donnell older women curate and articulate "collective memory" through "recovering human stories" in order to overcome familial and historical injury (79). The histories that are most obviously recovered are familial ones. Although the novel does not reference the black matriarch explicitly, older women perform similar duties, especially caring for younger generations. As has been seen, Carib explains that the voices within Thunder's head "would only stop when he found a way of understanding the spirits that lived inside him" to "stop the blue from crying red in between" (Collins 14). She tasks his great-grandaunt Mamag with the duty to tell the Malheureuse genealogical history to her great-grandnephew:

> The thunder he was hearing was the thunder inside him. Wasn't his alone, but the spirits letting him hear it and it would only stop when he found a way of understanding the spirits that lived inside him. 'You could only help,' said Carib, 'by telling him [Thunder] everything you know ... walk back with him over the Malheureuse story. Is he and others like him, here and to come, to stop the blue from crying red in between.' (13–14)

Carib links recovering familial histories with genealogical storytelling, substantiating Carolyn Cooper's claim that oral traditions, including genealogies, proverbs, and folk tales, act as "an authoritative knowledge system" in contrast with Paz's colonial law and book-learning (188). At the beginning of the novel, Carib appears to assert that "*only*" (my emphasis) older women's stories of genealogical 'blood' will assuage the debilitating voices and break the cycle of gendered and racialized trauma of Paz's colonial past and postcolonial present.

However, from an age studies perspective, Carib's invitation for Mamag to tell Thunder genealogical stories indicates a troubling foreclosure of older women's contribution to Paz's community and political development. First, Carib's insistence that genealogical stories are the "only" thing that will alleviate Thunder's suffering circumscribes Mamag's caring role as it is also the "only" way that Mamag could "help" him. Second, the instigation of intergenerational storytelling concludes Carib's purpose: "the line was finished, because Carib was fifty-ish and she had no children. When you see that, said Mamag, the work they come to do finish" (Collins 12). In this case, intergenerational storytelling contributes to a perverse reproductive futurist logic as older women's primary role is to pass on stories before they quite literally die out. So even if Carib represents "a rallying call for attention to history in a time of amnesia" (Donnell 77), then the black matriarch, and older women more generally, risk becoming restricted to "facilitat[ing] the island's memory" (DeLoughrey 252).

At this juncture, I wish to tease apart Collins's understanding of genealogical stories as a form of knowledge in the novel. Genealogy is typically associated with narrating blood relations. However, critics have noticed, with some unease, the link made between blood and land in *The Colour of Forgetting*. For example, DeLoughrey claims that "Collins draws upon the discourse of place" as a "unifying metaphor of national belonging" (259) rather than genealogy, yet she concedes that "Africans are depicted as having a dialectical engagement with the land" and concludes that Paz needs to forget aspects of its history to transition to an "Africanised" community (255). Conversely, Shalini Puri argues that landscape in Collins's creative work is "sometimes the visual equivalent of Creole [Caribbean people of mixed ancestry]" (15). Indeed, Mamag associates her familial genealogy with the earth, stating that "the Malheureuse name was in the mud from time" (Collins 51). She exposes the fallacy of prioritizing racialized hierarchies in a community wherein "everything is one thing" (192). I use the verb 'muddies' to emphasize the link made in the novel between history, blood and Paz's landscape. At first reading, older women in matriarchal roles in the novel seem to uphold a connection between genealogy, landscape, and memory.

Yet, at key points of intergenerational contact and care in the novel, it soon becomes apparent that older women cultivate a more complex system of knowledge and perception than simply being a container for family and community memories. Collins's aesthetics draw on the tradition of the Caribbean trickster to repudiate the idea that genealogical knowledges are a comprehensive means to ameliorate Paz's traumatic pasts and foreground other ways of surviving on the island. The Caribbean trickster is a folk figure, typically of West African origin, that came to the Caribbean through the transference of oral knowledge since African slavery (Marshall, *Anansi's Journey* 27–34). Emily Zobel Marshall argues that the trickster symbolizes postcolonial survival and resistance in the Caribbean ("Resistance" 210–12, 220). Tricksters, such as the spider Anancy of folk tales, may not be physically strong but have the powers of shape-shifting and bodily transfiguration, word play, wit, and an ability to cross between human and spiritual realities to disrupt and question the wider social order (Lavender III 110, 113–14; Rampaul 313–21). Tricksters have a presence in Paz's community, with Uncle Son-Son telling Ti-Moun Anancy stories as a child. Collins alludes to the Caribbean trickster via the repeated metaphorical motif of older women metamorphosing into the land, or more frequently, animals. Older women inculcate a way of 'knowing' that dissolves hierarchies of genealogical blood and selectively use the land as an animating metaphor for new forms of justice, community, and intergenerational care in postcolonial Paz. In short, older women do not simply recover and relate complex landed genealogical stories, but stress how knowledges need to be deployed tactically by young and old alike to inspire new ways of thinking and acting. As such, older women are invested in teaching younger generations the *means* to exact postcolonial change.

My interpretation is supported by the trickster-like representation of older women's bodies. During an altercation with Son-Son who is attempting to sell timber to the evicted Ti-Moun, Mamag is depicted as transforming into the landscape as she challenges her brother's claim to his nephew's land: "Mamag had planted herself in front of the mango tree on the hill. Her face was the brown of the cocoa trees around her. The yellow and red pattern of her headtie was like the red mace petticoat of the nutmeg peeping from the pod" (Collins 72–3). She transforms into a living embodiment of cocoa, nutmeg and mace, Paz's main cash-crops. Her transfigurative 'rootedness' disrupts the colonial economic and legal orders of the novel. Mamag's transformation recovers a connection and belonging to the land in contrast to the communities' racialized connotations of mace as a "blasted loupgarou [a Caribbean vampire]" exploiting black labour (Collins 100). After establishing her trickster-like connection to the land, she uses word play and wit to disrupt the supremacy of patrilineal white colonial law. She parodies Son-Son's insistence that "law is law" by asking rhetorical questions ("Who is you? Who is law?") and paraphrasing the Bible ("Be on your guard against the teachers of the Law" Collins 74–5),[10] before taking the terms of Son-Son's claims and using them against him: "you trespassing on my land! ... Alé [go], before I put the same law in you skin" (75). After the confrontation, Son-Son's makeshift counter collapses, which the narrator judges to be "because Mamag's words lean too heavy in the wind" (75). Mamag's embodied transformation into the land enables her to serve local justice against white patrilineal legal systems and begin to mitigate the collective hurt of familial dispossession from the land itself.

Older women also utilize rhetoric of trickster transformation to warn children of the dangerous entanglement between colonial laws and intrafamilial violence based on race and gender. Mamag metaphorically portrays herself as a shape-shifter when she tells the young Willive about the family history:

---

[10]   Mamag paraphrases Luke 20:46.

'That is family! That is law! ... If family and friend turn out good, is a
bonus. ... If you think I nice to you today, that good. But don't expect it
... Expect that I could turn viper tomorrow ... Is stranger that put their
hand and their head together, that help make it possible for your father to
make a living. He own blood make him eat the very bread that the devil
knead.' (70–1)

By comparing herself to a shape-shifting, predatory snake she dispels
easy assumptions about the healing potential of family relationships.
Instead, here genealogical knowledge means that one knows "the colour
of blood, how it flow and who is that cut the skin" but Mamag stresses
that the blood ties of familial kinship do not prevent the unpredictable
cycle of legally sanctioned, racially hierarchical intrafamilial violence
and betrayal (70). A new community outside consanguineous bonds is
necessary. Mamag's trickster performativity manoeuvres her out of her
expected role as a biological grandmother to become non-human and
strange. Distanced from the damaging triumvirate of blood, family,
and law, Mamag rhetorically aligns herself with a nurturing community of strangers, fellow islanders whom she deems to be outside of
biological kinship, to suggest new possibilities for an intergenerational
community of care.

Thunder's paternal grandmother Da's trickster-like capacity for bodily
transformation demonstrates how caring requires revised forms of communication between Paz's older generations and its younger people. She
resists ossification as an exotic and racialized 'other' by Thunder and his
school friends and foregrounds the potential of silence in intergenerational caring relationships. The narrative introduces Da when Thunder
conflates a painting of an African woman hanging in a wealthy school
friend's house with his grandmother: "an old woman, eyes distant and
brooding, trapped in charcoal ... he kept thinking: *Is Da*" (129). His
friend's parents are enraptured by the image: "could be Ashanti. Look at
that height! So tall! So thin! Elegant and unspeaking" (129). The painting's representation of a regal – and romanticized – African woman contrasts with Da's depiction as a transforming, reptilian creature:

Da never seemed to have words. Never seemed to have a thing to say.
Sometimes she tried. Looked at Thunder when he came close. Said 'Po-
po-i' [little one], with a smile and a half-stretched hand. But he would
giggle and stand there watching her. And Da would stretch her mouth
out, long and offended. 'Go,' she would say. 'Get away.' Hissing it ...
Sometimes her neck tried to disappear down inside her body. (129–30)

Her attempt to reach out and touch him denotes an endeavour to communicate with her grandson. Rather than fulfil the promise of intergenerational connection – as portrayed in the Bishop photograph – however, Thunder laughs at her. Without tactile reciprocity, Da's words were never imparted, and Thunder retrospectively recognizes this loss: "I wish I had known Da better ... I wish I had talked to her more" (199). With her reptilian hissing, stretching, shrinking neck and retracting body, Da reacts against being viewed as a mysterious, racialized curiosity. Instead, her personhood is constantly transforming and immutable. Her efforts to disappear into herself, as a tortoise might do into its shell, or her low hissing, reminiscent of a snake, occur when younger generations do not engage her on her own terms.

The trickster-like transformations subsequently foreclose Thunder's persistent requests for information as he learns to read. He continues to read aloud and asks her "Da, what is this word here?" to which she responds "'Look, child, leave me alone. Go, I say!' hissing it at him" (131). Just as her transfiguring body rejects an ossifying gaze, Da's hissing signifies a suspicion and dismissal of the written word and younger generation's expectations that she should impart wisdom. Later, Thunder reveals that he knew that Da could not read and his father states that her illiteracy "is why she never used to talk much. Especially with people that educated ... She used to feel, kind of stupid" (199). Read retrospectively, Thunder's innocuous request to be read to reveals colonial inequities: the engagement that Thunder offers is one that he knows his grandmother could not participate in. Her silence and refusal to speak in response then disrupts modes of book-learning and, in turn, 'teaches' younger generations about the importance of engaging older people in ways that are accessible, meaningful and comfortable for them.[11] Collins's aestheticized 'trickster pedagogies' disrupt the exoticization of the black older woman, as the women in the novel attempt to develop more equitable intergenerational caring relationships with their younger people.

The older woman's ability to transform paves the way for a new conceptual understanding of the connection between young and old. Collins deploys the trope of the crossroads to suggest that old and young need to share modes of embodied perception to 'read' the world around them. Crossroads are associated with tricksters, particularly the guardians Eshu and Papa Legba, who

[11] Indeed, Thunder appears to have learned his lesson years later when he overcomes years of estrangement from his father Ned. Thunder learns to negotiate with his father to visit the family doctor when the latter is ready to do so (Collins 199–200).

preside over crossroads linking the spirit and human world and carry messages between them (Marshall, *American Trickster* 18, 22, 37). Collins pursues a literary strategy by which embodiment and the senses constitute a crossroads between Paz's younger generations and older women, to demonstrate how both are essential for breaking the fatalistic impasse of Paz's postcolonial politics. Mamag argues that old age is commensurate with sensory loss:

> Mamag talked about getting old, and about the way people talked about old, old people who seemed to be losing their ordinary senses as if they were in a second childhood ... 'What you think it is? Is just that some don't forget yet and some just starting to remember. ... Child, sometimes in this second childhood people could hear the howling that come like a warning in the night clearer than those that lose their first childhood and not seeing their second one yet.' (Collins 87–8)

Mamag implies that older people become attuned to other forms of extraordinary sensory experience as they lose 'ordinary' senses and undergo another transformation. Old age becomes an intersecting crossroads of forgetting and remembering, which far from marking regression or decline, affords new ways of seeing and hearing. Collins's aesthetics delineate the material experiences of older people as a crossroads between different lived realities instead of the end stages of an individual life course. That older people can "hear the howling that come like a warning in the night" recalls Thunder's experience of "thunder roaring in his head" as both young and old perceive non-human forms of communication from Paz's spirits and the landscape itself (136). By likening old age to another childhood, Collins probes the possibilities for shared sensory experience and the potential to perceive – and, by understanding, perhaps resist – threats to their shared community and place.

Rather than emphasizing the significance of oral genealogical storytelling, it becomes more important for older women to attune younger people to these embodied modes of perception. Mamag concentrates on nurturing appropriate conditions so that younger children can also access new forms of learning through aural perception. While the narrative voice mentions that Mamag tells stories, there is no storytelling scene. Collins focuses on instances whereby Mamag attempts to inculcate new ways of thinking in her niece and great-grandnephew. She tells Thunder to:

> 'Sh-h-h! Listen. Listen.' And he would sit there with her listening to nothing. Nothing, that is, but the sound of the wind in the trees ... he didn't hear anything, but Mamag was always pleased that he had listened.

Mamag was always like that, leaving you with things to unwrap in your mind. (95)

Instead of divulging more pieces of familial history, the scene foregrounds the silent sharing of experience as young and old attempt to position themselves at a sensory intersection – a crossroads – between other voices on the island. Listening becomes a transformative sense as Thunder realizes that "nothing" is in fact multiple "things" that require careful listening and thinking to "unwrap" like a gift. By obscuring scenes of intergenerational telling and concentrating on scenes of shared listening, old and young participate together to synthesize new knowledges from the land.

The great-aunt also encourages the young Willive to cross and synthesize diverse narrative threads to make sense of competing narratives from a wide range of sources, whether they are 'folk' or belong to the natural world. In urging younger people to "listen," Mamag further widens conceptions of community to incorporate the narratives of non-human 'tellers':

And what Mamag couldn't talk, the way how she told it Willive weave a story from the threads she get from the talking. And when later she passed it on, was a story that Mamag told, is true, but was also a story that the wind told when Mamag paused to consider. (88–9)

The passage itself is dedicated to describing the 'who' over the 'what' of storytelling, demonstrating that older women are just individual tellers in a wider non-human society of knowledge. In focusing on the "way" that Mamag told stories, Willive learns "to play with the loose threads of Mamag's words" (89). The reference to weaving invokes the figure of the trickster weaver Anancy, who brings together diverse threads to understand the web of life (Benjamin 52). The weaving can be likened to another crossroads, where Willive begins to understand that "the wind telling the story that cause so much confusion. Trouble inside is not new story. Is story that there from time. Nation shall rise against itself" (Collins 27). The wind reveals a consistent history wherein Paz's community is repeatedly fractured from within. The cycles of catastrophe, while inaugurated by colonization, have been perpetuated by Paz citizens' claims to blood or land which ultimately cause further harm. In concentrating too exclusively on the 'future' each anti-colonial and then postcolonial activist group ultimately fails to address this systemic issue.

Trickster modes of perception consequently hold the key to collective survival in the relentless undertow of discord and division of Paz's society.

Cassandra, Willive's mother, knowingly builds on the liminal relationship between living and dead as a metaphorical means of survival. She conveys lessons taught to her by her great-grandmother:

> 'But, child, if you don't learn to play dead and even laugh as if you dotish [meaning 'senility' for old people or stupidity in children (Allsopp and Allsopp 200)] when the world knock you down, laugh just to witness you funeral, is kill they will kill you in truth. So play dead, me child, and learn to live. Child? Pick sense from non-sense. Play dead and learn to live.' (Collins 36)

Cassandra's great-grandmother metaphorically reinterprets the life course to suggest that occupying a state between life and death is a necessary means to experience the world. Trickery, masquerade, and humour enable one to interpret and survive in a violent, individualistic society. She advocates that her children strategically "play dead" as a way of judging the legitimacy of certain collective ways of thinking. 'Playing' dead, occupying a state between death and living, is presented as an instructive space of survival. The older women do not harbour idealistic visions of the value of community and familial comfort: rather, it is through playful deception that one can clearly assess the truth from the lie, so that living is an art that could be 'learned.' Such shared sensory experiences wherein young and old inhabit a crossroads between life and death are crucial to assessing Paz's current post-independence condition as part of a longer history of colonial conquest on the one hand, and a way of surviving it in the future on the other. Cumulatively, these new ways of seeing and listening offer an alternative to the unquestioning thinking in Paz's postcolonial present, where the absolutism of Marxist Black Power thought in the young is offered, in theory, as a solution to the enduring hierarchies of white power and land ownership, but risks erasing the island community's embodied knowledge in the process.

Collins develops these tentative structures of shared sensory perception to consider how bodily and sensory experiences of ageing towards the final stages of life might open opportunities to further forms of intergenerational learning. One benefit of such learning in this story is that it offers another important means to empower Thunder to address his psychophysiological condition. Mamag lives with age-related conditions: her sight is impaired, she requires a mobility aid to support her slow movements, and she is told by Willive that she is "getting forgetful" (93, 95). In his final exchange with Mamag, Thunder walks with her to a rock at the end of a row of houses and states that "your house is the last one in the line. Nowhere else to go after that" (95). She responds by moving to the back of the house:

> Lift her stick and lean forward to push back the branches of a peas tree plant there to the left of the rock. 'You see that, *petit garçon?* That track, people don't use it for a long time. But it there. It take you right down into the road on the other side. You could go down there and if you turn left under the thick bush down there, you coming out right under the old mill where those African people that still walking around used to grind the sugar cane and make sugar in the old days ... This same jookootoo track you see here. Bringing you out by all those places.' (95–6)

The passage echoes Mamag's exchange with Willive years earlier but with important variations. Instead of transforming into the landscape as she did during her argument with Son-Son, Mamag pushes aside the vegetation to reveal winding tracks. The pathways traverse a route to Paz's historical roots, negotiating and connecting uncultivated bush, former sites of plantation slavery, and processing plants worked by their 'African' descendants. Mamag cultivates a purposeful, controlled engagement with the past spirits living in the present, in contrast to other instances in the novel whereby the natural and spiritual landscape appear to terrorize the residents.[12] She uncovers a crossroads where the living and the dead intersect on the Paz landscape and makes this visible to the younger generation. Her speech shows that the community needs a way to see the histories encoded in the land. Mamag argues that the mud jookootoo track "always have somewhere else to go" (96). She urges Thunder to observe the "colour of mud" and its ability to change form after rain – "*Petit garçon*, tell people the colour of mud, how it does be when it dry and what happen when rain come" (96) – rather than recounting the colour of blood and divulging histories of familial trauma. The tracks in the land itself are immutable crossroads, with a capacity to reform to connect all of the different spaces and histories on the island as represented by the African spirits haunting the old sugar mill. Crucially, Mamag links the connective capacity of the land as a trickster-like crossroads between histories, spirits, the land and human settlement as another means to navigate Paz's traumatic colonial history, telling Thunder to "study you book, but life sense is not book sense, so study your head" (96). By looking at the crossroads, the routes, carved into the landscape by jookootoo, Mamag

[12] For example, residents report seeing fireballs (possibly soucouyants, female vampires) and the spirit of cut trees before the marketplace riot (Collins 158–9).

suggests that the land and people have the resources to resolve their own issues, which bypasses the need for any subsequent interference from the Great Country in Paz's affairs.

The pedagogic knowledge that Mamag imparts in this last scene with her great-grandnephew is offered at a time when her embodied reality as an older woman living with age-related conditions is figured by Collins as a temporal and sensory crossroads – the condition that she described to Thunder as akin to a second childhood. The passage is framed by descriptions of Mamag's slow steps and laboured breathing: she "mov[ed] one today, one tomorrow, because her legs weren't strong" and "sav[ed] her breath as she walked back, one today, one tomorrow" (95). The descriptions echo Mamag's earlier reflection that "[y]esterday is today is tomorrow" (94), referring to Paz's continuous cycle of violence and struggle over land possession. However, the destructive 'today' and 'tomorrow' pattern of familial trust and betrayal characterized by Mamag's rhetorical transformation into a viper earlier in the novel is replaced by slow, deliberate, and supported steps suggesting the sustainability of this new form of intergenerational care. The description of her "walking back" recalls Carib's invitation for Mamag to "walk back" over the family's history with Thunder at the beginning of the novel, but instead of merely *relating* genealogical histories, Mamag *embodies* both the present and the future. When she dies shortly after the exchange, her death is symbolized by trickster-like crossing and re-crossing of temporalities and locations. In her final moments "she recognised no-one. Just stared vacantly and kept talking about going to the river" and Carib tells Willive "it hard to see the body go … Mamag going to glory. And she staying with us to lead us to glory" (98). Her final moments may portray a form of 'forgetting' of blood kin, but Mamag continues to stress the movement of the river, which winds and connects different areas of Paz and the landscape. She is figured as 'going' and 'staying,' demonstrating how even after death, older women in the novel will contribute to ongoing forms of spiritual care and guidance for the future. Mamag's ageing body causes her to consider new ways of learning through careful observation of the land instead of the relation of genealogies. She offers this pedagogy to younger generations so that they may find a way to avoid repeating cycles of intergenerational trauma by attending to and interpreting the lived histories of the island which education and revolutionary ideologies cannot accommodate. In doing so Collins positions the older Caribbean women in the text as central to the future fortunes of postcolonial Paz as they forge a nuanced connection between the island's colonial histories, spiritual temporalities, and unique locations. This embodied knowledge is shown to represent an internal resource that can be used to promote healing and ongoing political development without the discourse of racial hierarchies and rigid political Marxism taken up by younger generations. Just as the NJM asserted that Grenada's future was "forward ever and backward never," Paz's postcolonial revolutionary government in *The Colour of Forgetting* buys into the tenets of reproductive futurism, in this case the conviction that children are destined to propel a new Afrocentric Caribbean nation into economic security and break the cycle of Paz's own traumatic and troubled history. These beliefs shore up intergenerational relations shaped by the presence of the 'black matriarch,' as older women are expected to be nurturing caregivers and to support Paz's younger people through genealogical storytelling. I read Collins's *The Colour of Forgetting* as challenging the notion of reproductive futurism by demystifying the ideological relationship between ageing, race, and intergenerational trauma. Collins exposes the fallacy of a postcolonial Caribbean nation where youth, progress, and intellectual book-learning are deemed the precursors of successful nation-building and integration into a developing world economy facilitated by the Great Country. The novel interrogates colonial systems of reading, writing, and education that perpetuate racialized violence and hierarchies, phenomena that endure in the new youth-led Marxist Black Power revolutionary government. Crucially, the novel dismisses the promise of reproductive futurism as an unrealistic panacea for Paz's cycles of intergenerational violence and wounding. At the same time Collins is careful not to limit the role of older women to healing genealogical storytellers. Indeed, the novel is deeply suspicious of any imagined or rhetorical attempt to link female ageing and intergenerational care with racialized appeals to genealogical inheritance. Instead, Collins's recourse to aesthetics associated with the Caribbean trickster considers how older women might inculcate new ways of learning and thinking based on shared listening and careful observation. Older women navigate intergenerational postcolonial trauma through their deeply embodied, sensorial engagements within new intergenerational communities of care. As the closing sequence on board the *Huddersfield* powerfully attests, Paz has not 'recovered' from its colonial and revolutionary inheritances; the baby is claimed by the ocean, while Carib issues a conditional statement: "Is alright as long as we see and we know and we remember" (Collins 213). If younger people are to succeed in democratizing and protecting Paz's communities (and by extension, for Collins, Grenada's) in spite of the competing pressures of postcolonial independence and neo-colonial economic dependency, they need to attend to interpreting and deploying the historical, intellectual, and epistemological 'resources' that older women embody and animate.

Works Cited

Allsopp, Richard, and Jeannette Allsopp. *Dictionary of Caribbean English Usage*. Oxford UP, 1996.

Benjamin, Shana Greene. "Weaving the Web of Reintegration: Locating Aunt Nancy in *Praisesong for the Widow*." *MELUS*, vol. 30, no. 1, 2005, pp. 49–67.

The Bible. Quartercentenary edition 1611, King James Version. Oxford UP, 2008.

Brizan, George, and Kwamina Brizan. *Grenada: Fortitude and the Human Condition*. Laventille, Republic Bank Limited and CL Financial Limited, 2001.

Collins, Merle. "Grenada: A Political History: 1950–1979." PhD dissertation. London School of Economics and Political Science, 1990.

———. *The Colour of Forgetting*. Virago, 1995.

———. "Understanding through Poetry: A Story of the Grenadian Revolutionary Journey." *Perspectives on the Grenada Revolution, 1979–1983*, edited by Nicole Phillip-Dowe and John Angus Martin. Cambridge Scholars Publishing, 2017, pp. 85–98.

Cooper, Carolyn. "'Sense make befoh book': Grenadian Popular Culture and the Rhetoric of Revolution in Merle Collins's *Angel* and *The Colour of Forgetting*." *Arms Akimbo: Africana Women in Contemporary Literature*, edited by Janice Lee Liddell and Yakini Belinda Kemp. UP of Florida, 1999, pp. 176–88.

DeLoughrey, Elizabeth M. *Routes and Roots: Navigating Caribbean and Pacific Island Literatures*. U of Hawai'i P, 2007.

Donnell, Alison. "When Seeing Is Believing: Enduring Injustice in Merle Collins's *The Colour of Forgetting*." *Madness in Anglophone Caribbean Literature: On the Edge*, edited by Bénédicte Ledent, Evelyn O'Callaghan, and Daria Tunca. Palgrave Macmillan, 2018, pp. 75–83.

Edelman, Lee. *No Future: Queer Theory and the Death Drive*. Duke UP, 2004.

Kuba, Abdul. "Women Nationalists in Nineteenth and Twentieth Century Ghana and Zimbabwe: Case Studies of Charwe Nehanda Nyakasikana and Yaa Asentewaa." *Journal of International Women's Studies*, vol. 19, no. 2, 2018, pp. 159–71.

Lavender III, Isiah. "Lebert Joseph to the Rescue: A Positive Trickster in Paule Marshall's *Praisesong for the Widow*." *Journal of Caribbean Literatures*, vol. 6, no. 1, 2009, pp. 109–24.

Marshall, Emily Zobel. *Anansi's Journey: A Story of Jamaican Cultural Resistance*. U of the West Indies P, 2012.

———. "Resistance through 'Robber-Talk': Storytelling Strategies and the Carnival Trickster." *Caribbean Quarterly*, vol. 62, no. 2, 2016, pp. 210–26.

———. *American Trickster: Trauma, Tradition and Brer Rabbit*. Rowman and Littlefield, 2019.

Meeks, Brian. *Caribbean Revolutions and Revolutionary Theory: An Assessment of Cuba, Nicaragua and Grenada*. Macmillan Caribbean, 1993.

Meltzer, Susan. "Decolonizing the Mind: Recent Grenadian Fiction." *Small Axe*, vol. 11, no. 1, 2007, pp. 83–94.

Port, Cynthia. "No Future? Aging, Temporality, History, and Reverse Chronologies." *Occasion: Interdisciplinary Studies in the Humanities*, vol. 4, 2012, pp. 1–19.

Puri, Shalini. *The Grenada Revolution in the Caribbean Present: Operation Urgent Memory*. Palgrave Macmillan, 2014.

Rampaul, Giselle. "Caribbean Tricksters at Crossroads: Davlin Thomas's *Lear Ananci and Hamlet: The Eshu Experience*." *Shakespeare*, vol. 9, no. 3, 2013, pp. 313–21.

Scott, David. "The Fragility of Memory: An Interview with Merle Collins." *Small Axe*, vol. 14, no. 1, 2010, pp. 79–163.

——. *Omens of Adversity: Tragedy, Time, Memory, Justice*. Duke UP, 2014.

Searle, Chris. *Grenada: The Struggle against Destabilisation*. Writers and Readers, 1983.

Senior, Olive. *Working Miracles: Women's Lives in the English-Speaking Caribbean*. James Curry, 1991.

7

Critical Interests and Critical Endings: Dementia, Personhood and End of Life in Matthew Thomas's We Are Not Ourselves

ELIZABETH BARRY

In his essay on "Ageing and Human Nature," philosopher Michael Bavidge contends that we can distinguish "between the end of our existence as animals, as human beings, and as persons" (41). There is no guarantee, however, that "these terminations will neatly coincide and harmonize with each other." He does not fully substantiate this contention, but I will examine here what seems to me to be at stake in such an idea, and explore its significance in relation to the end of life as it is experienced for people with dementia and those who care (in all senses) for them. I will establish how these endings align with certain philosophical positions on identity, and, with this framework in place, consider how far research on ageing and dementia, as well as its cultural imagining in fiction, might or might not support the idea of such different endings. In what Stephen Post has called the "hypercognitive society," what survives of personhood in dementia after memory and propositional speech are lost? When and how are we, in the words of King Lear, and in the title of Matthew Thomas's 2014 novel, *not ourselves*? And, if we come to this condition, how does this and should this bear on the question of our ending?

Bavidge alludes here to a central account of personal identity in recent philosophy. A dominant strain in liberal moral philosophy has been to find in human existence what distinguishes it from animality, to see human persons and animals as distinct. It has commonly followed John Locke's 1867 construction of personhood as requiring language, memory and 'reason': a person a "thinking intelligent being, that has reason and reflection, and can consider itself as itself, the same thinking thing, in different times and places" (Locke 287). Another line of thought, however, admits our animal existence as central to our identity – the 'animalism' argument. Whether or not we attain rationality for a part of our lives, our essential identity is as a (human) animal (see, for example, Olsen; Snowdon). Whatever we can or cannot *do*, this is what we *are*. Animalism does not deny the Lockean account of personhood: reason is attained, if it is, when we develop language and reflective cognitive capacities. We become human persons at this moment and may lose this personhood (without losing our fundamental identity) before we die. It may differ, however, in seeing the very beginning of life (our existence as foetus), or the very end, when rational capacities may have been lost, as nonetheless constitutive of and continuous with our essence as human beings. Bavidge's account differs from both these arguments in also positing a third term: that of human existence, which seems to sit somewhere between bare animal life and fully rational personhood. His essay leaves this third kind of existence largely unexamined, but I will, by the time I conclude this discussion, make some tentative suggestions as to how we might think about it.

Those following Locke into the domain of personal identity in recent thought, philosophers such as Alasdair MacIntyre and Ronald Dworkin, have developed his conception of personhood (as "reason and reflection") in terms of a *narrative self*, not only continuous over time, but able to give a cohesive account of its past actions, and shape its future according to its idea of its own character, intentions and values – what Dworkin has called its "critical interests" (137, and ch. 3, *passim*). Alasdair MacIntyre has argued (51–3) that the idea of personal identity presupposes the concept of narrative (and vice versa). The unity of human existence requires a capacity for narrative, an idea which is argued for in other intellectual domains, perhaps most famously by psychologist Jerome Bruner. This narrative is, furthermore, conceived of as teleological: as heading somewhere. Helen Small, reading MacIntyre in relation to old age in her masterful study of the topic, *The Long Life*, describes this phase of life as being seen, in MacIntyre's conception, as life's "culminatory stage," a stage at which we "shall be able to see its achieved unity" (Small 94). Life is, in MacIntyre's terms, not simply a story but a quest. Bavidge's conception of death, by contrast, presupposes that there are different narratives at play in the conception of an individual life, that they are not all linear in nature, and that not all of them are ultimately told or controlled by the individual in question.

The test case for these different conceptions of human existence is the condition of dementia, in which we may lose our ability both to maintain a coherent account of ourselves over time and to make rational judgements in the present. This condition tests arguments about personhood, as well as those about the ethics of decision-making, responsibility and ultimately the preservation or relinquishing of life itself. As Small suggests elsewhere in her study, advanced old age – and, in this discussion, the condition of dementia – might cause "difficulties for [any] general theory of how we should live, or how we should think about our values, interests, selfhood" (266). Does this phase of life, if we reach it, exist within or outside the bounds of personhood as it is conceived in different accounts? Does a human subject with the reduced capacities that dementia may bring about remain a person? And is there room (both conceptually and in terms of real decisions made in social and health care) for a category of existence – "human being," in Bavidge's terms, perhaps – that, though diminished, remains valued by and integrated into the social world?

This essay will begin by thinking about a case for the continuation of personal identity even in the absence of Locke's conditions for personhood. It will consider arguments in moral philosophy that emphasize critical values as well as critical interests in the service of a more expansive sense of selfhood. It will also take into account developments in thinking about the 'narrative' of the narrative self that might suggest a different and less insular conception of such a self. Finally, it will think about the possibilities for and challenges to conventional narratives, in the sense of literary plots, offered by dementia in relation to Matthew Thomas's novel *We Are Not Ourselves*. This story of the simultaneous ending and endurance of a human life engages conceptions of selfhood, autonomy, and value which bring Bavidge's forms of "termination" to human existence back into play, testing them out in the rich ecological context of realist fiction.

Some fictional treatments of dementia offer little middle ground between fully constituted personhood and animal existence. Michael Ignatieff, for instance, offers a pitiless binary in *Scar Tissue*, his novel about a son dealing with his mother's dementia: a conscious death in which the world remains "precious to us until the end," and an "unconscious" one in which we lose our grasp on the world, and "everything familiar becomes strange, everything known becomes unknown, everything true becomes false, everything loved becomes indifferent" (Ignatieff 198). Personhood is lost under the terms of this second eventuality, and there is no room in Ignatieff's narrative landscape for a redemptive view of human existence sitting between fully developed consciousness and an unreflective inertness. In taking dementia as its theme, the novel capitulates to this second vision, and in the guise of scientific objectivity, adopts a form of fatalism, as others have discussed (Small, Hartung). The narrator imagines that he can feel the genetic predisposition towards Alzheimer's disease, the cells "too small to see," in his own body and surrenders to them: "My fate has come to meet me. My journey has begun" (199).

Ignatieff's novel performs what age scholar Margaret Gullette has called a stance of tragic irony, in which one tells a version of one's story which emphasizes "how much of life is irreversible" (Gullette, *Safe at Last* xxv). As Marlene Goldman has pointed out, this goes as far as identifying with Oedipus in framing dementia as an irrevocable curse on the family (217). Thomas, on the other hand, turns his narrative against a fatalistic outlook, even though it too ends with Connell, the son, investigating his own genetic susceptibility to early-onset dementia. His father Ed's dementia is a harbinger of uncertainty rather than certainty in Thomas's narrative. If it ushers in a life of unknowns, painful and frightening as this is, there are also unexpected boons: ways of being that a narrowly delineated vision of one's future and a determination to control that future through sheer will have previously precluded. Ed's wife Eileen, relentlessly future-oriented, permits herself to look back at what might have been. And in so doing she realizes two apparently contradictory things. On the one hand, she embraces what has been: the implacability of the fate dealt to her and the relinquishing of control that it has forced upon her – or, from another perspective, allowed her. On the other hand, however, she also realizes that there are other stories to tell than that of material or social failure (neither of which has, by most people's standards, arrived in any case). It comes to light in the course of the novel that Ed has, in fact, over the course of their life together gently encouraged her to depart from the social script of her upbringing – to be content with values rather than goal-oriented interests, in the terms the philosophers offer. As the title suggests, among other connotations, this means that there are, for Eileen, also other people to be in the future. The story of Ed's ending becomes a story about the future effects of his legacy. One can enact a complex and discontinuous story, not just a linear quest or trajectory. The narrative of one's life can be not one singular story but a set of causes and effects, memories and influences, that reverberate through and colour one's own and others' lives, both past and present.

Personhood and the Narrative Self

The philosophy of personal identity as told by Dworkin and MacIntyre does not admit of the self that expands into other lives: dispersed amongst other people's attitudes and behaviours, active in others' pasts and futures. It does, however, propose a self that is extended over time. Following Locke, these thinkers have fashioned their idea of personhood to encompass not only enduring self-consciousness and self-recognition, but also the attendant capacity for moral agency: the ability to take responsibility in the present for one's past actions *as* one's actions. The subject who has lost these capacities, they suggest, lacks full personhood. Dworkin and others have thus argued from this idea of a diminished or cancelled personhood, what Daniel Davis calls an "ontological nullpoint" (376), that the rights of such a denuded subject might be suspended, even to the extent of denying life-preserving treatment (or actively practising euthanasia). Those with Alzheimer's disease, Dworkin argues in his controversial 1993 work *Life's Dominion: An Argument about Abortion, Euthanasia and Individual Freedom*, "are ignorant of self – not as an amnesiac is, not simply because they cannot identify their pasts – but more fundamentally, because they have no sense of a whole life, a past joined to a future, that could be the object of any evaluation or concern as a whole" (230). In this argument, they are no longer, in Daniel Dennett's evocative phrase, "cent[res] of narrative gravity" (103 *et passim*), and their lives are, in a very direct sense, no longer their own.

The "sense of a whole life" that could be the object of "evaluation or concern" which is critical to Dworkin's account of personhood is consistent with the idea (identified most strongly with Jerome Bruner) that the human subject is a narrative being. As humans we not only remember our past but connect the actions and events that comprise it, see patterns in them, and understand them to unfold according to a certain logic that informs our future behaviour. There is in such a view, as Samantha Vice has put it, "no innocent, brute experience or self-conception" upon which narrative is imposed (94). Narrativity is seen as constitutive of personhood in the same way that reason is, and forms an essential part of this reason. As Bruner writes: "life as led is inseparable from life as told – or more bluntly, a life is not 'how it was' but how it is interpreted and reinterpreted, told and retold" (708). In short, in the words of Charles Taylor, a "basic condition of making sense of ourselves [is] that we grasp our lives in a narrative" (47) – a process threatened by the significant loss of memory that dementia entails. As Bavidge puts it in the essay that opened this discussion, it is not the "odd memories of the distant past," often retained in dementia, that are seen to count, but "the ability to integrate past events into a meaningful progressive pattern of experience" (42) – and this those with dementia cease to manage.

Continental philosophy has, however, offered dementia research a somewhat different model of the subject. Sociological work on dementia has taken up the idea developed in a certain strand of phenomenology (principally the work of Maurice Merleau-Ponty) of the body-subject, suggesting that the body might retain certain pre-learnt kinds of capacity that it can continue to deploy even in the absence of propositional thought. The body for Merleau-Ponty is both material and intentional, literally incorporating the "cultural and spiritual" world that the subject inhabits, and thereby expressing not only instinctual and physical desires but feelings, tastes, habits and skills (see Carman 123). These habits and skills even encompass certain kinds of verbal utterance, complicating the distinction between mind and body, purposeful language and instinctive response. John Bayley in his memoir about his wife, the novelist Iris Murdoch, for instance, observed that Murdoch's "buried reflexes" meant that she could answer the door and deploy forms of social politeness and even grace when language and higher-order cognition were otherwise almost entirely lost (75–6). Habit and embodied memory can allow for forms of sociality that can, among other things, express attachment and sympathy, produce situational humour, tease, clown, and follow quite complex conversational conventions, even in the absence of autobiographical memory.

The strands of philosophical thought that find their way into ethical and sociological research into dementia do not, however, simply cleave into Anglo-American moral philosophy with its obdurate condition of rationality on the one side, and French philosophy with its (more expansive but more diffuse) idea of the embodied and affective subject on the other. Daniel Davis, for instance, has argued that the subject with dementia even fails the tests of personhood set by phenomeno-logical thought, not able to be the self-aware subject Heidegger would value, and finally even undergoing what Davis calls a "splintering" of its "sedimented layers of Being" (375), the experiential learning that Merleau-Ponty would argue has been laid down in the self. Others (see, for instance, Kitwood; Kontos) have countered this view, suggesting that embodied knowledge of this kind persists until very late in the progres-sion of the disease, well beyond the loss of linguistic competence. Their view of human life as relational, and identity as produced and main-tained intersubjectively, offers a way beyond the monadic self that is proven only by its own inward-turning processes of reflexivity.

While phenomenology might offer some support for the idea that existence might persist beyond self-reflective personhood and even bio-logical vitality, this discussion wants to take on the arguments of moral philosophy – and so the more stringent conditions for selfhood – on their own terms. It seeks to go beyond the concept of bare life (if, nonetheless, human life) held up by the animalist thinkers as important, to reconsider what constitutes a subject's central interests and values, and how these might be less vulnerable to loss of capacity than Dworkin contends. It will look at some of the divisions already present within the philosophy of identity in thinking about the self in dementia, in this respect, with a view to reflecting in its final section on how literature might negotiate these different ideas of selfhood, and how it might – crucially – set them in play in the dynamic and temporal framework of the life course.

One aspect of the 'unbecoming' that Ronald Dworkin sees befalling the demented subject is the idea, as has been seen, that this subject can form no new critical interests, that is, those concerns, beliefs and principles that dictate how one behaves and what one values. Without the creation of any meaningful new interests, he argues (and Helen Small gives a good account of this in *The Long Life* 128–30), one's treatment by others should abide by the critical interests one espoused when one was competent and relatively well, rather than the desires one expresses in the present (when one is ill and perceived to be not of sound mind). In one sense this suggests a discontinuity, a sort of ghost self that continues to exert a moral pressure alongside what Dworkin sees as the "diminished" self, and which can stand in for the present self. And this principle extends in Dworkin's argument (though it is difficult to see this becoming law in practice, at least in the United Kingdom) to the idea that one might give an advance directive when competent that one might be denied treatment, or even euthanized, when one reaches a certain point of incapacity. This would, followed rigorously, take place even if one is relatively serene in one's incapacity at the time.

Such a hypothetical advance directive is described as a Ulysses pact, a clause that binds one to a certain course of action in the future, whatever one's wishes in that future – in reference to Ulysses (the Latin version of the Greek Odysseus), who had himself bound to the mast of his ship in the famous myth (perhaps the *Ur*-narrative of Western culture) in order to resist the song of the beautiful Sirens, women who tried to lure him to a watery death in the ocean. Dworkin posits a kind of *reverse* Ulysses pact in which one might arrange one's death (rather than one's preservation) in the future in order to live with more composure in the present. And for all that this sounds drastic, Neil Gorsuch, discussing Dworkin's argument, gives the compelling example of an Oregon woman who, at a relatively early stage of dementia (still knowing what she was doing, and able to play tennis, for instance – though not keep score), was assisted by a radical US doctor to kill herself rather than face future decline: the prospect of reaching a point of incapacity and unawareness when she would no longer be able to make the decision to take her own life (Gorsuch 677). If she had had a Ulysses pact, Gorsuch suggests in illustration of Dworkin's position, she could have lived for a lot longer, in relative good health, rather than being forced to take her own life while she was still sure she was competent to make the decision.

In Matthew Thomas's novel, *We Are Not Ourselves*, the latter half of the story is given over to the development of early-onset Alzheimer's disease in the father of the family, Ed, and its effect on his wife, Eileen, the novel's protagonist, and his son, Connell. The novel offers several different perspectives on the persistence or otherwise of Ed's central identity, bringing Dworkin's ideas into play, while arguably offering an alternative view to that which lauds an individual's interests – critical or otherwise – above those of the collective (in this case, the family). Ed as a character is shown to be resolutely against euthanasia – a position stated in so many words in a conversation with his son, a scene at the mid-point of the novel, but relatively early in the dementia storyline. Connell assigns Ed the 'against' position in a (practice) debate about euthanasia, although Ed does not mount a complex argument from this point of view; part of the purpose of including this conversation is, we might assume, to show that he is already too affected by the disease to argue with the fluency of his son. Connell is aggressive as a debater, and also – in his enthusiasm for the argument and the logical application of his chosen perspective – startlingly unfeeling towards his father: "You want to know what the best neg example you could have, Dad? You are. With your Alzheimer's. Think about it. If we euthanized people at will, maybe you would have been taken out already. For the good of the herd" (364). Thomas does not return explicitly to this issue later, when Ed is more severely impaired, and the characters – even his son, who is periodically angry with his father for his illness and incapacity – do not show or seem to feel any desire, even fleeting, that he should die, let alone be put to death. This topic is, as Ed's voice itself is, conspicuous by its absence, however. Ed's simple and unshakeable moral conviction – "I don't believe in euthanasia, son" (363) – is a value to which they all seem tacitly to hold. Had Ed been a passionate advocate of euthanasia, in his case or for others, things might have been different, but as it stands for this small herd, at least, his critical interests in this respect are seen to coincide in an unspoken way with those of the rest of the family. He is seen as more than a singular individual – a position that this essay will examine at greater length below. Even when Connell feels that Ed has "gone" (542) as a father, or when Eileen too feels that any meaning-ful relationship with her has also "gone" (546), his interests are attended to, and he remains part of what Habermas called a "shared lifeworld" (2007); his marriage to Eileen, as she determines, one "that wouldn't die" (525).

Critical Interests and the Concept of Valuing

Ed's last phase of life might be viewed somewhat differently by virtue of another, contrary, strand of moral philosophy: a counter-argument made to Dworkin's position on critical interests from within the same philo-sophical tradition. Moral philosopher Agniezska Jaworska has taken issue with Dworkin's argument that one loses personhood in dementia, at least as far as personhood consists in the ability to form meaningful 'interests' and hold meaningful views about one's life. She cites fellow philosopher Rebecca Dresser, who disagrees so forcefully with Dworkin's view that past wishes should be respected over and above present ones that conflict with them, that Dresser denies – at least rhetorically – that this person in the present is the same person as the one who expressed those (past) preferences (Jaworska 108). In one sense, this seems to lend weight to the idea that personhood has not survived – that selfhood founders if the subject is not, in Locke's terms, "the same thinking thing, in different times and places" – but Dresser argues that this continuous 'narrative' self is a fiction even in a healthy subject. Jaworska takes up a different position, in any case, in contending that the person in the present, however changed and however incapacitated, exerts a "moral pull" which might (and, in Jaworska's argument, should) impel a carer to try to grant their needs and desires, whether they are a "fully constituted person" or simply a "conscious being capable of pleasure and pain" (108).

Jaworska may not quite want to argue that the subject with dementia is a "fully constituted person," but neither does she agree with Dresser that this is a completely different being from that which may have expressed more developed critical interests in the past. For Jaworska, some autonomy and even authority has survived the descent – as it is usually seen – into dementia. She aligns potential for autonomy with the "capacity to value, and well-being with living in accordance with one's values" (109). Jaworska also differs from Dworkin on the "minimal requirements" for both autonomy and authority concerning one's well-being, and therefore over the point at which someone's earlier values might be invoked to govern what happens to her, whether or not she can now appreciate them (109). Jaworska argues that Dworkin's qualification of "opinions about my critical interests" as "opinions about what is good for me" itself indicates that these are opinions about values. She discusses as evidence of the persistence of such valuing, an Alzheimer's patient who is aware of his condition and how it is affecting his speech, and who regrets this, saying "There you see the Alzheimer's at work," after trying and failing to produce a sentence. This case, as do others like it, shows that far into the progression of the disease, when the patient's production of speech is severely impaired, he or she can regret the loss of valued abilities. Such attitudes are not merely *desires*: if they were simply desires, one could work towards achieving (and thus eliminating) them. This is not appropriate in the case of a valuing, however. In Jaworska's example, the individual with speech problems is made sad by his loss of competence, but he does not desire to stop valuing being articulate or the authority and agency that fluent speech allows; he just wishes his relation to these things were different.

An example of valuing as a kind of continuity of self is found in Diane Keaton's 2011 memoir, *Then Again*, about her mother who lives with dementia. Keaton reproduces some of what her mother says about herself (and her home): "I mean, I've been here before, but I don't live here now, right, Diane? That isn't my cat, even though it looks like a cat I would have" (Keaton 227). She does not recognize her own house – but that observation about the cat, a clear and instantaneous connection with her own predilections and interests (and thereby a nuanced instance of self-knowledge), belies the comment she makes a few seconds later: "I'm afraid, because I'm not real familiar with me" (227).

These continuities in relation to likes, dislikes and things that one values are also observed in Bayley's memoir about Iris Murdoch. He describes Murdoch pouring her drink into the potted plants, now "wilting under the treatment": "But she never does this with a real drink, an alcoholic one. Sensible girl, her old fondness for bars still stands her in good stead" (Bayley 128). This may seem like a trivial kind of taste – but it is part of a pattern in Bayley's memoir (much criticized in other respects) of emphasizing the continuities in Iris's behaviour, interests and values – the expression of which might change in character, but not in kind – over the radical change on which such narratives usually focus. We might compare this to the editor of a book of dementia testimony, *Let the People with Dementia Speak*, observing of a participant that he paused a long time before expressing wishes or responding to questions – but never when the subject was whether or not he wanted a beer. In this work this reads as a salutary tale: we need to be aware that such pauses might be a sign of disinclination to engage rather than of cognitive delay; the expression of an ambivalence, the assertion of a wish or aversion; in short, an assertion of will. The individual with dementia can much more easily show to us such signs of meaningful engagement (and disengagement) if we look for them – if we think about what might have salience in his or her world and adapt our interaction accordingly. This world can reveal numerous instances of valuing if we recognize them as such.

Fiction can also model attention to such instances. One example is an incidental scene in the 1985 short story "Lichen" by Canadian novelist Alice Munro. In this story, Stella takes her former husband David to visit her ill and disabled father in his nursing home once a year. It is not clear that Stella's father has dementia as such, but he has a cluster of physiological and neurological problems following a stroke that include cognitive problems with memory and episodes of delusion. He can barely speak and follows conversation only intermittently – but to the attentive witness, his critical interests are still in evidence. On the occasion in the story, for instance, he gives David an "acknowledging sound," a "conversational offering," and listens to the younger man's talk about a car even while he cannot participate in it:

> This conversation seemed welcome. His father-in-law appeared to follow it. He nodded, and on his narrow, elongated, bluish post-human face there were traces of old expressions. An expression of shrewd and dignified concern, suspicion of advertising and of foreign cars and car dealers. There was even a suggestion of doubt – as in the old days – that David could be trusted to handle such things well. (Munro 51)

This character's values and attitudes (politically proper or otherwise) are maintained and communicated beyond speech, something that his daughter Stella – who visits every week rather than once a year – notes rather ruefully: "Daddy was so pleased to see you, David. A man just means more, to Daddy" (52).

In Thomas's novel, Ed's values too remain constant throughout the narrative, something exemplified in his attachment to his desk. The desk is one of the few things his cash-strapped father was able to give to him (rescuing it from an office clearout), and so the source of one of his few happy childhood memories, and he too protects it when Eileen might have thrown it out to make way for more elegant and expensive household décor. It represents paternal care, genealogical continuity and a commitment to work, all values central to Ed's life. When Connell takes casual and premature ownership of it before Ed's death, making an assumption about Ed's capacity to continue using it, and usurping the proper ceremony of handing it on, Ed is furious and upset, even though his awareness of other events and their significance is much diminished. When Ed comes upon his own academic and professional diplomas, at an advanced stage of his illness, he does not recognize them as his own hard-won successes – but his appraisal of them as representing "a lot of work" (410) is suitably approving and respectful. Even his continuing attachment to his baseball team, the New York Mets, is a particular instance of his general capacity for fierce and constant loyalty.

Thomas reminds us not only of the enduring nature of the capacity to value in Ed, but also the fact that, like his desk, his values are passed on to his son Connell. His love of music is shared with his son from an early age, and listening to music with Connell when he has lost the ability to speak unlocks not only the ability to feel pleasure and deep emotion, but also the retained capacity to keep time and appreciate complex musical rhythms. As Connell watches his father clap to the rhythm of a Mozart piece, he remembers going to concerts in Carnegie Hall as a child and watching "for his father's hands to come together with authority to know when he himself should clap" (557). Thomas also includes the device of a letter to Connell, setting out his father's feelings and hopes, read as it is designed to be after Ed's death – a familiar enough trope but one that has added significance here. This letter gives us access to Ed's inner thoughts – inaccessible not only towards the end, because of his disease, but also his whole life long because of his natural reserve. The novel is not principally from his point of view, but, as Katsura Sako argues in her perceptive reading (Falcus and Sako 172), suddenly not only his character but his role in the family and its story come to the fore. This narrative strategy, while perfectly plausible in a story about terminal illness, feels somewhat like a *deus ex machina* – an instrument of authorial agency, in narratologist Peter Brooks's terms (see, for example, Brooks 83–4), rather than agency in Ed himself. Precisely because we have heard so little from Ed in the course of the novel, this fluent, expressive and reflective address seems out of character – and perhaps even beyond this particular character. Nonetheless, this strategy on Thomas's part affords us an account of Ed's critical interests consistent with his behaviour in life. Coming as it does after his death, the letter also disrupts the downward trajectory of the story, the 'decline narrative' familiar to stories about dementia and ageing, as Sako's comments about "untimely" temporality suggest (Falcus and Sako 173). The letter moves us analeptically back for a space to the time when Ed was articulate, reflective, and properly paternal. It also looks forward, however: it demonstrates the capacity for a life to continue to exist and positively to influence beyond its term. The 'quest' of Ed's life is a quest not to achieve material success in his own lifetime but to pay forward into and improve his son's life, and therefore the trajectory it follows is a non-linear one, lived to some extent in the mode of prolepsis. His life has always (as long as his son has been alive, at least, and perhaps for the length of his marriage) been bigger than himself and therefore (potentially) longer than the term of his own life story.

Narrative Ends

The perspective of teleological linearity (the quest, the aims, the prospect of crowning achievements) in which the life course is customarily conceived in the thinking of MacIntyre – and perhaps more casually by most of us – is complicated by dementia time in more than one respect. John Bayley notes in *Elegy for Iris* the benefits of the strategy, in caring for those with dementia, of focusing on immediate but real interests rather than, implicitly, the carer's likely inclination to longer temporal perspectives: towards planning for the future, for instance, or recalling (and likely lamenting) the lost capacities of their loved one. He writes: "The Reverend Sydney Smith, a benevolent clergyman of Jane Austen's, used to urge parishioners in the grip of depression who appealed to him for help, to 'take short views of human life – never further than dinner or tea'" (Bayley 53). If such are the horizons of the experience of the subject with dementia, however, the question might present itself as to how far they can be the subject of a work of literature. The whole of a fiction does not often enact a time-travelling strategy as does Ed's letter. What notion of character and what narrative arc can encompass this condition that is at once highly unpredictable day to day, and nonetheless relentlessly linear in its larger trajectory? What temporality can impose itself in a narrative that is truly 'about' dementia, rather than using the condition as a plot device in which to wrap devastating family secrets, the key to the whodunit murder mystery, or repressed historical guilt (some of the familiar patterns of story in popular 'dementia' fiction – see Bitenc; Sako; Falcus and Sako)? Can dementia in the central character – in a real subject's life story as well as a fictional narrative of ageing – ever be anything other than the end point of the story?

Anthropologist Janelle Taylor has written of the widespread belief that life stories are brought to an inevitable end in this way, as evidenced by people's anecdotes and colloquial accounts of others' lives: "Over time, I have come to think that what is important about these stories is the way that evidence of dementia always serves to end them. It is as if someone with dementia never could any longer be part of any story that might continue – and if the life story is over, then the life must be over too" (J. Taylor 321). How then do narratives that deal directly and centrally with dementia negotiate this sociocultural assumption that one's meaningful, purposeful, significant living is over once the disease process of dementia is begun? Do they allow for a gap of some kind between life story and life? Or do they make a new kind of story out of life with dementia?

When reading Matthew Thomas's epic novel, which comes to centre, as has been seen, around the early-onset dementia of the protagonist Eileen's husband Ed, we bump up against such questions. And at first glance, we can indeed see the way in which dementia might derail conventional drivers of plot. One such driver is ambition, an imperative that, as Peter Brooks has argued, is "a dominant dynamic of the realist novel: a force that drives the protagonist forward, assuring that no incident or action is final or closed in itself until such a moment as the ends of ambition have been clarified" (Brooks 39). Eileen, from whose point of view for the majority of the novel we see Ed's decline, reflects upon the foreclosure of this story of ambition for Ed, the evaporation of this "force" in their lives: "After the diagnosis, [Ed] redoubled his efforts, staying late at the lab many nights. She knew she should have been proud of him for continuing to follow the faint trail of a fleeing ambition, and she was proud, sometimes, but she knew it would come to nothing" (332). Ed needs to keep working for a couple of years after his diagnosis in order to get to his '30-year mark' and qualify for a better pension, but this is the extent of his (and now Eileen's) ambition for his career, an observation made relatively early in the telling of his story, and one that shuts off the narrative possibilities of his work (as a science lecturer, who in another kind of story might have invented a cure for his disease, or – a little in the style of the HBO series *Breaking Bad*'s Walter White – done away with himself with a concoction of his own invention).

The illness also asserts its own contingency, resisting narrative meaning: "Why Ed? Why now? It hadn't happened for a reason but they would find something to glean from it anyway" (382). Alzheimer's disease mocks causality. It cannot find a place in a metaphysical system, a moral order. Even the scientific explanations available point for Eileen to heartless chance rather than intelligible meaning: "There was an obvious answer [to the question 'Why Ed?'] – it was random, senseless, genetic, environmental." They cannot be agents in this story; this is not the liberal story of transcending one's circumstances, or the capitalist dream – to which realist narratives have so long been harnessed – of making one's own way. The project of self-improvement that has driven the narrative of the novel so far, represented symbolically for Eileen by the unachievable dream of the perfect family home, is thwarted. From now on, they would deal in "gleanings," glimpses of redemption, insight, understanding into their situation and each other. In fact the naming of the illness is understood as both the answer to a riddle, and also an event of such improbability that it cannot be made sense of: "When [the doctor] was gone they sat mulling over the news. It was a paradox of sorts: nothing made sense unless it were true, and yet it made no sense whatever for it to be true" (323). It is the key that unlocks the narrative of the illness, the answer to the medical detective story, but this illness narrative cannot itself be fitted into any predictable or meaningful plan, be part of any larger story about their lives together that Eileen can, at this moment at least, conceive.

MacIntyre's perception of the narrative self as a quest of which old age is a culminatory stage is comfortably or uncomfortably close to the 'progress narrative' that has come to seem synonymous with the American Dream. Margaret Gullette has written illuminatingly of the script that this represents, in which one achieves career success, one's income increases year on year, and one's pension similarly builds to allow for a comfortable and affluent old age (Gullette, *Aged by Culture* 93–4, 143–5).

The self in this story is not simply a narrative self but, in Margaret Urban Walker's term, a "career self" (Walker 129), of which the one dominant narrative identity is professional (and by implication economic) life, and all activities are 'managed,' planned and budgeted for (in terms of time as well as money). This equates in Walker's argument to the culturally valued conception of self as unified, behaviour and goals coordinated, in the service of what John Rawls called a "rational life plan" or MacIntyre, as we have seen, a "quest." The vicissitudes of old age make this story uncertain, however. As a career self, Ed has undoubtedly 'failed,' and is no longer a fully constituted person (see H.L. Nelson 84). Ed has never colluded with this narrative in the first place, however. He has not taken career opportunities at odds with his critical values – exemplified by his dedication to teaching and the success of his students. He has never chased a bigger or more lavish home. Connell begins to see that his father's legacy is his "contribution to science": not just the effect he has had on his students but "the impacts those students had had, and would have on others" (Thomas 588). This ever-expanding sphere of influence is his father's "real estate."

This story, then, is less an ambition plot derailed than a critique of aspirations to social mobility and material success at the expense of values or disposition. Ed has modelled a virtue that does not conform to MacIntyre's model of a teleological narrative, a quest: his virtue is evidenced piecemeal, cumulative rather than culminatory, reactive and diffuse. His self resembles the alternative concept of selfhood derived from the feminist philosopher Hilde Lindemann Nelson's phrase "living life *seriatim*" (see J.L. Nelson 122–3; see also Chivers 79–96) – a series of episodic selves, valued in relation to their immediate context, rather than the overarching, self-identical, teleological self that is suggested by MacIntyre or Dworkin's account. Ed's temporality is cyclical in nature: the nurturing of successive generations of students, the familiar, repetitive rhythms of the Mets sporting calendar or the concert season at Carnegie Hall. Within these activities and events, there are small variations, and he changes in relation to them, but the framework they operate within is iterative; these horizons are closer to the 'short views' of Reverend

Smith than the expansive lifetime ambitions – masculine ambitions, in Lindemann Nelson's critique – that Eileen nurtures (to start with, at least) on his behalf.

Thomas's novel has worked from the beginning by bringing to the surface attitudes to one's life narrative and the identity that it forges. The characters self-consciously trade these different conceptions of the life course. Ed has always seen his identity as relational and embedded – he privileges teaching over individual research success, and sees the final meaning of his life in its influence on and continuity in that of his son, Connell. He refuses the opportunity to lead a research group, or to take on the deanship of Bronx Community College, where he works. Eileen's attempts to 'co-author' his identity are quietly but firmly rebuffed. Dementia arrives as what could appear as a trite moral device to make her reconsider her values in life – but Thomas gives depth and texture to this process. The effortful and isolated striving for an American model of success (home ownership in a desirable area, affluence, propelling her husband and son to career glory) is perforce set aside in a series of interrelated 'setbacks' underpinned by Ed's decline in capacity, unpredictable in shape but inexorable. Ed, and by extension the family, lose not only a proportion of their savings but the social capital that health represents. And yet the capitulation to a kind of 'decline narrative,' conceived of as a noble failure in society's eyes, is in fact felt by Eileen ultimately as something of a relief.

This is not then an ambition plot. There is a lot of love in this novel, but neither is it a love story as such. The courtship of the couple – the customary story in which the narrative dynamic resides in the drive for consummation of mutual desire – is dealt with in a brief chapter, and is seen initially at least as a rational decision on Eileen's part (to marry a steady, hardworking man from a similar background to her own) as much as a breathless romantic imperative. Indeed, the house has taken the place of romantic love object (as Marjorie Garber (42–4) in her cultural history of property has indicated it frequently does), in a story of seduction, pursuit, and even illicit deception (Eileen scheming to complete most steps of the house purchase without Ed's knowledge).

Yet an alternative love story emerges. Eileen has to make the transition from author to reader of her own story in order to effect the transformation, but in coming to accept Ed's illness and reshape her life according to its dynamic, she comes to recognize in her story a new kind of romantic plot (or perhaps a very old one). In a late chapter, told from her point of view, she determines never to remarry: "This was life: you went down with the ship. Who was to say that wasn't a love story?" (569). The ending to this story does not resemble a familiar narrative arc: it is neither the coming together of the pair in marriage, nor their being reunited (in recovery or in death) after a crisis or loss. The ending is instead for Eileen to feel fulfilled by fulfilling her duty of care towards Ed. "This," Thomas writes, "was his final gift to her: to silence her regrets about the paths she hadn't taken" (574). Eileen has tried so very hard to eliminate chance from her life. In the end, however, contingency is not eradicated by a singular, forward-moving, linear narrative trajectory (of ambition or desire) but in looking backwards and identifying value in spite of – and in – chance and compromise. Retrospection is the logic of realist narrative *par excellence*, even if the revelations here are modest. The retrospective eradication of contingency is for Eileen, so consumed by her emotional investment in a better future for most of the novel, ultimately the happy ending.

The conclusion of this novel, in this way, makes sense of the middle of Bavidge's three kinds of termination (and by extension three kinds of existence) that we might be seen as humans to have (person, human and animal): the termination of *human being*. Ed has died as *person*, "his gaze," as Thomas puts it, is at the end "vacant, without any bouts of clarity" (558); he has died as *animal*, the pneumonia in his prone body causing him to drown in mucus. As *human being*, however, he is simultaneously dead (bestowing his final gift symbolically on Eileen in giving her an ending to the story of their relationship; leaving a last letter for his son Connell to read), and alive – a ghost in the house that they still share by virtue of Eileen deciding to stay on. He is the ghost of the "former future she might have had" (575), as Thomas puts it, a ghost in the second seat next to Eileen that she buys when she goes to a Mets baseball game alone ("the empty seat for Ed" (598)). This third category (the human) represents our intersubjective identity: perhaps the only meaningful identity we have in reality, and one which terminates perhaps only long after our death, with that of our loved ones.

Ed continues to be many things after the termination of his animal existence. He is the legacy of his genetic code in the body of Connell and Connell's children, a genealogical and biological afterlife that can be both positive and negative. Yet he is also a letter, a desk, an empty seat at a Mets game. His death marks the premature end of a certain quest that is not his own, that of Eileen, who felt that to succeed as a good wife was to spur her husband to material success and status. In fact, Eileen's quest – to be a good wife – was achieved without her realizing it, before she had realized it, without material proofs, and in a form she had not envisioned. MacIntyre's model of life as *telos* is modified by the temporality of narrative: the fact that none of its terms, from character to action, are static. Where we end up will modify the story of where we started, how far and where we have come, and what value it has for us. Things will, in other words, look a bit different from the position of old age.

Works Cited

Bavidge, Michael. "Ageing and Human Nature." *Dementia: Mind, Meaning, and the Person*, edited by Julian Hughes et al. Oxford UP, 2006, pp. 41–53.

Bayley, John. *Elegy for Iris*. Macmillan, 1999.

Bitenc, Rebecca. "Representations of Dementia in Narrative Fiction." *Knowledge and Pain*, edited by Esther Cohen et al. Rodopi, 2012, pp. 305–29.

Brooks, Peter. *Reading for the Plot*. Clarendon Press, 1984.

Bruner, Jerome. "Life as Narrative." *Social Research*, vol. 71, no. 3, 2004, pp. 691–710.

Carman, Taylor. *Merleau-Ponty*. Routledge, 2008.

Chivers, Sally. *From Old Woman to Older Women: Contemporary Culture and Women's Narratives*. Ohio State UP, 2003.

Davis, Daniel H.J. "Dementia: Sociological and Philosophical Constructions." *Social Science & Medicine*, vol. 58, 2004, pp. 369–78.

Dennett, Daniel. "The Self as a Center of Narrative Gravity." *Self and Consciousness: Multiple Perspectives*, edited by Frank S. Kessel et al. Psychology Press, 1992, pp. 103–15.

Dresser, Rebecca. "Life, Death, and Incompetent Patients: Conceptual Infirmities and Hidden Values in the Law." *Arizona Law Review*, vol. 28, no. 3, 1986, pp. 373–405.

Dworkin, Ronald. *Life's Dominion: An Argument about Abortion, Euthanasia and Individual Freedom*. Alfred A. Knopf, 1993.

Falcus, Sarah, and Katsura Sako. *Contemporary Narratives of Dementia: Ethics, Ageing and Politics*. Routledge, 2019.

Garber, Marjorie. *Sex and Real Estate*. Pantheon Books, 2000.

Goldman, Marlene. *Forgotten: Narratives of Age-Related Dementia and Alzheimer's Disease in Canada*. McGill-Queen's UP, 2017.

Gorsuch, Neil M. "The Right to Assisted Suicide and Euthanasia." *Harvard Journal of Law & Public Policy*, vol. 23, 2000, pp. 600–710.

Gullette, Margaret Morganroth. *Safe at Last in the Middle Years: The Invention of the Midlife Progress Novel*. U of California P, 1988.

——. *Aged by Culture*. U of Chicago P, 2004.

Habermas, Jürgen. "The Language Game of Responsible Agency and the Problem of Free Will." *Philosophical Explorations*, vol. 10, 2007, pp. 13–50.

Hartung, Heike. *Ageing, Gender, and Illness in Anglophone Literature: Narrating Age in the Bildungsroman*. Routledge, 2016.

Ignatieff, Michael. *Scar Tissue*. Farrar, Straus and Giroux, 1993.

Jaworska, Agnieszka. "Respecting the Margins of Agency: Alzheimer's Patients and the Capacity to Value." *Philosophy and Public Affairs*, vol. 28, no. 2, 1999, pp. 105–38.

Keaton, Diane. *Then Again*. Random House, 2011.

Kitwood, Tom. "The Experience of Dementia." *Aging and Mental Health*, vol. 1, no. 1, 1997, pp. 13–22.

Kontos, Pia. "Embodied Selfhood in Alzheimer's Disease: Rethinking Person-Centred Care." *Dementia*, vol. 4, no. 4, 2005, pp. 553–70.

Locke, John. *Essay Concerning Human Understanding*, edited by P.H. Nidditch. Oxford UP, 1975, Book II, ch. 27, §9.

MacIntyre, Alasdair. *After Virtue: A Study in Moral Theory*. U of Notre Dame P, 1984.

Munro, Alice. *The Progress of Love*. Chatto & Windus, 1987.

Nelson, Hilde Lindemann. "Stories of My Old Age." *Mother Time: Women, Aging and Ethics*, edited by Margaret Urban Walker. Rowman & Littlefield, 1999, pp. 75–95.

Nelson, James Lindemann. "Death's Gender." *Mother Time: Women, Aging and Ethics*, edited by Margaret Urban Walker. Rowman & Littlefield, 1999, pp. 113–29.

Olson, Eric T. *The Human Animal: Personal Identity without Psychology*. Oxford UP, 1997.

Post, Stephen G. "The Concept of Alzheimer Disease in a Hypercognitive Society." *Concepts of Alzheimer's Disease: Biological, Clinical and Cultural Perspectives*, edited by James C. Ballenger. Johns Hopkins UP, 2000, pp. 245–56.

Rawls, John. *A Theory of Justice*. Harvard UP, 1971.

Sako, Katsura. "Dementia and Detection in *Elizabeth Is Missing* and *Turn of Mind*." *Contemporary Women's Writing*, vol. 10, no. 3, 2016, pp. 315–33.

Small, Helen. *The Long Life*. Oxford UP, 2007.

Snowdon, Paul. "Animalism and the Lives of Human Animals." *Southern Journal of Philosophy*, vol. 52, no. 1, 2014, pp. 171–84.

Taylor, Charles. *The Sources of the Self*. Cambridge UP, 1989.

Taylor, Janelle. "On Recognition, Care, and Dementia." *Medical Anthropology Quarterly*, vol. 22, no. 4, 2008, pp. 313–35.

Thomas, Matthew. *We Are Not Ourselves*. Fourth Estate, 2015.

Vice, Samantha. "Literature and the Narrative Self." *Philosophy*, vol. 78, 2003, pp. 93–109.

Walker, Margaret Urban. *Moral Understandings: A Feminist Study in Ethics*. Oxford UP, 2007.

8

Self-Help in the Historical Landscape of Ageing, Dementia, Work and Gender: Narrative Duplicities and Literature in a "Changing Place Called Old Age"[1]

DAVID AMIGONI

Wendy Mitchell's memoir *Somebody I Used to Know* (2018) is not in the first instance a narrative about becoming old. Wendy Mitchell is only fifty-eight when her purposeful world of fulfilling professional work, keeping fit and single-parent family life begins to blur and lose definition. She goes to see her doctor to seek a diagnosis following a nasty, unexplained fall when running. Her doctor shrugs and unthinkingly accounts for it with one word: "age" (ch. 1). Mitchell's narrative records a process of investigation that eventually produces a diagnosis of cognitive decline: specifically, young-onset Alzheimer's (ch. 3). Prior to this, her doctor had unthinkingly read profound cognitive impairment as though it were simply a consequence of 'age,' or a taken-for-granted descent into longevity as inevitable physical decline. Indeed, even when she knows that her condition cannot be accounted for by age alone, the conventional stereotypes of old age are precisely the images that haunt Wendy Mitchell as she recalls picture-writing the dementia-to-come: "men and women at the end of their lives, old and white-haired ... blank stares, the *helplessness*" (ch. 3, emphasis added).

Despite – or perhaps because of – this anticipated and perceived helplessness, however, Mitchell in fact writes a work of self-help. She tells a compelling story about sustaining rather than losing selfhood. Her narrative therefore participates in the wider tradition of self-help narrative that

[1]   I am grateful to Drs Sian Adiseshiah, Amy Cully and Jonathan Shears for the invitation to present an early version of this essay at the "Narratives of Old Age and Gender" conference, 12–13 September 2019, British Academy. Sincere thanks to Wendy Mitchell for her thoughtful and critically constructive feedback on that paper. Sincere and heartfelt thanks too to Drs Elizabeth Barry and Margery Vibe Skagen for their excellent editorial advice, support and patience.

has a long literary and cultural history. What this essay will uncover is the way in which the self-help tradition itself has come to include ageing as one of its key concerns, and how, conversely, the writers of stories of ageing and decline often participate in this generic tradition, intending to help their readers as well as themselves.

The self-help narrative has been and continues to be an important contributor to the literature of ageing and gerontology (academic and popular) in ways that I shall seek to explore in this essay. The historical frame is important: we are, as Joan Bakewell observes, in the midst of experiencing "a changing place called old age" (the phrase from my title) because of changing attitudes to ageing; but also the appreciation of specific demographic challenges posed today. However, these first became acutely visible from the early nineteenth century through discussion of Thomas Malthus's influential treatise on population. As Andrea Charise has argued, this established the idea of a significant later-life cohort (xxxiv). Consequently, my essay argues that this 'changing place' has been a long time in the making. In advancing this point, the essay will explore the ways in which literary conventions – in particular Romantic literary conventions for representing age – interact with other modes of self-inscription, and other critical discourses, in this historical landscape. These discourses include the key identity-shaping category of work, or labour. Work, styled in the Victorian period as 'the Gospel of Work' by writers such as Thomas Carlyle and Samuel Smiles, has always held a revered position in the self-help landscape (Briggs 116–39). These discourses also include specific modes of inscribing gender. The voices of women are a less frequently encountered part of the self-help pantheon but their emergence exerts a critically resonant shaping and contesting effect on the genre as a whole: and especially in its contribution to the understanding of ageing. This essay will consider the historic overlap between narratives of self-help and narratives of ageing and how recent accounts of ageing might be read in this light. I will explore recent narratives by Carl Honoré (2018) and Joan Bakewell (2006), comparing them with early twentieth-century narratives by G. Stanley Hall and Harriet Paine. Both G. Stanley Hall's founding statement of gerontological science, *Senescence: The Last Half of Life*, published in the United States in 1922, and Harriet E. Paine's *Old People*, published in the United States in 1910, and curated into a commentary by Hall, can be linked to our understanding of the "changing place called old age" today.

Somebody I Used to Know and Contemporary Self-Help

I will begin with Wendy Mitchell's contemporary memoir of losing and regaining control in the face of dementia, to draw out the particular shape that self-help might take (at least in some circumstances) in older age. Ageing with a dementia diagnosis, in particular, and so in some sense atypically (though cognitive decline is increasingly, and perniciously, taken as *the* image of advanced old age), poses challenges to the notion of 'self' upon which the self-help tradition rests. Mitchell's work asks the question, indeed, of whether a narrative about dementia can tell a story about age *per se* at all. It is necessary to observe the biological, medical and ontological distinctiveness of ageing and dementia as conditions – and yet narrative performs duplicitous work in this context. That is to say the changes narrated in *Somebody I Used to Know* both are not, and at the same time *are* about ageing and shared cultural conventions and stereotypes for representing later life. Ageing and dementia blur here into a state of duplicitousness: in other words, ageing and dementia are not the same here, but they are mistaken for one another, and the latter imposes a premature version of the former that makes Mitchell strange to herself.

This doubling effect is therefore also perforce at the heart of Wendy Mitchell's narrative of dual selfhood, a narrative that had its origins, as well as its continuous elaboration, in an online blog. There is a shadow self: one that was once in control and known, but is only intermittently present in the self of the 'now,' still spoken of but variable in manifestation ("which me am I today?"). Duplicity, in its archaic sense of the state of being double, accounts for the narrative moment when ageing and dementia become one another in Wendy Mitchell's imagination. The more modern, pervasive and somewhat negative valence associated with duplicity is simultaneously present in the narrative movements that explore the self. For these invoke a sense of misrecognition: things being other than they appear to be (I look like the old me, but I might not be; I don't behave like the old me, but I might be). Arguably, the more modern sense of duplicity is even present in the misrecognition that places dementia in the same category as ageing. In any event, helplessness, the loss of independence, is the fear that underpins the narrative even as the narrative emphasizes coping and resourcefulness.

Following her diagnosis, and in the face of her fears, Wendy Mitchell takes steps to help herself in acts that seek to secure the very self that is slipping away. She goes online. She finds videos of role models who have dementia but have found ways of living with the condition that belie the stereotypes of decline and deficit. Loss of identity through retirement from work is associated with the most profound erosion of self: Wendy Mitchell retires early from her demanding job as a non-clinical team leader organizing work rosters in the British National Health Service. Memory, organizational prowess and attention to detail made her successful in her professional role (she is nicknamed 'the guru' at work; Mitchell ch. 1). But these are the very things that are being stripped away from her, so while she heroically strives to carry on in her job, early retirement is accepted with acute and understandable sadness and resentment (ch. 8).

The idea of work is central to Mitchell's memoir. The idea unfolds in complex acts of narration tracing patterns of misrecognition and recognition when work has to be relinquished at a number of levels. Paid work is memorialized as a publicly validated activity generating milestone-related pride (*"Do you remember your first day of work? … that day felt like the first of the rest of your life,"* ch. 8). Work is removed from the domestic, familial sphere (the clinic sits beyond 'whooshing' electric doors that admit access) and therefore creates a structural doubling of roles that further fuels the crisis of self-erosion. Domestic work in the home, habitually misrecognized (especially to the disadvantage of women) as non-work by gendered social convention, is mourned when its status as work is grasped and realized. Memories of home decoration, gift-making, and garden maintenance – sleeves are rolled up to wallpaper and to repair a second-hand bike for Christmas, undergrowth is hewn back – are recognized as crucial features of the work that she performs to make a comfortable, secure, attractive and loving environment for her girls. As Mitchell's narrating self speaks to her past self she come to know that *"you worked hard to hide these things from the girls"* (ch. 4). Here the hard work of single-parenthood is acknowledged as being subject to concealment and misrecognition by the very determination to sustain that secure environment, to hide the effort and cost that it takes to create the comfort. Concealment, a sense of benign duplicity, is itself another form of hard work. This is already work that is not recognized as such by society; it is all the harder when she has to conceal the growing toll such work takes as she finds her capacities being challenged by her initially undiagnosed illness. Wendy Mitchell's dementia steals her capacity for work in so many senses.

Work stands out as identity-defining: when it is relinquished, the consequences are devastating: "My career made me feel valued, but now I feel worthless" (ch. 8). To recover self-worth, she throws herself into a new kind of work: she comes to advocate for those who experience dementia; she involves herself in research projects that aim better to understand the condition and improve the lives of those who experience it. To support her in this endeavour she works hard to adapt elaborate systems of inscription in the form of *aides-mémoire* on colourful Post-it notes. As a result of a quirk of individual neurological wiring, she retains, remarkably, her skill as a typist: so she types, incessantly, on an iPad, to compensate for the cognitive functions that are seeping away from her deteriorating neural networks. This massive enterprise in self-help is launched in the first instance in a heroic effort to hold onto her identity-defining professional job. While this first effort fails, she goes on to channel this intensive labour of self-archiving into blogs and interventions into social media that form the basis for her memoir.

Wendy Mitchell has written a popularly acclaimed, sophisticated and complex example of memoir.[2] She has also written a narrative that participates in a sub-genre of life writing that comes recognisably from the 'self-help' tradition. Although self-help is often associated with the advice and conduct manual and is by no means always set forth in memoir, the self-helping behaviour that Wendy Mitchell records can find a home in that genre. As an individual she is challenged by a severe and deteriorating condition. She perseveres to solve problems to manage her dementia; but not, notably, to overcome it. For self-help stories can also invite exploration of the limits of self-determination. In her turn, Wendy Mitchell writes a narrative in which the complex re-making of her individual self is performed in part through the assistance of other people. The journalist Anna Wharton helps her to conceive and shape the story of the doubling of selves that becomes the memoir, described by Wharton as "a ball of wool" that has to be untangled (Mitchell and Wharton). As 'ghostwriter,' Wharton adds to the layers of duplicity and the shadow selves present (Mitchell, Acknowledgements; Mitchell and Wharton). Social groups, charitable networks and research initiatives constitute communities of self-sustainment for Wendy Mitchell's new, divided but purposeful selves. Inscriptive tools and technologies are the means that enable the extension of her selves into those communities. As readers follow Wendy Mitchell's self-sustaining work with the Post-it note and the iPad, they become aware of the complex labour involved in Mitchell's making of literature: from notes designed to act as a proxy for memory; to blog-posts; to the reading and discussions that lead to crafted narrative; to the wider readings and discussions that these in turn prompt.

In going beyond the classically defined boundaries of the individual self, Mitchell's story is one in a long line that uses the interface between disability, ageing and (paradoxically) self-help to complicate and see in a

---

[2]   The memoir has been a Radio 4 "Book of the Week," https://www.bbc.co.uk/programmes/b09rj35w; as well as featuring as part of the Richard and Judy Book Club, https://www.richardandjudy.co.uk/books/Somebody-I-Used-to-Know/738.

new light the productive fractures, fissures and duplicities in the apparently sovereign individual self. Even Samuel Smiles, the original Victorian popularizer of the format, could see that his title *Self-Help* (1859) was in danger of becoming a source of misrecognition. It did not, he pointed out in a "Preface" to the revised edition of 1866, extol "a eulogy of selfishness"; rather, the stories of self-help that he told were inextricably linked to help from, and also for, "neighbours," or wider familial and social networks (Smiles vi).

The Victorians and Beyond

Mitchell's work, then, has a long lineage. In the nineteenth century, 'self-help' came to refer to metaphorical journeys of independent self-improvement where the individual self is styled as the source of problem-solving and improvement. 'Self-help' is, as we have begun to see, a genre; but also, a publishing and dissemination phenomenon. The first usage recorded by the *Oxford English Dictionary* was by Thomas Carlyle (1831). Carlyle styled self-help as "the highest possession": vaunted as the most elevated form of self-possession, the phrase became an extensively used term in the later Victorian period, on both sides of the Atlantic, following the publication and wide dissemination of Samuel Smiles's phenomenally popular *Self-Help* in 1859.[3]

The original *Self-Help* by Samuel Smiles offered advice to youth: particularly to the nineteenth-century generations who needed guidance through the precarious mid-Victorian landscape of work and its vast economic and social insecurities. They were to be guided by exemplary lives, in the form of biographies of the great masters of engineering (Stephenson), industry (Wedgwood) and statecraft (Peel). The exemplars were both of sterling value – this is *the* person that you should aspire to be like – yet in seemingly endless supply: the exemplary potter, engineer

---

[3]   For an account of the 'self-help' concept in the development of Smiles and mid-Victorian thinking, see Adrian Jarvis, *Samuel Smiles and the Construction of Victorian Values* (Alan Sutton, 1997). *Self-Help* was published by John Murray; it went through four editions in the first month of publication alone (November 1859) and sold 20,000 copies in its first year. By 1904 (the year of Smiles's death) it had sold one-quarter of a million copies; it had been reprinted forty-seven times to that point. For more on this, see Peter W. Sinnema, "Introduction" to Smiles, *Self-Help* (Oxford UP, 2002), pp. xvi, vii. Smiles's book was an international phenomenon in its own time. As he pointed out in the Preface to the revised edition of 1866, the book had been reprinted in the United States, as well as being translated into Dutch, French and German.

and statesman would be followed by a whole range of other exemplars from just about every field of work. The self-help exemplary life pre-dated Smiles. Significant numbers were published in 'improving' early nineteenth-century magazines such as the *Penny Magazine* (of the Society for the Diffusion of Useful Knowledge). The vogue for the self-help life was further promoted by Smiles's success. The repetition effect of this abundant provision – and assumed impact – was the narrative stock-in-trade of the self-help genre: it did not make for sophistication in its quest for, and assumptions about, the transformative power of reading. Repeating the advice frequently would be sure to effect the necessary change in the unformed, but aspiring, youthful self.

Self-help has been gradually, and now widely, adapted to account for the ageing self: self-help journeys have come to frame the experiences of ageing in much of the contemporary popular literature about the meaning of growing old. To take a contemporary example, the journalist Joan Bakewell takes her readers along on her own journey to experience "the changing place called old age" in her 2006 book *The View from Here: Life at Seventy* (ch. 1). The age-conscious reader who occupies the 'place' we have come to call 'old age' is an identity that is open to self-helping solutions because the thinking that constitutes that place is manifestly changing as deficit models of later life are questioned and challenged. Age UK, for instance, offers "10 Tips for Ageing Better." And Carl Honoré, the author of *Bolder: Making the Most of Our Longer Lives* (2018), has published "12 Rules for Ageing Boldly." His advice to "Keep on Learning and Experimenting" exemplifies, perhaps, the sense that ageing does not fix us; instead, it becomes a new driver of self-formation (Honoré's website). His book *Bolder* reinforces this message: "These days, what matters more and more is not when you were born so much as how you think, talk, look, move, exercise, dance, dress, travel, play" (Introduction). Such advice aims to have an impact on the reader by prompting some change of thought or behaviour. Indeed, we can see evidence of thought formation or reinforcement: electronic platforms are useful for registering both affect and effect. In my Amazon Kindle version of the text, the highlighter function tells me that Honoré's advice received thirteen highlights (Introduction): readers may actually be using the text to shape their self-styling as they think about ageing.

Honoré's exploration of ageing also provides a recent example of popular writing that participates in the self-help space, incorporating as we have seen its customary discourses of both gender and work. Honoré presents his intervention as a journey that begins with the author's own changing perception of ageing as a facet of his masculine self-identity.

Discovering that he is, at forty-eight, the oldest person in a hockey tournament "knocks the wind out" of him: the energy and competitiveness of hockey is his way of "putting off" thinking about ageing and the assumed negativity that surrounds its onset. The following journey is specifically a form of self-help, enabling this male author "to learn how to age better and how to feel better about ageing" (Introduction). Though work is not included in Honoré's list of later-life-style resources, it is an important focus. When we encounter work for older people, it centres on the contribution of women: Honoré's visit to the Cho Heng Rice Vermicelli Factory in Thailand is effectively the first stage on his journey, and a globally resonant one. The factory prides itself in employing older workers, and he focuses in on Darunee Kramwong, a seventy-three-year-old cleaner, grandmother and erstwhile lover. Honoré observes that "she feels like one of the gang at Cho Heng, and is proud that younger colleagues seek her advice on both cleaning and romance." The "aim … [of] this book," Honoré contends, is "to harness the Kramwong Effect," by which he means the rounded authority in life experience offered by this older woman with a positive outlook derived substantially from her working life in older age and the relationships that it enables (*Bolder* ch. 1).

The appeal to an ageing working woman as role model here contrasts radically with the origins of self-help stories, even if it corresponds in this respect to the later exemplars which I have mentioned. In 1859 Smiles's stream of exemplar figures were all men of seemingly boundless energy. Indeed, 'energy' is one of the most frequently used words in Smiles's text and this is, perhaps, part of an implicitly masculine field of connotation into which Honoré unconsciously taps as he charges around the hockey pitch, keeping the fear of enforced helplessness at bay. Honoré's encounter with Darunee Kramwong at the vermicelli factory in Thailand provides its readers with an alternative perspective on later-life energy and its sources. In Kramwong, Honoré finds exemplary energy in the sustainment of a valued and affirmed self, embodied in a late working life. The narration of a woman's life experience here emerges as a critically resonant discourse. When combined with a focus on work – central to the Victorian self-help tradition but also vital to contemporary demographics of ageing – such voices connect to multiple modes of literary and non-literary discourse for exploring the experience of age-related change and other so-called 'deficit' conditions such as dementia, age-related illness and other modes of geriatric disability (Phillipson et al.).

The self-help narrative's relationship to gendered ageing is thus a way of challenging the deficit model that casts a large shadow over the experience. Yet the path to Honoré's 'Kramwong Effect' is a rocky one: the obstacles to successful healthy and purposeful ageing – the fear of illnesses and limiting changes that may threaten to remove capacity and enforce dependency – continue to haunt narratives about age. The ambivalences that follow from this recognition and continue to pervade the experience of ageing remain present in the self-help narrative, adding to its duplicitous effects. At the core of this narrative – inaugurated by the original Victorian version – is a fear of helplessness and, to counter this, a moral commitment to independence of mind and means enshrined in particular versions of 'character' (a key word for the Smilsean tradition).[4]

Self-help in the context of ageing has thus proved to be a resonant and complex discourse for exploring the multiple and varied ways in which the experiences of change associated with ageing confront and contest sources of identity formation. Work is one such source: but so are gender and geriatric disability (dementia, blindness, deafness). It is also important to acknowledge, as another source of identity formation, the resonant place of influential Romantic literary conventions in shaping attitudes to ageing. Romanticism itself has bequeathed a double legacy. As Charise argues through the course of her innovative 2020 book *The Aesthetics of Senescence*, Romantic and Victorian writing inaugurate a powerful public debate about ageing that spanned the nineteenth century. However, key Romantic poetic conventions could also fix, homogenize and limit ageing identities. The point then is to explore the ways in which these double legacies surrounding self-help and women, Romantic literary conventions, and work as a powerful source of identity formation were curated and contested by early twentieth-century narratives that were beginning to articulate possible models of self-sustainment to populate "the changing place called old age."

Narrative Curation: Ageing, Work, Gender and Literature

Self-help narratives have exercised a curatorial function to provide a means for exploring the relationship between ageing, literature, and work from the later nineteenth century to today. This enables us to see ways in which today's self-help narratives about ageing recapitulate some of the moves of the earliest texts of academic gerontology as a discipline; for instance, G. Stanley Hall's *Senescence*, which also participated in and helped to curate the self-help genre as part of the early twentieth-century public understanding of ageing. Thus, while 'old age' is truly a 'changing place'

---

[4]   Samuel Smiles published *Character* in 1874, effectively a sequel to *Self-Help*.

for those living in the twenty-first century, the terms within which the changes have come to be comprehended and negotiated were being put in place over a century ago.

This is evident when we reflect on the place of work, gender and literature in Joan Bakewell's sense of the "changing place of old age" as a central context for the advice she offers. The hybrid form of Bakewell's *The View from Here: Life at Seventy*, placed as it is between reflective advice and memoir, is an especially good example of these possibilities. Bakewell, a journalist, has also become a significant public advocate for older people and her narrative had its origins in a newspaper column (in the UK's *The Guardian*). *The View from Here* addresses work as a key factor in changing opportunities and needs in later life, recognizing that "We shall all certainly have to work longer, the whole economic house of cards will collapse unless we do." Yet Bakewell also resolves this economic imperative into a positive element of self-help through enhanced self-worth: "we need to plan for part time, less hectic working lives, in jobs that society needs and welcomes, yet in which we also feel needed and valued" (ch. 1). Critical reflections on received images of old age are also curated by Bakewell's memoir format for these may be held to promote the continuing misrecognition of older people, preventing them from being seen as productive, skilled and valued participants in the work force. Bakewell accounts historically for her own changing attitudes to ageing as represented in these images, shaped as they have been by generational relations, and altering opportunities around education, culture, work, gender – and literary education. In a telling moment, Bakewell's memoir-mode recalls how, as a twelve-year-old child in 1947, she wrote a poem to her seventy-year-old grandmother, born in the 1870s. Bakewell's narrative curates this juvenile text, even commenting on the "faultless copperplate" in which "a stooped, white-haired figure ... walking with two sticks" is addressed. Bakewell's curation of her own juvenile text reconstructs the context of this expression on the occasion of her own arrival at the seventy-year milestone. Thus, the reader is made aware of a doubling effect in the juxtaposition of these milestone moments for two seventy-year-old women, separated by history. The diction of the juvenile poem, with its reflections on "life's dwindling rays" (ch. 1), is drawn from the elegiac tones of the Victorian poet Tennyson. There is homage to higher-status literary genres such as the Victorian elegy but Bakewell's later-life perspective on this literary tradition, internalized at a young age, is ambivalent, mixed as it has been with a critical sense of intergenerational distance. We can discern the degree of misrecognition that Bakewell's seventy-year-old self can see in the elegiac styling of her grandmother at seventy from her childhood pen.

This moment of duplicity in Bakewell's text may be viewed as a reca-
pitulation of movements that are recorded in an early text of academic
gerontology that participated in the self-help genre. It is important here
to focus on the early transatlantic history of the interdisciplinary study of
ageing by looking at G. Stanley Hall's seminal work *Senescence: The Last
Half of Life* (1922); an interdisciplinarity that continues into the gerontology of our own time.[5] *Senescence* while dealing with the difficult "transition from leadership to the chimney corner" so that "the press notices of
my withdrawal read not unlike obituaries" (ix): in other words, late life
was doubled disconcertingly with end of life.

Hall's ambivalences enabled him to reflect on ways in which older
people feel "set aside" by a younger generation through particular thought
processes that convert age into a catch-all and duplicitous source of all
deficits when "Shortcomings that date from earlier years are now ascribed
to age" (ix). In a moving passage in which Hall reflects on the experience
of taking on and then relinquishing a position of leadership in later life
where his need to be creative was pushed to its limit, he reaches for the
elegiac tradition through Tennyson's poem "The Brook" (viii). He does
this through a contrast between the symbolic power of endurance represented by a source of flowing water, and the symbolic finitude of the
individual human life under the regimes of ageing and death that point
to the inevitability of termination and succession. The contrast between
institutional continuity and individual human transience needs appreci-
ating in the context of Hall's recognition of his retirement or fall away
"from leadership to the chimney corner": it is identified with end of life
via the model of Tennyson as the leading Victorian exponent of the elegy
and inheritor of the Romantic tradition. In his seminal *Disciplining Old
Age* (1996), Stephen Katz noted the intense subjective "ambivalence" of
Hall's *Senescence* towards the experience of ageing, underlined by this
generic borrowing. For Katz, this ambivalence paradoxically "prevented

---

[5]   As Miriam Bernard, Mo Ray and Jackie Reynolds argue in their Introduction
to *The Evolution of British Gerontology*, the field of study constitutes an 'interdis-
cipline' that has taken shape at the interfaces between medical, scientific, social,
humanistic and technological knowledge (Policy Press, 2020). Indeed, the case
that I have made here for the relationship between popular self-help writing and
the complex knowledge formations comprising gerontology also draws on the cultural constellation at the heart of Andrea Charise's new account of the "aesthetics
of senescence." Her thesis advances an innovative historical account of the relationship between literary representation, age as a feature of the nineteenth-century
discovery of demographics, and the constellation of public issues and disciplinary
development that made a critical conception of age studies possible.

it from becoming gerontology's first modern textbook" (94). From my perspective, the ambivalence at the heart of Hall's use of the self-help format proved strangely enabling: it facilitated the complex exploration of ageing as a contest of meanings both in itself and in relation to gender, as well as conditions such as cognitive impairment, blindness and deafness. Indeed, Hall's chapter, "Literature Written by and about the Aged," which appears after the first chapter tracing historical views of older age, is a good example of a curatorial act that facilitates this exploration. Tellingly, as Hall mapped "the second half of life," he placed writing about the experience of age first and prior to his analysis of the biological basis for researching later life. In doing so, Hall surveyed a canon of writings that had come to represent the Anglo-American experience of ageing in the nineteenth century. The poetry of Tennyson, Arnold and Whitman was prominent; but so too was a survey of the burgeoning transatlantic canon of self-help literature about the ageing process that had accumulated between *circa* 1870 and 1920.[6] The very first work he surveyed in "Literature written by and about the Aged" was Harriet E. Paine's *Old People* (1910).

The participation of Paine's text in the self-help genre of advice and exemplarity established by Smiles is indicated in some of her chapter titles; 'character' was a central category for Smiles and Paine writes a chapter entitled "The Last Lesson in Character." Paine compiled two chapters: one about blindness which she entitled "Darkness" (VIII); and one on deafness which she entitled "Silence" (IX). In both of these chapters, the exemplar stories relate the experiences of older people who first mourn the loss of their sensory capacity; then display cheerfulness and fortitude as they meet the challenge of a dark or silent world. These experiences of darkness and silence, on the face of it elements that echo the imagery of the elegiac tradition, in fact prepare the reader for Chapter XI entitled "The Inner Life of the Old." Darkness, silence and isolation are in fact seen by Paine to prepare older people for being the ideal recipients and cultivators of the best, contemplative aspects of inner life. The final chapter, however, is entitled simply "Sunset," which helps older readers towards a consoling end, marked by an extinguishing light. It also, incidentally, prefigures the twelve-year-old Joan Bakewell's derivative elegiac image of "life's dwindling rays" addressed to her seventy-year-old grandmother. The seventy-year-old Bakewell, we recall, rejects this figuration of termination, seeing it as a denial of self-help while pointing out that her grandmother lived until eighty-six (Bakewell ch. 1).

<hr>

[6]   As a feature of the transatlantic circulation of printed material Hall also surveyed titles published in Britain such as Mortimer Collins's *The Secret of a Long Life* (1875) and Nicholas Smith's *Masters of Old Age* (1905).

Hall describes Paine as "a retired maiden teacher": her now 'retired' professional status is blended, as if naturally, with her 'maiden [unmarried]' status (Hall 102). It is significant (despite the blend of sexism and ageism) that Hall began his survey with a book by a retired member of a growing (but embattled) class in early twentieth-century American academic life: the cadre of women teachers and researchers in the educational work force (Aljberg Graham 733–59). Paine had been educated at Wheaton when it was a women-only seminary; she went on to teach at colleges in Massachusetts, including a return to Wheaton. The liberal arts curriculum that she taught required a training in the sciences as well as literature (she had read her scientific naturalists, including Darwin and Herbert Spencer). The profession of teacher provided opportunities for travel (she spent time in Europe, learning French and German), as well as for writing and publication. Paine's *Old People* was a posthumously published example of a popular writing career that found expression through the self-help genre.[7]

Paine's book appeared with a biographical notice written by Alice Brown, a former pupil of Paine's, and this format produced a subtle contest of voices between women of different generations from an emergent and gendered professional class. Brown had gone on to become a novelist and writer, rather than an educator, so there is a sense of both a generational and occupational separation that opens up here – the younger, educated woman of imaginative fiction looking at the elder didactic writer and educator, by whom she had been taught. Brown purports to give a sober biographical portrait of a woman in her early sixties, but she frames this portrait with the language of the grotesque (for which there seemed to

---

7   Paine's dates were 1845–1910, so *Old People* was published in the year of her death (1910), at the age of sixty-four. Her biographer, Alice Brown, indicated that she had actually written it in her late fifties. Brown manages, in that elegant yet curiously lumpen tradition of nineteenth-century women writing about women, to make Paine into a dutiful, if somewhat terrifying (to her pupils), servant of God and the teaching profession. In fact, in being the only daughter of the Reverend John Chester and his wife, Eliza Folger Paine, she descended on her mother's side from a network of eminent New England Puritan families (including the Folgers who eventually endowed the Shakespeare Library). Paine was, thus, New England intellectual aristocracy, from a family on a par with the James family (William and Henry).

Paine had written self-helping advice texts before; in 1890 she published *Girls and Women* under the pseudonym of 'E. Chester' which followed the surname of her father and (probably) the initial of the first name of her mother. She took the surname of her mother's line in her last/late writings. For the Gutenberg version of *Girls and Women* see http://www.gutenberg.org/files/20362/20362-h/20362-h.htm.

be something of a vogue in the fiction of the period) to capture the view of her subject's ageing body.[8] Brown generates an ambivalent perspective as she focuses on the grotesque feebleness of Paine's "lined" body and face, yet also describes the latter as "noble" (Brown in Paine xxv). Not in spite of but through these bodily changes, Brown presents Paine as the epitome of "spiritual" life in bodily death, a beautiful "emaciated saint" spoken best by poetry (xxxi). Indeed, Brown mobilizes a rich range of nineteenth-century literary conventions in a duplicitous act that ambivalently voices and misrecognizes the suspicion that early twentieth-century Western cultures reserved for the embodied reality of ageing, professional-intellectual women. Paine's energetic working life in education and scholarship is captured in George Eliot's phrase to describe Dorothea (*Middlemarch*): Paine should be recalled for her "unhistoric acts," quietly delivered but unrecognized in the dominant field of masculine achievement (Brown in Paine xxi). Reaching for Wordsworthian Romanticism, Brown also styles her teacher as an embodiment of the poetry of temporal loss and decline offset by inner, imaginative gain that is signified through allusions to 'Tintern Abbey' (Brown in Paine xxvii). It is striking to recall the way in which Joan Bakewell in *The View from Here* came to distance herself from her poetic address, written at the age of twelve, to her grandmother at the age of seventy. Rendered in a derivative version of these expressive conventions, if it urged self-help, then it was in the form of an accepting, contemplative withdrawal and death.

Paine's own writing met the challenge of representing women of age in similar terms to Brown: women are at this time figured as being in place mostly to serve and be sympathetic. However, Paine's voice produces some subtle variations in tone. She reaches into a different metaphoric economy, which utilizes her training in biology and geology. This enabled her, when necessary, to sidestep the literary conventions and traditions on which Brown depends. Paine had read Charles Darwin's *Beagle* narrative and was disturbed by his report of the destruction visited upon older Fuegian women of the Patagonian tribe that figures in the narrative: hunter-gatherer brutalism, perhaps, refracting for her some more subtle tendency in her own culture (Paine 49). Drawing on her own educational formation, Paine did not take from her scientific reading reductive ideas about inevitable biological degeneration but instead foregrounded examples of conservation and even renewal that the natural world offered. For instance, Paine begins her narrative recalling an encounter with a

---

[8]   See Arnold Bennett, *The Old Wives' Tale* (1908). Bennett borrowed the language of the grotesque that he uses for depicting ageing bodies from Mrs W.K. Clifford's *Aunt Anne* (1892); see also Amigoni (pp. 181–96).

vivacious, publicly engaged ninety-year-old woman. To explain her great energy, Paine reaches for an analogy from the discipline of physiography, the science of the formation of geological features: waterfalls, Paine observes, are generally a property of younger rivers – but movement of the riverbeds can produce them again in "old rivers," and "so in the case of my old lady's vivacity. New work had been given to her in her old age, and it lent her in turn the sparkle of youth" (19). "Work," Paine argues in a nod to the self-help tradition, is the analogue to the geological fault that energetically disrupts the ageing riverbed. It is worth noting that this is a qualitatively different image of water flow/age/late life when compared to the elegiac, Tennysonian image of "The Brook" on which Hall draws in his reflections on his own retirement/end-of-life.

Paine's chapters on late-life work and earning a living (IV, V) are prescient: they would not look out of place in today's policy discussions of active ageing and later-life work. In fact, she proposes a scheme that looks a lot like what we now know as Peter Laslett's ideas about the emergence of the third age and its pedagogic services (University of the Third Age): superannuated teachers teaching adults in small towns. For Paine this would overcome the problem of wasted capacity because "At present there is a great and unnecessary waste in the resources of the nation because old people who cannot do much are not given the opportunity to do what they can" (Paine 103). Paine's conceding an 'innate' limitation of older people is perhaps of a piece with her public acceptance of the limited opportunities for women: but she offers sound reasoning for the importance of both as a resource, as well as examples of their vitality and value.

It is also important to note that G. Stanley Hall, who styled Paine as a "retired maiden teacher," clearly saw the importance of the case that she made for the social benefit of labour when he acknowledged in his account of her book that "the weapon against loneliness is work" (Hall 104). This is one of the ways in which Hall's ambivalent act of self-helping curation in *Senescence* was critically resonant. It placed the older elite, male professorial college president and the (much less publicly esteemed) older female college tutor into discursive contact as mirror images of one another in the identity-eroding space of enforced retirement. We know that Hall responded negatively to his own removal from a position of responsibility; we can speculate, given Paine's defence of continuity of the working life, about her own ambivalent experience of the end of her working life. In this encounter between Hall and Paine, there were misrecognitions of purposes and principles along the way, which arose from conflicted imagined identities that were both orientated towards, and suspended between, the expectations of later life, the challenges of cognitive and sensory decline, and the battleground of gender. However, the imperative and allure of work, rooted as it was in the shared commitment of this pairing to education, secured a kind of textual camaraderie between them.

Conclusion: Typing the Self, Duplicity and Connective Work

In placing the interrelations between self-help and ageing at the centre of my exploration, I have argued for the centrality of work to self-identity, and examined the ways in which a working role (whether or not a professional one) can be sustained in older age and in the face of cognitive impairment. I have further argued that the duplicitous moments of narration where these conditions double and generate misrecognitions can produce cultural insight. Self-help, as Samuel Smiles recognized, is itself a conceptual source of misrecognition in that, contrary to the drift of its name, it is orientated as much towards others as it is to the self. The networks of support that extend beyond the self feed back into a sustainable and enriching form of selfhood that both gives and receives through teaching, advising and writing. Literature is important to these goals. While, as we have seen, literary traditions and legacies can generate misrecognitions around the experience of later life and cognitive impairment, literature as the act or indeed work of inscription generates other possibilities. I shall conclude by returning to Wendy Mitchell and the place of typing – the mechanics of inscription, the skill contingently left intact despite the work of dementia – in sustaining a complex selfhood that can perform connective work.

It is fitting to conclude by examining the complexity of the doubling effects, and the way they confound expectations, as presented in Wendy Mitchell's narrative of her two selves. These expectations are challenged by the act of inscription itself. Fast-moving fingers become the means by which technology is mobilized to function as the bridge between embodiment and the signs of cognition, text and meaning production, behind which elements readers expect to recover a classically received image of mind (replete with memory, in control of itself). However, the fact that dementia is now touching so many in later life – individual lives lived under the condition as well as families, friends and carers touched by the experience – also means that an understanding of the condition should be widely shared: an aspiration that may be extended by electronic social media.

One of the sterling features of Wendy Mitchell as blogger and tweeter – she is a great role model – is her ability to re-tell her story of self-help and supportive advice in different formats. If the Victorian self-help narrative was ubiquitous in its reproducibility (from Smiles's text in multiple editions to the magazines and serial formats that deluged the world with self-help narratives), it can be argued that the opportunity offered by social media is its ability to frame and repeat an important message. Thus, in a recent tweet, Mitchell tells again the story of "why typing is the key to my survival ... of [sic] that skill disappears ... so do I" (Twitter, 27 August 2019). She even includes a poem on a link to her blog "Which Me Am I Today?":

When I type
Words come freely
Fingers work quickly
No sign of dementia ...
I can pretend
I can be normal
Just like you

Unlike Alice Brown on Harriet E. Paine, or Joan Bakewell (aged twelve) on her ageing grandmother, Wendy Mitchell's poem does not gesture to or derive authority from the nineteenth-century elegiac tradition in framing its loss or the consolations for it. Instead, the poem is about the act that brought it into being: the speaker reflects on her typing skills as a form of duplicity (here, notably its non-archaic sense, for things to appear as other than they are) associated with an age-related degenerative condition: seemingly one thing, actually another. This complicates our responses to ageing, as well as to dementia as a neural degenerative condition contingently linked to it. This complication links back to the story of Wendy Mitchell's reactions to her circumstances, and her self-helping determination to outwit them, that she tells in her memoir. In fact, it gently challenges those sceptical observers who see the outward evidence of her skill, agency, and purposefulness: who cannot believe that they are in the company of someone living with dementia because of Mitchell's refusal to live by the image of the greying, passive, silent, *helpless* ageing stereotype.

Works Cited

Albjerg Graham, Patricia. "Expansion and Inclusion: A History of Women in American Higher Education." *Signs: Journal of Women, Culture and Society*, vol. 3, no. 4, 1978, pp. 759–73.

Amigoni, David. "Active Aging in the Community: Laughing at/Thinking about Victorian Senescence in Arnold Bennett's *The Old Wives' Tale* and Its Theatrical Afterlife." *Interdisciplinary Perspectives on Aging in Nineteenth-Century Culture*, edited by Katharina Boehm, Anna Farkas, and Anne-Julia Zwierlein. Routledge, 2014, pp. 181–96.

Bakewell, Joan. *The View from Here: Life at Seventy*. Kindle ed., Atlantic Books, 2009.

Briggs, Asa. "Samuel Smiles and the Gospel of Work." *Victorian People: A Reassessment of Persons and Themes, 1851–1867*. Penguin, 1990, pp. 116–39.

Charise, Andrea. *The Aesthetics of Senescence*. SUNY P, 2020.

Hall, G. Stanley. *Senescence: The Last Half of Life*. D. Appleton, 1922.

Honoré, Carl. *Bolder: Making the Most of Our Longer Lives*. Kindle ed., Simon and Schuster, 2018.

——. "12 Rules for Ageing and Living Better," http://www.carlHonoré.com/12-rules-for-ageing-and-living-better/

Katz, Stephen. *Disciplining Old Age: The Formation of Gerontological Knowledge*. U of Virginia P, 1996.

Laslett, Peter. *A Fresh Map of Life: The Emergence of the Third Age*. Weidenfeld and Nicolson, 1989.

Mitchell, Wendy. *Somebody I Used to Know*. Kindle ed., Bloomsbury, 2018.

——. "Which Me Am I Today." https://whichmeamitoday.wordpress.com/

Mitchell, Wendy, and Anna Wharton. "How Do You Write a Memoir When You Can't Remember?" *Granta*, 5 April 2019, https://granta.com/how-do-you-write-a-memoir-when-you-cant-remember/

Paine, Harriet E. *Old People*, with an Introduction by Alice Brown. Houghton Mifflin Co., 1910.

Phillipson, Chris, et al. "Uncertain Futures: Organisational Influences on the Transition from Work to Retirement." *Social Policy and Society*, vol. 18, no. 3, 2018, pp. 335–50.

Smiles, Samuel. *Self-Help: With Illustrations of Conduct and Perseverance*. John Murray, 1908.

"10 Tips for Ageing Better." Age UK, www.ageuk.org.uk/information-advice/health-wellbeing/mind-body/10-tips-for ageing-better/

Thane, Pat. "The Liberal Party and Family Welfare, 1906-1922." *Cercles*, vol. 21, 2011, pp. 1–10.

9

Toying with the Spool:
Happiness in Old Age in Samuel Beckett's
Krapp's Last Tape

PETER SVARE VALEUR

From the time of its publication, it has been frequently claimed that the protagonist in Samuel Beckett's short play *Krapp's Last Tape* (originally published in 1958, and later translated by the author into French) is a "pathetic old man" (Knowlson and Pilling 84), "helpless and awkward" (Reinton 92), his life "a string of aimless, inconsequential, and monotonous events" (Brustein 192). Krapp's habits, it has been pointed out, are stale and tedious, his mind in decline, and he has been seen as a media junkie addicted to his tape machine – his "masturbatory agent," as Beckett calls it in a note (*Theatrical Notebooks* 67). In addition, his name suggests "residue and waste" and that "the dregs are all Krapp has left at the end of his life" (Campbell 64). As a sixty-nine-year-old, he is described in the stage directions as "a wearish old man," "hard of hearing," "very near-sighted," with a "cracked voice," and with a foible for bananas and alcohol.[1] A rather comical figure, his appearance might make us think of Beckett's well-known quip "nothing is funnier than unhappiness" (Beckett, *Dramatic Works* 101). This unhappiness is closely connected with his old age.

One of the central tenets of Beckett scholarship is that his works tend to represent processes of *worsening* and states of *worseness*, what the French philosopher Alain Badiou has called "empirage."[2] The way Beckett often describes old people as physically and mentally decrepit makes this age seem an eminent figure of this process. Kathryn White, in her book

[1] All quotations will be from Samuel Beckett, *Krapp's Last Tape, and Other Shorter Plays*. Faber, 2009.

[2] In his *Petit manuel d'inesthétique*, Alain Badiou speaks of the "exercices d'empirage" in Beckett's works. The word comes from the French translation of Beckett's marvellous late text *Worstward Ho*; in French, *Cap au pire*. According to Badiou, Beckett's works follow various strategies to bring out this "worseness" of things (see Badiou 137–87).

Beckett and Decay, thus argues that Beckett's "representation of the aged is a horrific study of the implications of growing old and the undesirability of reaching those twilight years, when all we have to look forward to is bad health, isolation and the overwhelming need to reach the grave" (White 22). Other researchers have, however, been less negative, seeing old age less in terms of biology and death. Elizabeth Barry, who rightly argues that "old age – or at least the tropes associated with it – are everywhere in Beckett," highlights the relationship between old age and narrative, referring to Beckett's own statement (in a conversation with Lawrence Shainberg) that "with old age, the more possibilities diminish, the better chance you have" (Barry 206). Barry sees this claim in terms of how in *Molloy* and *Malone Dies*, Beckett uses the lapses of memory and concentration associated with old age to challenge narrative unity, and to think more deeply on the nature of temporal structures.[3] In this article, which shares with Barry the interest in literary form, I want however primarily to pose the question about old age and happiness. Indeed, a prominent feature of Krapp is what the text repeatedly calls his "happy smile," and his ability to get pleasure out of listening to his tapes.[4] As I argue in this essay, this pleasure is far from insignificant, as it shows how – despite the general "worsening" or "severity of ageing" (White 22) – Krapp is still happy.

To approach the question of happiness in Krapp, this essay takes its cue from a stoic insight about *solitude*, seen as a way that the individual can be 'together with itself,' free from the disturbing presence of others. As Montaigne puts it, "the greatest thing on earth is to know how to belong to oneself," and he remarks that this is a privilege particularly given to old people who no longer need to "live for others," but can cultivate their own self.[5] Krapp, I argue, fits this idea of solitude, a solitude where he is not so much miserable as "together with himself" and thus, as it has been said,

---

[3]   Barry's article is printed in a special edition of *Samuel Beckett Today/ Aujourd'hui* devoted to old age in Beckett ("Clinics and Poetics: Beckett's Theatre and Aging," vol. 28, no. 2, 2016).

[4]   Happiness in old age is a central topic in Beckett's drama, for instance in *Happy Days* or the dialogues between Nell and Nagg in *Endgame*. Here Nell at one point says: "Nothing is funnier than unhappiness," and Nagg exclaims: "Happy! Don't you laugh at it still? Every time I tell it. Happy!" (Beckett, *Dramatic Works* 101f).

[5]   "La plus grande chose du monde c'est de savoir être à soi." In the same essay, entitled "De la solitude," Montaigne writes about solitude as a way for the self to be together with itself: "Nous avons une âme contournable en soi-même; elle se peut faire compagnie, elle a de quoi assaillir et de quoi défendre, de quoi recevoir, et de quoi donner. … C'est assez vécu pour autrui, vivons pour nous au moins ce bout de vie" (Montaigne vol. 1, 416ff).

"two-in-one,"[6] speaking to and enjoying himself. I thus disagree with White who claims that the play illustrates the "severity of ageing in an atmosphere where isolation takes precedence, and memories serve to reinforce the horror of the present" (White 22). Rather, what I want to show is that Krapp experiences what the play calls the "relish" of entertaining a relationship with himself. This claim is predicated on the fact that Krapp has made an archive of recordings from various stages of his life, and has thus fashioned himself into different "selves," or better put, different *age-selves*.[7] Or as Suzanne Lafont puts it: through his tapes Krapp redoubles himself, his "personnage se dédouble en plusieurs" (Lafont 183). The old Krapp's engagement with these other "selves" is often sympathetic, imaginative and playful, giving him pleasure. To analyse the way Krapp engages with his "dédoublements" and the pleasure this gives him, the essay looks at three dimensions relevant to it: the technology of time, the simultaneity of old age and childhood, and the play of imagination.

"What is a year now?" Krapp and Time

Beckett's piece is a "*mono*drama for *two* voices" (Dukore 351) where we hear the taped voice of Krapp at thirty-nine (called TAPE in the text) and the present Krapp at sixty-nine (called KRAPP in the text). In addition, Krapp at thirty-nine refers to a recording of himself made about ten or twelve years earlier. The play thus points to three ages of Krapp: Krapp as young, mature, and old. Of particular importance is the difference in mentality and worldview between the mature Krapp of thirty-nine and the old Krapp of sixty-nine. While the mature Krapp of thirty-nine is an intellectual governed by what might be called a *carpe diem* approach, the old Krapp is preoccupied with the past, yearning for happiness, and, as we will see, in some instances astonishingly imaginative.

---

[6] This expression comes from Hannah Arendt, who distinguishes solitude from loneliness: "As Epictetus sees it (*Dissertationes*, book 3, ch. 13), the lonely man (*eremos*) finds himself surrounded by others with whom he cannot establish contact or to whose hostility he is exposed. The solitary man, on the contrary, is alone and therefore 'can be together with himself' since men have the capacity of 'talking with themselves.' In solitude, in other words, I am 'by myself,' together with my self, and therefore two-in-one, whereas in loneliness I am actually one, deserted by all others" (Arendt 625).

[7] I agree largely with Ulrika Maude, who in her analysis of the technology of the tape recorder sees the tapes "as an opportune trope for identity, because of their simultaneously permanent and mutable nature: they epitomize both the stative and active aspects of subjectivity" (Maude 65).

Let us start with the recording Krapp made of himself when he was
thirty-nine, more precisely on his thirty-ninth birthday. In this, he talks
about his former life and that happiness is no longer a prime objective:
"Flagging pursuit of happiness," he laconically states (6[8]). Other pressing
ideas are now on his mind:

> Here I end this reel. Box – (*Pause.*) – three, spool – (*Pause.*) – five. (*Pause.*)
> Perhaps my best years are gone. When there was a chance of happiness.
> But I wouldn't want them back. Not with the fire in me now. No, I
> wouldn't want them back. (12)

For Krapp at thirty-nine, his "best years" are gone, and with them the
"chance of happiness," but there is no need to try to restore them, since
he now feels "a fire" inside himself. What is meant by this term? Earlier
in the same recording, Krapp had spoken of his "vision" and "that I suddenly saw the whole thing," and abruptly he had noticed "the light of
the understanding and the fire" (8f). Moreover, he had mentioned that
he had celebrated his birthday "before the fire," while he "jotted down a
few notes on the back of an envelope" (5), seeking to write what he calls
his *opus magnum*. There are clear indications, then, that "the fire in me
now" points to the thirty-nine-year-old's quest for knowledge, his yearning for "the light of the understanding," perhaps also his wish to write a
book. The "fire" which now seems to govern his existence is thus the fire
of the intellect.

It is useful to put these utterances in an intellectual context. Krapp at
thirty-nine might remind the reader of Descartes, a philosopher Beckett
knew intimately, and who was the subject of one of Beckett's earliest
works, the lengthy poem *Whoroscope* (1930).[9] In one of the notes he
attached to this poem, Beckett refers to Descartes's preoccupation with his
birthday: "[Descartes] kept his birthday to himself so that no astrologer
could cast his nativity" (Beckett, *Collected Poems* 244). The point about
the 'secret' birthday of Descartes evokes that of Krapp. Yet the Cartesian
allusions go further. At the beginning of his *Méditations métaphysiques*
from 1641, written at a time when he was around forty-five years old,

---

[8]   All subsequent page numbers will refer to Beckett, *Krapp's Last Tape.*

[9]   Beckett had worked extensively on this French philosopher when he was
at the École Normale from 1928 to 1930, and many scholars have argued that
Cartesianism heavily influenced his work, particularly his earlier texts (see for
instance the substantial discussion in Harvey 3–60). Harvey argues that one of
the things that particularly attracted Beckett to Descartes was the "idea of discontinuous time" (52). This idea is, of course, highly relevant to *Krapp's Last Tape.*

Descartes had insisted that he wanted to rid himself of all prejudices and, through the sole means of rational thinking, start from scratch ("commencer de nouveau"). Furthermore, he maintains that he has reached "an age so mature" that he cannot hope to be better fitted at a later stage to write the book over which he has long procrastinated (Descartes 57). The book starts with Descartes demonstrating his philosophy of doubt: he asks if he can trust his sense perceptions; might they not be delusions? For instance can he have any reasonable doubts that "Here I am, seated in front of the fire, wearing a dressing gown, and having some paper in my hands" ("que je sois ici, *assis auprès du feu*, vêtu d'une robe de chambre, *ayant ce papier entre les mains*, et autres choses de cette nature" (Descartes 59, emphasis added)? This setting of course recalls Krapp's birthday when he was seated "before the fire" while "jotting down a few notes." Given Beckett's sustained interest in Descartes, it is not fanciful to see the shadow of this thinker in the portrait of the middle-aged Krapp.[10]

Krapp at thirty-nine is thus in some ways *like* Descartes at forty-five: like the early Enlightenment philosopher, he wants to "commencer de nouveau," without the burden of the past. His concluding statement – "the fire in me now" – is testimony to his optimism and embracement of the now. But compare this to Krapp at sixty-nine, and we find a formidable change has taken place. While Krapp at thirty-nine, in the fashion of Descartes, renounces his past, Krapp at sixty-nine seems to have nothing better to do than to repeatedly listen to his old recordings of himself, playing them through with a kind of despairing obsession. In one of the most crucial and indeed telling statements of the play, Krapp at sixty-nine sets out to clarify his own situation:

> Nothing to say, not a squeak. What is a year now? The sour cud and the iron stool. (*Pause.*) Revelled in the word spool. (*With relish.*) Spooool! Happiest moment of the past half million. (10)

---

[10]   Let us also note that Krapp's so-called "vision" recalls the famous visions of the French philosopher, told by the biographer Adrien Baillet in his influential 1691 study *Vie de Descartes*, a book Beckett knew well (see Pilling 34). Baillet points out that Descartes' search for the truth "gave violent agitations to his mind as to kindle a fire in his brain: he experienced a kind of enthusiasm which exposed his already tired soul to all kinds of dreams and visions" ("La recherche qu'il voulut faire de ses moyens, jeta son esprit dans de violentes agitations ... de telle sorte que *le feu lui prît au cerveau*, et qu'il tomba dans une espèce d'enthousiasme, qui disposa de telle manière son esprit déjà abattu, qu'il le mit en état de recevoir les impressions des songes et des *visions*" (Baillet 81, emphasis added).

When the actor Patrick Magee asked Beckett what Krapp's phrase "The sour cud and the iron stool" meant, he allegedly got the following reply: "Rumination and constipation" (Knowlson and Pilling 35). To ruminate means to regurgitate the past, chewing it over in apparently endless repetition. To be old, Krapp seems to be saying, is nothing else than to chew cud, to live one's life on repeat. Life has become routine, a tedious habit.[11] In this situation, as Kathryn White claims, the "tapes provide escapism." Moreover, "a very real sense of human tragedy" (White 24) hangs over Krapp. His old age seems to be miserable, even doomed.

However, this is less simple than at first glance. We see this when we look at what I take to be the key word of the play, namely "spool," or rather, as Krapp insists, "spooool!", and which he relates to his "happiest moment." With its associations to skeins and threads, the word evokes the *Moirai* or Fates, the mythological figures who controlled the thread of life, and who were the incarnations of destiny. These figures were sometimes seen as old and their laws related to iron (which recalls Krapp's "iron stool"). Ovid, for instance, points out that it is impossible to break "the iron decrees of the ancient sisters" (Ovid 421).[12] However, Krapp's reference to the spool does not necessarily imply that he is doomed or that his life is subjected to the Fates and their evil influence. Rather, it could be claimed that Krapp himself entertains the position that the Fates entertained in the myth, inasmuch as by means of his spools and tapes, Krapp is himself capable of governing the thread of his life. Consider his question "What is a year now?" A year is something that goes round. In this sense, it is exactly like the spools that turn around in his tape machine. For Krapp, the time of his old age – "the year now" – is *like* a spool. And of course, spools can be played forward but also be wound back. Krapp thus presents a vision of his old age as circular rather than linear: to grow old is of course to go forward in time, but also to go backwards into the past. The past is not only the point from which one departs, but also a destination. This echoes classical notions, among others Seneca's view

---

[11]   In his essay on Proust, Beckett wrote extensively about how routines and habits can define a human life: "The laws of memory are subject to the more general laws of habit. Habit is a compromise effected between the individual and his environment, or between the individual and his own organic eccentricities, the guarantee of a dull inviolability, the lightning-conductor of his existence" (Beckett, Proust 18f).

[12]   "rumpere quamquam / ferrea non possunt veterum decreta sororum," in Ovid, *Metamorphoses* XV, ll. 780–1.

of life as circular, namely as a process where man, in his old age, goes back over his traces.[13]

For Krapp, it seems that through technology, he can control his own life, and more precisely his own past, in a way which recalls the Fates and their handling of the life thread. As we have seen, Krapp can manipulate time and history by means of the spools. Not only can he turn back time by winding the spool backwards, but he can also create pauses, cuts and repetitions. This technological manipulation of time shows, first of all, that Krapp's sense of ageing might be different from more traditional approaches to old age. One of the most frequent of these definitions holds that old age consists in a *scarcity of time*. Thus Montaigne, for instance, saw old age as a period of life in which time failed him and he was no longer free to dispose of it in the same way as earlier: "Le temps me laisse; sans luy rien ne se possede" ("time leaves me; without which nothing can be possessed") (Montaigne, *Essais* vol. 3, 365). Our last age is the age that gives us the least time, Montaigne argued.[14] For Krapp at sixty-nine, it is clearly different. He has saved up an enormous amount of time on his collection of tapes, so that rather than losing time, the process of ageing, to him, means acquiring ever more time. Apparently recording himself rather frequently, thus "eternalizing" his various ages by externalizing them to the tape, Krapp can be said to pluralize his time, or, better: he *produces* more time than he originally had at his disposal. Krapp has – as Seneca exhorted any wise person to do – quite literally saved and amassed his time.[15] And because he has so much of it, he can also allow himself to *skip* it. When listening to his tapes, he constantly winds them

[13]   Thus Seneca (epistle 17) defined the life of man as consisting of circles: "One span of life is divided into parts; it consists of large circles enclosing smaller. One circle embraces and bounds the rest; it reaches from birth to the last day of existence" (Seneca 69).

[14]   For Montaigne, the lessening of time corresponds to the lessening of the vital parts of the body. A famous anecdote in *Les Essais* III, 13, recounts Montaigne's experiences with a dead tooth. This points to the general tendency of human life, he argues: the parts of the body die gradually, and the process of ageing is constant reduction: first the nerves die, then the teeth etc.; the body is halved, then quartered. This gradual dying is however not something to be feared; on the contrary, it means that the death hour of old people is mostly peaceful because most of the body is already dead anyway: "la dernière mort sera d'autant moins pleine et nuisible: elle ne tuera plus qu'un demi, ou un quart d'homme" (Montaigne vol. 3, 515).

[15]   The *locus classicus* is Seneca's first letter to Lucilius, where he insists that it matters to save time for one's own good, and have a lot of it at hand in old age. Seneca's reasoning is that the wise person should be careful not to spend all one's powers at once (Seneca 3ff).

backwards and forwards because he does not want to hear everything, only those bits which he deems important (these he chooses to listen to many times over). But Krapp is also impatient. The monotonous life he leads – "the sour cud and the iron stool" – means that he is also eager to *cut or shorten time* (by winding the tapes forward, for instance), to get quickly to what he wants. It is thus not only that Krapp goes backwards – he goes backwards by speeding forwards.[16] Paradoxically, old Krapp seems to have both too much time and too little time at his disposal. In this way, it could be said that Krapp, like the Fates, manipulates and plays with the thread of his life.

Furthermore, Krapp's technological sense of time stored up on his tapes shows that time is not so much something he lives or spends, but of which he disposes. Time, to Krapp, has become property, a collection. Collections are places for things taken out of the sphere of circulation and use. In this sense, Krapp evokes other literary protagonists from the modern era. Take for instance the hero in Charles Lamb's 1825 story "The Superannuated Man." This text is significant because it throws light on the status of old people in a modern world of salaried retirement. After a life restricted to working in an office, the fifty-year-old hero retires with a good pension:

> It was like passing out of Time into Eternity, for it is a sort of Eternity for a man to have his Time all to himself. It seemed to me that I had more time on my hands than I could ever manage. From a poor man, poor in Time, I was suddenly lifted up into a vast revenue: I could see no end of my possessions: I wanted some steward, a judicious bailiff, to manage my estates in Time for me. (Lamb 84f)

Lamb's hero is clearly happy, and he regards it as a blessing to be free from work.

Krapp's sense of happiness is however different, for unlike Lamb's hero, he does not want to be free from the past, but to re-live it. In a key passage in the text, the sixty-nine-year-old laments: "Be again, be again. (*Pause.*) All that old misery. (*Pause.*) Once wasn't enough for you" (11). This sounds rather nostalgic, with Krapp hoping that by listening to the tapes he can re-live the past: to "be again." Yet considering Krapp's use of the word "misery," there is also something else at stake here. For why

---

[16]   This willingness to speed forward in order to gain the past, is something that Krapp shares with the modern era. Voltaire once wrote: "Nous sommes venus tard en tout. Je l'ay dit et le redit. Regagnons le temps perdu" (quoted in Blumenberg 218).

would he want to re-live "all that old misery"? I would argue that his utterance signals his hope that by manipulating the tapes he can reconfigure the miserable past (which he elsewhere called his "best years") into happiness. As we have seen, Krapp is someone who by recording, ordering and winding the spools not only plays the past (as it is recorded on his tapes), but manipulates and changes it. In this sense, the phrase "be again" must be understood not simply as a repetition of the same, but as repetition of something different. For Krapp, looking back does not mean to re-live the "old misery," but to experience what he called "the *chance* of happiness," the *promise* that the past carried with it. Listening to the tapes, with their snapshots from his past, renews this promise, and this is because the tapes can be manipulated. Defining his past on the basis of the tapes, Krapp feels that the past itself can be changed and manipulated: things can be different.

We see this clearly in a scene the old Krapp is particularly drawn to, namely his amorous encounter with a girl in a boat that he recorded as a thirty-nine-year-old:

Upper lake, with the punt, bathed off the bank, then pushed out into the stream and drifted. ... We drifted in among the flags and stuck. The way they went down, sighing, before the stem! (*Pause.*) I lay down across her with my face in her breasts and my hand on her. We lay there without moving. But under us all moved, and moved us, gently, up and down, and from side to side. (9)

The scene embodies what Krapp at thirty-nine calls a "moment," an emphasized and privileged term in his vocabulary, and illustrative of his *carpe diem* mentality. A "moment," to him, is something *shared* with another: "Moments. Her moments, my moments," as he puts it (8). Yet what makes such "moments" stand out from time? The formula of "all moved, and moved us" suggests an answer: what takes place in such moments is experiences that are pregnant with potentiality: everything can happen, as he and the girl are in thrall to the movement of the water. They are part of a dynamic they feel they cannot control, a situation of unpredictability. In this potentiality lies a promise, a "chance of happiness," a suggestion that something can happen. Re-playing this scene – the old Krapp plays it twice on the tape recorder – is itself a way of actualizing this promise. For by re-playing and re-winding his spools, he so to speak brings this very "moment" into propitious movement once more. The spools, and the way they can be wound back and forth in endless variations, are themselves media of movement, of energy, of plastic potentiality. We remember

Krapp's exclamation "Spooool! Happiest moment of the past half million." With his spools, Krapp can energize and innervate the moments from the past. This energy is manifest in the language itself with the extension of "spool" into "spooool" and the superlative "happiest." Not only the spools are moving, but the language, too. If we moreover take into account the spool in terms of the thread of life, we can even say that Krapp unwinds and *prolongs* the thread by adding the extra *o*'s. Compare this to the Krapp of thirty-nine, and we find an intriguing difference. For whereas Krapp at thirty-nine was only interested in the "now" and the present, the old Krapp thinks about all his life, not only or primarily in nostalgic terms, but with a view to changing it. The old Krapp's credo is thus not the traditional one of Cartesianism, but rather the following: "I spooool, therefore I am (again)."

As we have seen, then, Krapp's two age-selves are clearly distinguished: while Krapp at thirty-nine is dismissive of his past and perceptive of the "fire in me now," Krapp at sixty-nine desires to "be again." This fundamental distinction must have been on Beckett's mind when he chose to start the play with the following paradox: "A late evening in the future. KRAPP's den" (3). The point is of course that this conflates, into an enigmatic statement, the two different versions of Krapp: first, Krapp at sixty-nine, whose old age is seen in relation to being "late," and then Krapp at thirty-nine, who still has a "future."[17] Beckett thus creates a highly suggestive image that brings into focus the dynamic mode of ageing. As we will see in the next section, this connection of older and younger ages manifests itself in other ways in Beckett's play.

Old Age and Childhood as Simultaneous Ages

In an article on old age in Beckett's works, Suzanne Lafont writes: "to age is to make appear the virtual child (the possible child) which accompanies the actual age" (Lafont 181,[18] my translation). She understands ageing not as the arrival at the end, but as an opening up of a process, where the individual can at any time produce a new and different being from what he or she was before. The process of ageing, she argues, unleashes a

---

[17]   Another traditional definition of old age: to be bereft of future. The German philosopher Ernst Bloch contrasts old age and its loss of future, with the "magic of the long backgrounds," that is the wealth of future open to those that are twenty years old (Bloch 40).

[18]   "Vieillir, c'est faire advenir cet enfant virtuel (c'est-à-dire possible, présent en puissance) qui accompagne l'être actuel" (Lafont 181).

latent power – a "child" – inside the individual. Moreover, according to Lafont, Beckett's texts are full of connections between old persons and children, to the extent that there sometimes seems almost a conflation of the two ages. She sees the "couple matriciel" of the old person and child in Beckett's work not in terms of a model of chronological and successive ageing, with the one age following after the other. Rather, old age and child are simultaneous and connected modes of being. For an old man might bring out the child inside him, the "enfant virtuel." But Lafont, whose article is quite abstract, only briefly refers to *Krapp's Last Tape*. This section will explore her suggestions about the simultaneity between the ages and the happiness it entails, by looking at one particular scene in the play.

The scene in question takes place at the beginning of the play when Krapp (sixty-nine) enjoys mustering his collection of tapes:

> (Briskly.) Ah! (*He bends over ledger, turns the pages, finds the entry he wants, reads.*) Box … three … spool … five. (*He raises his head and stares front. With relish.*) Spool! (*Pause.*) Spooool! (*Happy smile. Pause. He bends over table, starts peering and poking at the boxes.*) Box … three … three … four … two (*with surprise*) nine! good God! … seven … ah! the little rascal! (*He takes up the box, peers at it.*) Box three. (*He lays it on table, opens it and peers at spools inside.*) Spool … (*he peers at ledger.*) … five … (*he peers at spools.*) … five … five … ah! the little scoundrel! (*He takes out spool, peers at it.*) Spool five. (*He lays it on table, closes box three, puts it back with the others, takes up the spool.*) Box three, spool five. (*He bends over the machine, looks up. With relish.*) Spooool! (*Happy smile.*) (4)

The monologue shows Krapp going through his apparently well-organized collection of spools, the order of which he has pedantically noted down in a ledger. Again, the key word is "spoool." Often this exclamation is interpreted as a proof of the decrepit, senile state of Krapp's mind (Knowlson and Pilling 19). However, I think that this word, and the "happy smile" that accompanies it, is more important than sometimes assumed, being the very catalyst of Krapp's imagined community with his former self. It creates, in him, a sense of togetherness in the stoic sense of being "together with himself." As we will see, it is through this word that Krapp imaginatively defies his loneliness, seeing himself as a participant in a shared community with a different age-self.

First of all, let us note that Krapp's pleasure in this passage derives from reading his ledger. In other words, Krapp is not only a listener to his tapes, but also a reader, and the way he enjoys the sensory properties of the word "spool" points to what Roland Barthes has called the *plaisir du texte*, which in Krapp's case consists in his extreme identification with what he reads. Nor is Krapp only a reader, he is also a writer, who apart from having written his ledger also at one point talks about writing a *magnum opus*. This point is relevant when we consider that the word "spool" derives from the German noun "Spule" which, according to the Grimm dictionary, is used in weaving – and which therefore of course evokes the life thread of the Fates – but also has a connection to writing a text: "spul: *federspule zum schreiben: pennula* ain spool, eyn spule, spul, *instrumentum scriptoris*" (in Latin the equivalent was called *glomus textorius*). The "spool" is thus etymologically related to the writer's pen, a fact that of course makes Krapp's – and Beckett's – fascination with the "spooool" quite understandable.[19]

Furthermore, as has been remarked by Siccama (1999), the passage alludes to the famous case study in *Jenseits des Lustprinzips* where Sigmund Freud discusses the game played by the young boy Ernst. Freud recounts that at several instances he had noticed the eighteen-month-old toddler play with a spool, a "Holzspule" which was attached to a thread and which he threw away from himself while uttering a long "O": "ein lautes, langgezogenes *o – o – o – o*." The mother, Freud tells us, interpreted this sound to mean "Fort" ("away"). By means of the thread, the child was able to also retrieve the missing spool, always welcoming it back with "ein freudiges 'Da'" ("a happy 'there,'" Freud 12f). According to Freud, this play of the disappearance followed by its retrieval of the spool was Ernst's attempt to master the unpleasant situation of his mother's absence. As Freud sees it, Ernst through his repeated play reflects and so to speak works through the painful moment when his mother leaves him. His initial despair is turned into what Freud calls a joy or "Lustgewinn" when by his own making, he is able to retrieve the spool (the symbol of the missing mother). This achievement means, further, that the child posits himself, as Freud puts it, "zu Herr der Situation," because he is no passive victim of his mother's coming and going, but, within the field of his game at least, can dictate the proceedings. Freud's conclusion is that Ernst's game represents an essential trait in children generally, namely

---

[19]   There are suggestions that Beckett was aware of this. For why else should Krapp at one instance refer to the so-called "weaver-bird" ("Spule" – to weave)? From a dictionary, Krapp reads: "the vidua or weaver-bird … Black plumage of male … (*He looks up. With relish.*) The vidua-bird!" (7). The phrasing of the stage direction "(*He looks up. With relish.*)" is exactly like the one when he utters "Spooool!"

their mimetic behaviour, their wish to *imitate* the older. Or as he puts it: "their play is influenced by the wish prevalent at this age: to be grown-ups and able to do what the grown-ups do" ("all ihr Spiel (steht) unter dem Einflusse des Wunsches, der diese ihre Zeit dominiert, des Wunsches: groß zu sein und so tun zu können wie die Großen," (Freud 15)).

We can see a clear affinity between the little child getting enjoyment out of his game with the "Holzspule," and Krapp's exclamation "Spooool." Yet while Ernst, in Freud's estimation, wanted to grow older, Krapp holds the inverse desire: he is rejuvenated, willingly playing the game of his own infantilization. The point is thus that Krapp does what Ernst does, but in the opposite way: while the child imitates older individuals, the old man imitates childhood. Such an identification with small children can of course be a quite pervasive trait in extreme old age. For Krapp, this imitation is double. Talking to his spools, Krapp names them "little rascal" and "little scoundrel." Through this affectionate chiding, Krapp stages himself as simultaneously a child ("Spooool!") and as the master of the situation ("little scoundrel"). In this, he not only plays the child but *plays the grown-up*. Krapp thus creates an imaginary community between his own different age-selves. In the merry exchange moving from "Spooool!" to "little scoundrel" to "Spooool!" to "little rascal," the perspective constantly shifts: between Krapp being a child joyfully teasing the grown-up, and Krapp being a grown-up gently chiding the child. Both age-selves are preoccupied with the other, caring for each other, and inviting responses from the other, and it is indeed difficult to say whether the "happy smile" which appears twice in the passage belongs to Krapp the child or Krapp the grown-up. As for the spools, they could be seen as transitional objects through which Krapp is able to establish an imagined community connecting his older and younger self in a playful configuration. Happiness is an essential dimension of this community.

What all this shows, is that through the game of the spool, old Krapp is able to derive happiness from a miserable situation – just like little Ernst, as described by Freud. His spools are toys similar to Ernst's "Holzspule," and through these, Krapp overcomes the determinism of age: he can be both young and old, joyfully alternating between the positions. In a note to the text, Beckett qualified Krapp in the following way: "Tendency of a solitary person to enjoy affective relationships with objects, in particular here with the tape recorder" (Beckett, *Theatrical Notebooks* 205). As we have seen, through the affective relationship with these spools, Krapp can in fact re-enact his childhood – a past he elsewhere discarded as "that old misery," but which he now refashions into one of joy. The toys enable him to imagine the possibility of a different past from the actual one, not one of "misery," but rather one in which the "chance of happiness" was present.[20] In this way, the scene confirms Lafont's argument about the simultaneity of old age and childhood: the process of ageing brings out "l'enfant virtuel" – and a happy child at that. This process has its foundation in his exclamation "Spooool!" "Spooool" seems indeed a magical word, an 'Open, sesame!' allowing Krapp to feel and imagine himself at a different age. Reading in his ledger and opening the boxes is for Krapp like the opening of a magic universe, an imaginary world. And this world is governed by rather mysterious forces, as we see in the opaqueness of the numbers mentioned in the passage. No wonder the text points to Krapp's "surprise."

Krapp and the Play of Imagination

One of the most famous literary depictions of old age can be found in Shakespeare's allegory of the seven ages in *As You Like It*. The passage begins in the following way:

> All the world's a stage
> And all men and women merely players.
> They have their exits and their entrances,
> And one man in his time plays many parts,
> His acts being seven ages. (Shakespeare 227)

The allegory ends with the "last scene," old age:

> Last scene of all,
> That ends this strange eventful history,
> Is second childishness and mere oblivion,
> *Sans* teeth, *sans* eyes, *sans* taste, *sans* everything. (Shakespeare 229)

Beckett's play, with its many references to lateness, lastness, theatricality and play, is a more or less clear allusion to this passage from Shakespeare. What is at stake in these verses, however, is something rather paradoxical.

---

[20]   Walter Benjamin once noted that toys are not only for children, but also for older people and their attempts at imagining themselves as young. As he puts it: "Das Spielzeug ist … Auseinandersetzung, und zwar weniger des Kindes mit den Erwachsenen, als der Erwachsenen mit ihm" (Benjamin, "Spielzeug" 144). Krapp's collection of spools – or toys – is particularly relevant here. As Benjamin claims in another essay, collectors collect items in order to dream themselves back into a past world considered better than the one they live in (Benjamin, "Paris" 241).

The point is that old age is a "scene," a spectacle, but that the protagonist, or rather actor, has nothing by which to present himself: no teeth, no eyes, "*sans* everything." This might mean that old age is nothing in itself, or more precisely, that old age is a persona or mask, but that this mask is also the absence of a mask, because it has nothing with which to equip itself. What, then, is old age? Notice that Shakespeare does not write "sans *any*thing," but "sans *every*thing," thereby suggesting that old age, even though apparently nothing in itself, can be 'everything.' Evidently, old age is a "scene" that offers much for the imagination, since despite its apparent nothingness, it can also be thought to be 'everything.' The actor who plays "the last scene" does not so much play with any actual props (teeth, eyes, etc.), as she or he plays with the imagination of the reader or spectator.

In fact, this curious play of the imagination is also manifest in Beckett's play, although not in quite the same way as in Shakespeare. When listening to the recording he made as a thirty-nine-year-old, the old Krapp had exclaimed: "I have just been listening to that stupid bastard I took myself for thirty years ago" (10). Krapp significantly uses the phrase "took myself for," suggesting that as a thirty-nine-year-old he created a persona that was perhaps not quite attuned to his identity. Such bias and confusion as regards identity – the whole oscillation between appearance and identity, or what has been called the "masquerade of old age"[21] – is equally manifest in the way Krapp at sixty-nine comes to the fore. Take, for instance, the introductory stage directions where Krapp is presented as "a wearish old man," "hard of hearing," "very near-sighted," and with a "cracked voice." The text then points to his clothes: he wears a "rusty black sleeveless waistcoat" and "rusty black narrow trousers too short for him" (3). The point that his trousers do not fit underscores a central feature, namely that there is something comically 'unfitting' about him, making it difficult to pin him down. That the text starts by describing his clothes, is rather significant; indeed, very often we tend to think of age according to how people dress.[22] But in Krapp's case the clothes don't fit. With the text's

---

[21]   In an article on Ovid's *Metamorphoses*, A.D. Nikolopoulos has shown to what extent "ageing as disguise" marks this work. Age like gender is "a masquerade," where the gods simulate old age through clothing or false wrinkles (53f). In itself, this is not quite a metamorphosis, but it nonetheless operates on the physical appearance of the body in the same way as true metamorphosis, according to Nikolopoulos.

[22]   As for instance pointed out by the historian Pat Thane. According to Thane, there exist three approaches to old age in modern times. First, there is what she calls the *functional* old age, which is "reached when an individual cannot perform

emphasis on his clothing, we might even begin to reconsider his so-called "wearish" oldness, too: is this adjective, with its fleeting evocation of the verb "to wear," itself a wholly adequate and fitting description of him?

The suggestion of something unfitting about Krapp is conspicuous not only in terms of his clothing, but of his behaviour. Take Krapp's reference to someone he calls Fanny, a "bony old ghost of a whore" (11) with whom he seems to have had several sexual encounters. Fanny had asked Krapp: "How do you manage it, she said, at your age?" (11). This question indicates that for Fanny, Krapp looks old, but, sexually, he is not at all "old" ("old," according to what has been called the functional definition of old age).[23] Krapp's answer is rather sarcastic: "I told her I'd been saving up for her all my life" (11).[24] The ageist stereotype that the old are impotent, here promoted by the old Fanny, is evidently undermined. In fact, Krapp's response takes us back to the verses from Shakespeare with its suggestive conflation of lack on the one side (*"sans"* anything) and potentiality (the opportunity to be "everything") on the other. Old age is not what it seems.

But the point about Fanny becomes even more interesting if we see it in light of the immediately preceding passage, where Krapp points to a novel he has just read, namely Theodor Fontane's *Effi Briest*. Here is the passage in full:

> Scalded the eyes out of me reading *Effie* again, a page a day, with tears again. Effie … (*Pause.*) Could have been happy with her, up there on the Baltic, and the pines, and the dunes. (*Pause.*) Could I? (*Pause.*) And she? (*Pause.*) Pah! (*Pause.*) Fanny came in a couple of times. Bony old ghost of

---

the tasks expected of him or her, such as paid work." *Chronological* old age is when old age is determined according to calendar years, and is "a bureaucratic convenience, suitable for establishing age limits to rights and duties, such as access to pensions or eligibility for public service." Finally, there is also *cultural old age* which occurs "when an individual 'looks old,' according to the norms of a society, and is treated as 'old'" (Thane, 98). Thane here explicitly mentions clothing: one can dress as an old person.

23   See note 22.

24   This might be a crude reference to Seneca, who said about old age: "I advise you to keep what is really yours; and you cannot begin too early. For, as our ancestors believed, it is too late to spare when you reach the dregs of the cask. Of that which remains at the bottom, the amount is slight, and the quality is vile" (Seneca 5). To save up time, one needs to start early. See also Campbell: "Crap also means 'the dregs of ale', and with this we again have the idea of residue and waste. The dregs are all Krapp has left at the end of his life: the life is ending, the cup has been drained and only dregs, the used and useless, remain" (Campbell 64).

a whore. Couldn't do much, but I suppose better than a kick in the crutch. The last time wasn't so bad. How do you manage it, she said, at your age? I told her I'd been saving up for her all my life. (*Pause.*) (11)

In the novel, the heroine Effi briefly entertains a not very happy relationship with a lover, and this episode leads to tragedy when her husband discovers the love letters. Krapp projects himself as the lover of Effi. By so doing, he so to speak changes or fictionalizes the very fiction itself: he alters the unhappy situation into a situation that holds the promise of happiness, of the potential of a "could have been happy with her." Krapp's imaginative response to Fontane's novel reminds us of what George Steiner has said about grammatical forms such as subjunctives, optatives and counter-factual modes, namely that because they allow us to alter the world, they offer "a nucleus of potentiality" and are as such "the passwords of hope" (Steiner 5). Evidently, old Krapp plays with the imagination rather than the fact; he ponders the possibilities, not the actualities. In this way, he approaches Fontane's work – *and* his own life – aesthetically rather than empirically. He considers not the ugliness and grim tragedy of Effi's situation, but the potential and unrealized beauty of it, and he embraces the unrealized chance of love.

Yet the passage is not altogether positive, of course, for Krapp wavers between the affirmative and hopeful "could have been happy with her" and the more sceptic "Could I? (*Pause.*) And she?" This pondering leads him to think about Fanny. But here, too, Krapp's utterances are far from clear-cut. There is understatement in the phrase "The last time wasn't so bad," with the negation suggesting the opposite, namely that, from a certain perspective, it was quite good. Again, Krapp plays with the idea of changing the bad ("all that old misery") into something better, of transforming the past. Shakespeare, we remember, spoke of old age as "the last scene," which in Beckett has become "the last time." This "last time" is by no means seen as particularly negative or miserable, for Krapp's answer, "I told her I'd been saving up for her all my life," even if it is read as sarcastic, indicates the possibility of something fulfilling, as the uncharacteristically lyrical and even romantic moments in this text (so rare in Beckett's work) seem to imply. In this way, the "last time" indicates that potential for "everything" which the allegory in Shakespeare suggested as consistent with old age.

This rather positive view is moreover resonant with some of Beckett's own claims regarding old age. I have already briefly referred to Beckett's conversation with Lawrence Shainberg. In this, Beckett argues:

It is a paradox, but with old age, the more possibilities diminish, the better chance you have. With diminished concentration, loss of memory, obscured intelligence ... the more chance there is for saying something closest to what one really is. ... A child needs to make a sand castle even though it makes no sense. In old age, with only a few grains of sand one has the greatest possibility. (quoted in Barry 206)

While symptomatically linking old age to childhood, Beckett sees the former as "the greatest possibility." Other examples from Beckett seem to point in the same direction. Elizabeth Barry quotes a claim in *Molloy* that we become "a little less, in the end, the creature we were in the beginning, and the middle." According to Barry, however, "to be less oneself (or even less *tout court*, diminished in some physical or mental aspect) is not necessarily a bad thing for Beckett, of course, but the whole weight of his narrative experiment rests on our assumption as readers that it is" (Barry 208). In fact, the "lessness" of old age – and of childhood – does contain possibilities. Or with Beckett: "the greatest possibility."

To what degree is this "greatest possibility" present in Krapp? Here we might first go to Augustine, another author that Beckett knew quite well and from whom he took notes in his reading.[25] In short, Augustine held that bodily existence is inherently sinful and thus a deviation from the eternal divine regions. The bodily and mundane sphere is ruled by time, and time, as Augustine contends, makes everything un-like itself, confusing the order of the divine. This claim found a particularly poignant formula in *Confessions* where Augustine launched the term *regio dissimulationis*, meaning a place of exile, illusion and incoherence, where nothing is identical with itself.[26] Augustine had taken this term from Plato's *The Statesman* and its so-called myth of the reign of Cronus (Castoriadis), a myth that deals with old age in intriguing ways. It concerns the relation-

[25]   On Beckett's interest in Augustine, see Stefano Rosignoli. As Rosignoli points out, it was Pusey's 1876 edition and translation of *Confessiones* from which Beckett took notes. For traces of Augustinian thought in *Krapp's Last Tape*, yet seen from a wholly different perspective than the ones presented here and without reference to old age, see Tsushima.

[26]   In the seventh book of *Confessions*, Augustine writes: "Thou art my God, to Thee do I sigh night and day. Thee when I first knew, Thou liftedst me up, that I might see there was what I might see, and that I was not yet such as to see. And Thou didst beat back the weakness of my sight, streaming forth Thy beams of light upon me most strongly, and I trembled with love and awe: and I perceived myself to be far off from Thee, in the region of unlikeness" (7, 16, 121). For more on this concept, see Margaret W. Ferguson's brilliant article "Saint Augustine's Region of Unlikeness: The Crossing of Exile and Language" (1975).

ship between the humans and the gods. Plato tells that initially the gods did not care much for the human race, and that they let it do more or less what it wanted. However, as this gradually led to the world becoming ever more messy and chaotic, the gods felt something needed to be done: they turned time backwards so that instead of growing older and dying, the humans instead grew continually younger, regaining childhood. This was when the god Cronus was in charge of the human race, and his reign lasted very long, indeed Plato calls it both "timeless and ageless" (Plato 65). During this reign, the human race was happy. This, however, changed when the gods turned back time, so that the humans once more grew older. By so doing, the humans admittedly regained the sovereignty that they had so sorely craved, for they were no longer dependent on Cronus, but this also involved getting older and therefore weaker and unhappy. This, according to Plato, plunged the human race into new confusion, and what he calls the "boundless sea of diversity" (273d). From this, Augustine took his phrase "region of unlikeness."

Evidently, a quick reading of Plato and Augustine would suggest that old age is the best example of the ravages of time, since it makes us, with Beckett, "a little less the creature we were in the beginning." Old age makes us different from ourselves, destroying our identity, positioning us in the region of unlikeness.[27] However, as Geoffrey D. Dunn has recently shown, Augustine considered old age through an eschatological lens as not only entailing mental and physical diminishment – and thus increasing non-identity and unlikeness – but also as a means for the individual to prepare itself for eternal life, and so to gradually release itself from the sinful body. Shakespeare's verse "*sans* teeth, *sans* eyes, *sans* taste, *sans* everything" makes immediate sense here: it is when one is free from those things related to the body that one has the greatest possibilities. In his article, Dunn especially highlights the connection in Augustine's *De vera religione* between the six ages of humankind and the Biblical idea of

> the seven stages of the new person, which are calculated not in terms of age but of progress and perfection in the spiritual life. The seventh stage is eternal life, and before it, in the sixth stage, the person 'passes from every kind of change into eternal life, to the extent of forgetting the life of time, now that he has been perfected in the form and shape which was made to the image and likeness of God.' (*De vera religione* 26, 49; Dunn 46)

---

[27] Beckett considers in great detail this notion of time in his study on Proust. Proust himself describes the connection between old age and inexorable time in the famous "Bal des têtes" which concludes *A la recherche du temps perdu*.

In this way, the "lessness" of old age is not necessarily a bad thing, because it might mean taking leave of those things that Augustine saw as bodily and therefore sinful. Old age might be a way to prepare for another life. Is this what we find in *Krapp's Last Tape*? Even if the play is far from promoting a Christian worldview, it certainly has eschatological connotations, as we saw with its initial statement: "A late evening in the future." As I have shown in this essay, "the greatest possibility" which Beckett saw represented by old age comes to the fore in Krapp. This is a play about the *potentiality and future of old age*, about what Lafont called the nature of ageing: to bring forth the virtual child. As we saw with Krapp's manipulation of the spools, the past is not so much something actual to him, as something virtual, containing a promise, a possibility, a "chance of happiness." Krapp's idea of life is not exclusively the miserable life that actually was, and which he referred to as "All that old misery," but that which *could have been*: *a possible life*. Given his cyclical understanding of time, the past might become the future, or more precisely: the bad past might become a great future. As we have seen, in his imaginative dealings with Effi Briest, with Fanny, with the woman on the boat, or simply with himself, he constantly aspires to uncover what George Steiner called the "passwords of hope."

Works Cited

Arendt, Hannah. *The Origins of Totalitarianism.* Penguin, 2017.

Augustine. *The Confessions*, translated by E.B. Pusey. Parker, 1876.

Badiou, Alain. *Petit manuel d'inesthétique.* Seuil, 1998.

Baillet, Adrien. *La vie de M. Descartes*, première partie. Paris, 1691.

Barry, Elizabeth. "Samuel Beckett and the Contingency of Old Age." *Samuel Beckett Today/Aujourd'hui*, vol. 28, no. 2, 2016, pp. 205–17.

Beckett, Samuel. *Proust, Three Dialogues.* Calder, 1965.

———. *The Complete Dramatic Works.* Faber, 1990.

———. *The Theatrical Notebooks of Samuel Beckett. Vol.3: Krapp's Last Tape*, edited by James Knowlson. Faber, 1992.

———. *Krapp's Last Tape and Other Shorter Plays.* Faber, 2009.

———. *The Collected Poems*, edited by Sean Lawlor and John Pilling. Faber, 2012.

Benjamin, Walter. "Spielzeug und Spielen." *Erzählen. Schriften zur Theorie der Narration und zur literarischen Prosa*, edited by A. Honold. F.a.M., 2007, pp. 143–7.

———. "Paris, Hauptstadt des XIX. Jahrhunderts." *Passagen. Schriften zur französischen Literatur*, edited by G. Raulet. Suhrkamp, 2007, pp. 233–47.

Bloch, Ernst. *Das Prinzip Hoffnung*, Bd. 1. Suhrkamp, 1973.

Blumenberg, Hans. *Lebenszeit und Weltzeit.* Suhrkamp, 1986.

Brustein, Robert. "Krapp's Last Tape." Review in *New Republic* 1960. Reprinted in *Samuel Beckett. The Critical Heritage*, edited by Lawrence Graver and Raymond Federman. Routledge, 1979.

Campbell, Julie. "The Semantic Krapp in *Krapp's Last Tape.*" *Samuel Beckett Today/Aujourd'hui*, vol. 6, 1997, pp. 63–72.

Castoriadis, Cornelius. *On Plato's Statesman.* Stanford UP, 1999.

Descartes. *Méditations métaphysiques.* Flammarion, 1992.

Dukore, Bernard. "*Krapp's Last Tape* as Tragicomedy." *Modern Drama*, vol. 15, no. 4, 1972, pp. 351–4.

Dunn, Geoffrey D. "'With Length of Days I Will Gratify Him.' Augustine, the Psalms, and Old Age." *Scrinium*, vol. 15, no. 1, 2019, pp. 44–61.

Ferguson, Margaret W. "Saint Augustine's Region of Unlikeness: The Crossing of Exile and Language." *The Georgia Review*, vol. 29, no. 4, 1975, pp. 842–64.

Freud, Sigmund. *Jenseits des Lustprinzips. Gesammelte Werke*, Bd. 13. Fischer, 1999, pp. 1–71.

Harvey, Lawrence. *Samuel Beckett: Poet and Critic.* Princeton UP, 1970.

Knowlson, James, and Pilling, John. *Frescoes of the Skull: The Later Prose and Drama of Samuel Beckett.* Grove Press, 1980.

Lafont, Suzanne. "Un Air de Déjà Vieux." *Samuel Beckett Today/Aujourd'hui*, vol. 28, no. 2, 2016, pp. 179–92.

Lamb, Charles. "The Superannuated Man." *Prose Essays*, edited by B. Perry. Doubleday, 1871, pp. 80–91.

Maude, Ulrika. *Beckett, Technology and the Body.* Cambridge UP, 2009.

Montaigne, Michel. *Les Essais*, vol. 1. Libraire Générale Française, 1972.

———. *Les Essais*, vol. 3. Libraire Générale Française, 1972.

Nikolopoulos, A.D. "Tremuloque Gradu Venit Aegra Senectus: Old Age in Ovid's *Metamorphoses.*" *Mnemosyne*, vol. 56, no. 1, 2003, pp. 48–60.

Ovid. *Metamorphoses*, Books 9–15, translated by Frank Justus Miller. Loeb, 1984.

Pilling, John. *Beckett before Godot*. Cambridge UP, 1997.

Plato. *The Statesman/Politikus*, translated by H. Fowler. Loeb, 1962.

Reinton, Ragnhild Evang. *Minnekrise og Minnebilder. Litterære Erindringer fra det 20.århundre*. Novus forlag, 2015.

Rosignoli, Stefano. "Dreaming through the *Confessions*: On the Intertextuality of the Augustinian Excerpts in Samuel Beckett's 'Dream' Notebook." *Journal of Beckett Studies*, vol. 25, no. 1, 2016, pp. 39–55.

Seneca. *Epistles 1–65*, translated by R. Gummere. Harvard, 1917.

Shakespeare, William. *As You Like It*. Arden, 2006.

Siccama, Wilma. "Beckett's Many Voices. Authorial Control and the Play of Repetition." *Samuel Beckett. Today/Aujourd'hui*, vol. 8, 1999, pp. 175–88.

Steiner, George. *Grammars of Creation*. Faber, 2002.

Thane, Pat. "Social Histories of Old Age and Aging." *Journal of Social History*, vol. 37, no. 1, 2003, pp. 93–111.

Tsushima, Michiko. "'Memory is the Belly of the Mind': Augustine's Concept of Memory in Beckett." *Samuel Beckett Today/Aujourd'hui*, vol. 19, 2006, pp. 123–32.

White, Kathryn. *Beckett and Decay*. Continuum, 2009.

Afterword:
When Age Studies and Literary-Cultural Studies Converge: Reading "The Figure of the Old Person" in an Era of Ageism

MARGARET MORGANROTH GULLETTE

To be wise these days about age and ageism, one starts (as these essays do) from the proposition that all of life is relational. Life itself often depends on this fact. Social support must start with the newborn infant and, as the Covid-19 era of excess deaths in later life painfully reminds us, must continue throughout life to the best possible end (Gullette, "Avoiding"). To those with increasing cognitive impairment, neglect worsens every phase of the condition. Without adequate support, no human being can form a self, maintain selfhood, or make progress however defined at any age. "Selfhood" is often an individualist concept – when what we need, in Elizabeth Barry's words, is "a way beyond the monadic self" (p. 134), an unshakeable belief in the existential value of *the self-in-connection*. To be human is to need support; to be human is to offer it.

This ethical stance leads to the overarching reasons why age studies needs literary-cultural studies. And vice versa. Age and all its intersections across the entire life course are still, to put it mildly, ill defined. Old age remains the most mysterious phase of existence, and ageism the most acceptable bias of society. In the Age of Alzheimer's, even the boon of democratized longevity can be made to seem frightening. "Anxiety about what may come ... is [often] located in the figure of an old person," Sarah Falcus correctly notes in her essay here (p. 71). People believe universalizing statements about later life and about old people that are incorrect, ahistorical, acultural, asocial – and damaging. Without persistent close attention to the cultural and historical conditions in which people grow old, there is no way that *everyone* – including the most vulnerable – can remain, as they should, "within our social embrace" (Taylor). Representation in creative writing, and its analysis in literature and cultural studies, need to offer precisely this sort of attention. In tandem, they can improve our society's ability to think age and defy ageism by casting doubt on perverse if conventional "truths."

Reading Fiction: Its Dangers and Our Disappointments

Some people believe imaginative literature, more or less. Naively, long before the resurgence of critical study of character and identity, I used to take fictional personas as real. As a girl and even as an English Literature student who contrived to *major* in the novel, I tried to model myself on aspects of the characters I admired: the Girl of the Limberlost, Jane Eyre, Edmond Dantès, Dorothea Brooke. I was able to choose from among many models because the Bildungsroman of Youth was, and still is, a crammed genre. But whenever little information about a fraught subject is available, the risk of generalizing from single instances is great.

Given the ageist lacunae and distortions I have alluded to, can we trust literature to carry anomalous, ambiguous, contrarian, and necessarily partial truths into its depictions of later life? We should be wary. Writers have the blessing, and dare I say, the curse, of being free to choose which unpredictables to explore, which intersections to ignore, which stereotypes to assert. "[T]he Poet, he nothing affirms, and therefore never lieth" (Sidney 235). Philip Sidney was wrong. The problems for writers are greater if they grow up in a society where their subjects are othered in some way – which can happen when the understudied category of age intersects with race, gender, sexuality, class, and other intersections – if these writers lack counterbalancing insights. Where nothing is affirmed, as in fiction or drama or film, any collection of utterances or any narrative structure may freely imply and thereby mislead.

I reread Richard Ford's *The Lay of the Land* (2006) recently to see how he kept his first-person (white) narrator, Frank Bascomb, interesting for so many pages at the age of fifty-five. (Ford has written several novels about Frank Bascomb at earlier ages.) A little older than Frank, Ford accomplished the task imaginatively, relying mainly on the many voices hidden within a single body that strolls the beach, muses philosophically, sells real estate, gets treatment for prostate cancer, brawls, and observes the world around him. Frank is a 'round' character in E.M. Forster's term, whose age is not foregrounded. But Frank's 'friend' Wade, who is represented as eighty, is a mass of 'flat' qualities keyed to 'old': he smells, his false teeth slip, he sinks irrationally into belligerence. Frank thinks: "Old people, no matter what anyone says, do not make the best company when spirits flag" (Ford 211). "I sometimes think of old people as being *like* pets" (Ford 312). Rüdiger Kunow, an age critic in American literature, suggests to me that "peripheral [characters represented as old] would also offer interesting material because they pose the question of why the author made them be old in a perhaps less reflective way that he/she would have brought to the main character" (Kunow, email). The danger of othering an ancillary character may be greater if they are meant to seem funny. Or (a point I'll come back to) when the character is older than the writer. In midlife (although no longer looking for 'models'), I remained eager to find protagonists who were my own age or older, regardless of whether they shared any of my other characteristics. Disappointment has often been my lot, as I acquired gerontological illuminations and came to my own theories about age culture. As I grow older yet – I am now in my seventies – so do many of my preferred protagonists. I also read on the basis of buzz, of course, and draw the line at the preposterous (one-hundred-year-old men who climb out of windows). Still, age changes our reading preferences and interpretations,[1] and may do so more definitively for cultural critics in age studies. I imagine that other readers have also read their way past the formulaic genres. Rom-coms about young people, coming-of-age stories, midlife *Bildungsromane*, dramedies about the adulteries and dysfunctions of midlife people, all have to reach a very high bar not to bore me. I am disgusted with stories showing people with cognitive impairments (crudely lumped together as 'dementia') in which suicide is treated as the inevitable option. I want fresh plots and pastures new.

This quest for pleasure and information about characters somewhat like me has led to some unexpected, rewarding results. The Canadian film *Still Mine*, a romance about married love in old age, when the wife is starting to lose her memory, with its startling sex scene and bold disregard of local building codes, charmed me (see *Ending Ageism* 159–62).[2] I picked up the quietly moving *Going, Went, Gone* (2017) by Jenny Erpenbeck, in part because her central figure, Richard, was an East German, a retired professor, and a lonely widower at a loose end. Erpenbeck uses Richard's dawning commitment to young African migrant men as a thread to tie the story to state power and private justice. I took a chance buying Paulette Jiles's *News of the World* simply because its hero was "seventy," and thus discovered a National Book Award finalist who deserved the honour in every way. It's a prose poet's version of Reconstruction history, set in the wild Reconstruction era of 1870s Texas. Captain Kidd takes on a

---

[1]   On "the dynamic relation between age and narrative," see Port, "Rereading the Future," *PMLA*, vol. 133, no. 3, 2018, 640–6. That *PMLA* issue includes other vanguard essays about reading and age. See also the chapter on rereading Jane Austen's *Emma*, in Gullette, 2011: 167–82.

[2]   2. *Still Mine* (2012) was directed by Michael McGowan; the leads were played by James Cromwell and Genevieve Bujold. It won Best Motion Picture from the Canadian Screen Awards.

quest, to escort a true kid, a ten-year-old white girl raised as a Kiowa who no longer speaks English, south through chaos to her remaining family. (What Jiles does with the dimes that Captain Kidd charges to read the news in each frontier town he visits, is worth reading the novel to learn.) It's a double 'journey,' in which both display their skill sets and increase their wisdom. Each of these older figures, in fact, is a self in relation to another more vulnerable character, who in exchange helps the protagonist grow (Gullette, "Saviors and Survivors"). I relished seeing how the needs of the relationship fostered resilience, curiosity, persistence, or bravery – qualities so often limited to characters represented as young.

Age is important in every one of these works of art, without being foregrounded. It can suggest a challenge, physical or social, which builds genuine suspense. Age can be suggested without being at all times the character's dominant identity. Other identities, like race, gender, or class, are not necessarily always uppermost in our subjectivity, so this subtler creative approach to age should not come as a surprise. What any reader draws from such works about being old is nondidactic, particularized. Another fine old saying applies: 'In nothing do people differ more than in their aging.'

Far from apologizing for my reading penchant, I want to share it widely. Why should old people, alone among targeted subgroups, not turn to representation to ask for 'more people who look like us' (but who are of course in other ways different), also *written*, most likely, by people who look like us? Feminists, including me, early on decided to read books by women, by predilection and for practical reasons – so more women would be encouraged to write, would be able to find publishers for their books, and get them bought and read. And prized.

Eventually, rooting around for well-written novels that might also be about people like me in age, I began to notice how rarely they turned up on lists of fiction prizes. (If more did win, that might be an encouragement to writers to produce them.) Perhaps they are rarely published? For films, AARP presents a list of what it calls "Movies for Grownups," which star actors over fifty and include "Best Grownup Love Stories." The nonprofit feminist organization VIDA ("Women in Literary Arts. We Count") literally counts the authors of selected print publications in order "to highlight the lack of diversity in publishing, in gender, in race, in ethnicity, in sexuality, in disability, etc." Notice that age disappears inside "etc." I for one notice age inequality in book reviews and literary prize culture – exemplified by the "Thirty Under Thirty" attitude of *Granta*.

Could some big-data experts apply to best-seller and prize lists what you might call "a diversified VIDA count" focused on age? Whatever their methodology, they could count the age of the protagonists, say, everyone over fifty or sixty, and the age of the writers.[3] Such counts might uncover pipeline problems in publishing. I suspect it is harder to find an editor as you age. If you start writing fiction only when you have grown old, is that a handicap? Do agents acquire 'new' novelists who are not new in years? Jiles was born in 1943, so she was close to Captain Kidd's age when she wrote *News of the World*. Richard Ford was around sixty when he devised Frank Bascomb at fifty-five. As John Updike also did with Rabbit Angstrom, or Drabble with her many female protagonists, writers tend to invent protagonists *younger* than they are. It's not a rule – Erpenbeck was born in 1967 – but for most it may be a wise decision. Ceridwen Dovey explains why, in a *New Yorker* article analysing why she started and then stopped writing a novel about old people when she was in her thirties:

I found I had modelled my characters on the two dominant cultural constructions of old age: the doddering, depressed pensioner and the ageless-in-spirit, quirky oddball. After reading the first draft, an editor I respect said to me, "But what else are they, other than old?" I was morti-fied, and began to ask myself some soul-searching questions that I should have answered long before I'd written the opening word.

The first was: Why did I so blithely assume that I had the right to imagine my way into old age – and that I could do it well – when I would approach with extreme caution the task of imagining my way into the interior world of a character of a different gender, race, or class? Had I assumed that anybody elderly who might happen to read the book would simply be grateful … and forgive my stereotyping?[4]

After a lecture in 2019, Richard Ford, now seventy-five, told me that he soon plans to start his next novel about Frank Bascomb, whom he will now represent as being seventy. Ford will no doubt decide that once you are living it, seventy is as fascinating as any other age; will he therefore have Frank regret his harsh sentences about Wade, uttered when he was a jejune fifty-five? Or will Frank at seventy encounter a ninety-year-old who is rebarbative Wade redivivus?

[3]   In 1977 Mary Sohngen did a count of eighty-seven novels published between 1950 and 1975 with a protagonist over sixty, and provided an annotated bibliog-raphy, in "The Experience of Old Age as Depicted in Contemporary Novels," *The Gerontologist*, vol. 17, no. 1, 1977, pp. 70–8.
[4]   In fact, in 2000, Barbara Kingsolver described such a couple – he a pes-ticide-using curmudgeon, she a sweet-tempered environmentalist – in *Prodigal Summer*. In "What Is Old Age Really Like?" Ceridwen Dovey quotes age scholars Sarah Falcus, Lynne Segal, Helen Small, and me, as well as many creative writers.

Writers not only have to go on writing, they also have to succeed in getting published – a high bar – before enough of them arrive at the age when they can write plausibly about later life. (Writing symbolically or allegorically is a separate issue.) Many writers drop out along the way. Despite the fact that we hear endlessly about a 'tsunami' of old people (many of whom, we are also told, buy books), publishers may feel there is not a big enough audience for fiction about old people.

"Age studies" has no pipeline problem, fortunately. Some of its early adherents, its vanguard figures, are mentoring and producing outstanding work. And younger people are moving in, eager to comprehend this understudied dimension of life and to offer their fresh contributions. Undergraduates and graduate students enter the field from many directions: aside from critical, social, cultural and humanistic gerontology, of course, and literature, cultural studies, history and philosophy, they emerge from anthropology, sociology and psychology (where entire courses on "ageing" are taught), women's studies, and from medical humanities, nursing, architecture, technology, postcolonial studies – wherever age is becoming noticed as a neglected aspect of being or a category of social construction, and in a far wider variety of institutional and geographical locations than before.[5] The two scholarly networks on age, European (ENAS) and North American (NANAS), encompass researchers on five continents, who meet in a joint conference every three years. The International Network for Critical Gerontology produces newsletters and accepts blog posts. The Dementia and Cultural Narrative Network also sends out monthly updates.[6] *Radical History Review*, like *Essays and Studies*, is producing a themed issue. Academic publishers are adding book series focused on age. Within only a few years, 'ageism,' long ignored amid other social prejudices, has become a mainstream topic. Age studies is emerging as a multidisciplinary, intersectional, and global field (see my

---

[5]   To take one small instance of international reception where I happen to have data: Readers of my writings reside in countries where, before 2019, I had none: Bangladesh, Bosnia-Herzegovina, Estonia, Ethiopia, Finland, Ghana, Hungary, Italy, Korea, Pakistan, Slovenia, South Africa, Tunisia, and Uganda. Data from Researchgate and Academe.edu.

[6]   To join the listservs, see the websites: NANAS: http://agingstudies.org/NANAS/; ENAS: www.agingstudies.eu/; International Network for Critical Gerontology: https://criticalgerontology.com/. The Dementia and Cultural Narrative Network will soon be adding a publications section: dementia.and.culture.network@gmail.com or https://dementia-culture.wixsite.com/network?f-bclid=IwAR2WptukvAEFGYoMcLMQ4WnyFcZwzwBZXtWG3z7D56b3knZ-vyigII6pRsy8 or www.facebook.com/DemNarrCulture/.

"What Is Age Studies?"; Katz; Pickard). Post Covid-19, it may be filled at times with activist urgency.

Meanwhile, the feelings of disappointment with age-related fiction, its production and reception, are not to be dismissed. Disappointment is a stage of grievance. Reform starts with feeling and stating grievances.[7] Age studies – nothing if not critical – can participate in this reform.

The Thrill of the New Turn to Age Studies

Some of the essays you hold in your hands try in fascinating and original ways to get far beyond rectifying falsehoods. They bring insights that expand the possibilities of reading well, understanding culture, influencing readers and writers, and liking older people better a priori. These essays emphasize the *contexts* of a particular text: its political and cultural history, a writer's personal limitations or ambivalences. Jacob Jewusiak, for example, invents the term, "the grandparenting of empire" to describe a move Rudyard Kipling makes in *Kim* (1901), where a Tibetan lama occupies the position of elder, while an Irish boy fills that of youth. Kipling substitutes a grandparent–grandchild dyad for the paternalistic one, to "make power appear … a matter of choice rather than coercion" (p. 87) for political ends.

Themes helpfully recur from essay to essay. David Amigoni finds a memoir, by a woman diagnosed with cognitive impairment, so focused on using social networks that she complicates "the classically defined boundaries of the individual self" of typical self-help narratives (p. 153). Samuel Beckett's solitary, morose old men may seem to deny that monads have windows at all. But Peter Svare Valeur, in "Toying with the Spool," imaginatively points out that Krapp, living alone with his toys, his many boxes of audio-tapes, "is a multiple subject, consisting of a variety of different age-selves." The current one is occasionally amused and even "happy." The tapes provide Krapp with the support – which he relishes – of those earlier erotic and literary selves. And, I add (with my long-term interest in the odd ways that writers show progress) that however harshly Krapp's Oldest Self judges his *past* selves – "that stupid bastard I took myself for thirty years ago" – the Oldest Self takes its *current* powers of judgement and pleasure as superior. This complacency about being older-and-wisest is, I daresay, widespread.

---

[7]   See "A Declaration of Grievances," the last two pages of my book, *Ending Ageism, or How Not to Shoot Old People*, which also appears on dedicated websites, including https://static1.squarespace.com/static/5638bad6e4b07c4dab7a60a2/t/59b6556312ab-d93aa2c22000/1505121636851/A+Declaration+of+Grievances.pdf.

Sarah Falcus's observation that "Ageing is central to the dystopic imagination," leads her to explore a genre she names "demo-dystopias," in which humanity's disastrous futures are allegedly "brought about by demographic change or that make population matters a salient concern." Older people are blamed for every decline, from globalization and job loss to climate change. Arguably, these novels can express deeper hostility to old people than either the realistic decline novel or the existential play.

* * *

Every time literary and cultural studies move into a new area (gender and sexualities and sexism, disability, race and racism, ethnicity, LGBTQ studies, critical legal theory), the results for the investigators and the fields have been bracing. The intellectual advantages (distrust of conventional interpretations, the raising of doubt, perceptions that break open the mind) emerge *pari passu* with the emotional advantages. Every small step forward is an expansion of empathy for the othered, a step forward for readers and scholars into a deeper sense of "how to feel" and who is embraceable. So it has been, and will continue to be, from the turn to age studies.

The authors in this anthology don't use a rhetoric of "suspicion" – at one time a popular scholastic term for "rubbing in what writers fail to know and cannot represent" (as Rita Felski wittily wrote in "Context Stinks" (574), about teaching students how to discuss texts). But age critics are unlikely to assume a condescending attitude when doing our necessary interpretive work. Disclosing what writers fail to know means linking cultural issues to literary texts, and this is not easy. In describing how writers unknowingly inscribe "the master narrative of aging," Rüdiger Kunow quotes Fredric Jameson's suggestion "that a certain complex of cultural problems (in this case age) can be shown to express itself not just in the treatment of subject matter but in structural consequences as well" (Kunow, "The Coming of Age" 300–1).

Some of these complex formal issues – among others, authorial tone, excessive similarities among characters, even plot events – can be illustrated through the rather banal ageism of Margaret Drabble's *The Dark Flood Rises*. The main protagonist, Fran Stubbs, is supposed to be a gerontologist, indeed, a salaried expert, although I noticed that she never shows "first-hand empathetic familiarity" with the needs of the elderly as a group (6). Nor is she deeply concerned about climate change. Fran herself, and other characters, male and female, mostly in their mid-seventies, Kathleen Woodward summarizes, all "regularly reflect on ageing, *the central preoccupation of their lives*" (p. 42, emphasis added). Woodward points out that

while age-studies scholars have been at pains to show that ageing is not
solely physical, but a phenomenon shaped by gender, race and class, in
Drabble's novel it is presented "first and foremost" as a biological process:
"Ultimately how peculiar and empty and white is the vision of ageing in
the novel" (p. 45).

Yet for many people lucky enough to arrive there, "three score and ten"
holds no legendary terrors. Foregrounding thoughts of their physiological ageing, in fiction about people still only in their seventies, is indeed
"peculiar." It is rare for writers to do this even about characters who need
"care homes," aka sheltered housing for the elderly. Like characters far
younger, such older, often disabled, folks are usually shown to have a great
many matters, and passions, and projects, on their minds, other than the
decline associated with their life stage (Gullette, "Against 'Aging'"). I can
say this with some confidence, because, in order to produce an annotated
bibliography of them for an absorbing guide about the advantages of
continuing-care retirement communities, *The Big Move*, I read many such
novels in different genres, from John Updike's *The Poorhouse Fair* to Tim
Sandlin's *Jimi Hendrix Turns Eighty* (Gullette, "Annotated Bibliography"
79–90).[8]

Like others who historicize age-related writing, Woodward correlates
Drabble's "empty ... vision" with post-Thatcher Britain's atomism, "compounded by the collapse of care on the part of the [neoliberal] state,
rendering it altogether reasonable to fear old ageing" (p. 46). Finding
"triumph" nevertheless in Drabble's "collision of ordinary human time
[with] time punctuated by inevitable if unpredictable large-scale catastrophe," Woodward then takes the discussion well beyond the novel to open
up interesting prospects for age studies to intersect with climate activism
in the Anthropocene.

Since my focus here is the way writers can let unreflective bias influence form and undermine empathy, I am not 'grateful' for Drabble's
novel, despite its being written by a person of appropriate age about
characters of appropriate ages. (It could be counted on a diversified VIDA
list, but that would be misleading.) Several characters repeat that old
people are "selfish." Longevity (as in some dystopian novels) is "disastrous" (18). In casual conversation with younger colleagues, with whom
Fran prides herself on hanging out, she observes without irony while

---

8   The central section of *The Big Move* is written by Anne M. Wyatt-Brown,
a humanistic gerontologist who describes honestly how she had to overcome her
own internalized ageism when she moved into a continuing care retirement community, or CCRC. *The Big Move* is very much about self-in-relation to others.

dabbing a shrimp in sauce, that "women live too long ... We need a plan to get rid of us" (18).

For a reader of Drabble's early fictions, her youngish heroines' breezy tone used to bring light-hearted relief from their miseries. It hinted that women would overcome. In later life Fran combines nonchalance with depressiveness. The novel sounds dismissive about being old-and-healthy yet still alive. We are even led not to care or know, Woodward points out, how Fran dies. I suspect that younger readers who recognize Drabble's pessimism may be pleasantly surprised by themselves if they turn seventy – especially if their ability to care for others and for the planet has grown. Meanwhile, they may be taken aback by the offhand-edness with which Fran expresses internalized ageism and Drabble so often has her recede behind other characters and finally disappear amid a list of others who have died.

Ageism inflects not only the novel's tone and structure, but Drabble's use of her own memory and past fictions. Fran remembers a period, such as Drabble long wrote about, when being young and a mother was tormenting (15), but it doesn't occur to Drabble that Fran's current situation – as an older, competent, postmaternal woman, without imposed responsibility – compared to her period of youthful female angst, could be what Saul Bellow famously called a contrast-gainer (61). (No matter how flawed, uninteresting and unattractive two people are, one of the pair always makes the other look better.) Drabble once had a theory of life-course progress, but it is useless to this novel, dedicated to one healthy, active, middle-class character's causeless sense of decline.[9]

In some of its literary forms, ageism sidles toward ruthlessness, and abets the policies of ruthlessness, by fixating on a human category it chooses to represent as useless, unwanted, superfluous. Hate-speech against the old can sound so ordinary and banal – to borrow from Hannah Arendt – that it is invisible. Yet a reader who is theoretically innocent about how decline ideology infiltrates literature may still be disturbed by an instinct that this particular dark title, that ordinary con-versation over shrimp cocktail, or this structure of jumping from one old peripheral character to another as if none was interesting enough to linger on, is hurtful, perhaps even violent. Or say that, as an agewise reader, I feel personally immunized from explicit or implicit ageism (I in fact do not; I feel potentially crushable by a concatenation of onslaughts), I may still suspect that others can be psychologically damaged.

---

[9]   The "dark flood" refers not just to tsunamis of old people, but also to Africans trying to migrate to Europe.

From within our various multidisciplinary perspectives, age critics take for granted that readers need to get from us not only interpretation of texts and exploration of contexts, but also careful, educated evaluation. What initially excited me about literary-cultural studies of age was finding critics looking again at 'classic' texts that were still being taught, or newer texts likely to be taught, and offering them a quizzical, feminist, anti-ageist look. Revisionist literary/cultural readings, emerging from committed critique, can make sense of works that could be troubling. Take Margaret Atwood's "Torching the Dusties": is this dystopian satire, about a mob of young people setting fire to an old people's residence as an act of economic revenge, likely to inculcate precisely what it warns against? Before the Covid-19 pandemic, some students who self-identified as an age cohort may have used the retort "Okay, Boomer." Post-pandemic, called by some the "boomer remover" (Aronson, "'Covid Kills Only Old People'"), will this violence still seem emotionally plausible to them, or a repugnant fable written for a benighted era of unconsciousness? Will age studies and social change make teaching such a text unnecessary?

Our current conjuncture includes explicit cultural warfare against so-called 'political correctness.' It should not deflect age critics. 'P.C.,' used as a vulgar epithet rather than a term of praise, ignores the valuable results of consciousness-raising. Once we have achieved heightened sensitivity to others and knowledge of the contexts they survive, we cannot help but use those feelings. Once woke, people may stay woke. Until the next fresh burst of enlightenment opens our eyes even wider. The humanities need age studies because fresh consciousness is itself thrilling.

But this promise of progress in thought comes posted with a warning and a prophecy. In many events of our time – to bracket the pandemic, and name only the global financial crisis, the politics of Brexit or Trumpism, the climate apocalypse, the attacks on the social safety nets – certain groups have found ways to scapegoat the people wearing older bodies. As the interests behind ageism notice our revisionist critique and anti-ageist energy, their backlash against us may emerge defiant and vocal. Formerly, intellectually curious scholars joining age studies learned to ask, time and again, in field after field, in topic after topic, "What's *age* got to do with it?" That was an invitation to look harder into texts and contexts for what was missing. But sometimes 'age' really has nothing to do with it, except as an attempt to weaken a movement by and on behalf of older people. Now age critics must ask that same question sceptically, maybe even caustically. The newly enlightened enter a rougher world than they may have imagined. Some will march into the world of words to make a difference, wherever age is either ignored or newly set up to matter more brutally than it should. Some will become renowned for solidarity, fighting in a "war" that until now has barely been declared.

Works Cited

Aronson, Louise. "'Covid-19 Kills Only Old People.' Only?" *New York Times*. March 22, 2020. https://www.nytimes.com/2020/03/22/opinion/coronavirus-elderly.html.

Bellow, Saul. *Humboldt's Gift*. Penguin, 1975.

Dovey, Ceridwen. "What Is Old Age Really Like?" *New Yorker*, 1 October 2015.

Drabble, Margaret. *The Dark Flood Rises*. Picador, Farrar, Straus and Giroux, 2016.

Felski, Rita. "Context Stinks." *New Literary History*, vol. 42, no. 4, 2011, 573–91.

Ford, Richard. *The Lay of the Land*. Alfred A Knopf, 2006.

Gullette, Margaret Morganroth. "What Is Age Studies?" *Aged by Culture*. U of Chicago P, 2004.

——. "Annotated Bibliography of Further Reading: Fiction." *The Big Move: Life Between the Turning Points*, edited by Anne M. Wyatt-Brown, et al. Indiana UP, 2016, pp. 79–90.

——. "Avoiding Ageist Bias and Tragedy in Triage." *Tikkun*, April 14, 2020. https://www.tikkun.org/avoiding-bias-and-tragedy-in-triage.

——. "Against 'Aging' – How to Talk about Growing Older." *Theory, Culture & Society*, 21 December 2017, www.theoryculturesociety.org/margaret-morganroth-gullette-aging-talk-growing-older/.

——. "Contrived Generational Wars Disguise the Failure of the American Dream." *Boston Globe*, 13 October 2019, www.bostonglobe.com/ideas/2019/10/11/beware-labels-contrived-generational-wars-disguise-failure-american dream/BwpcAnlGfHVsctTkpCX8tK/story.html.

——. *Ending Ageism, or How Not to Shoot Old People*. Rutgers UP, 2019.

——. "Saviors and Survivors, Mentorship as Rescue." *Rediscovering Age(ing) through Narratives of Mentorship: Essays in Cultural Gerontology*, edited by Núria Casado-Gual, et al. Transcript Verlag, 2019.

Katz, Stephen. "What Is Age Studies?" *Age Culture Humanities* 1, 2014.

Kingsolver, Barbara. *Prodigal Summer*. Harper Perennial, 2000. https://ageculturehumanities.org/WP/what-is-age-studies/.

Kunow, Rüdiger. "The Coming of Age: The Descriptive Organization of Later Life." *Representation and Decoration in a Postmodern Age*, edited by Alfred Hornung and Rüdiger Kunow. Universitätsverlag Winter GmbH Heidelberg, 2009, pp. 295–309.

——. Email correspondence. 6 December 2019.

Pickard, Susan. *Age Studies. A Sociological Examination of How We Age and Are Aged through the Life Course*. Sage, 2016.

Port, Cynthia. "Rereading the Future." *PMLA*, vol. 133, no. 3, 2018, pp. 640–6, www.mlajournals.org/doi/abs/10.1632/pmla.2018.133.3.640.

Sidney, Philip. *Sir Philip Sidney: A Critical Edition of the Major Works*, edited by Katherine Duncan-Jones. Oxford UP, 1989.

Taylor, Janelle. Episode Twelve: "Friendship Beyond Dementia." *The Anthropologist on the Street*, 3 October 2017, https://anthropologistonthestreet.com/2017/10/03/episode-12-friendship-beyond-dementia-the-anthropology-of-aging-with-dr-janelle-taylor/.

"Women in Literary Arts. We Count." Vida: Women in Literary Arts. 2019. www.vidaweb.org.

Wyatt-Brown, Anne M., et al. *The Big Move: Life between the Turning Points*. Indiana UP, 2016.

Index

References to footnotes consist of the page number followed by the letter 'n.' followed by the number of the note. Entries for essays and contributing authors in this volume are shown in small capitals.